AMERICAN LIKE ME

AMERICAN LIKE ME

Reflections on Life Between Cultures

Edited by **America Ferrera**

with E. Cayce Dumont

GALLERY BOOKS

New York   London   Toronto   Sydney   New Delhi

G

Gallery Books
An Imprint of Simon & Schuster, Inc.
1230 Avenue of the Americas
New York, NY 10020

First Gallery Books trade paperback edition September 2019

GALLERY BOOKS and colophon are registered trademarks of Simon & Schuster, Inc.

For information about special discounts for bulk purchases,
please contact Simon & Schuster Special Sales at 1-866-506-1949
or business@simonandschuster.com.

The Simon & Schuster Speakers Bureau can bring authors to your live event.
For more information or to book an event, contact the Simon & Schuster Speakers Bureau
at 1-866-248-3049 or visit our website at www.simonspeakers.com.

Interior design by Davina Mock-Maniscalco

Manufactured in the United States of America

20   19   18   17   16   15   14

Library of Congress Cataloging-in-Publication Data is available for the original hardcover edition.

ISBN 978-1-5011-8091-0
ISBN 978-1-5011-8092-7 (pbk)
ISBN 978-1-5011-8093-4 (ebook)

For Baz,
and every child everywhere,
with my hope that you seek, and find,
reflections of your deep worth and truest value.

Contents

INTRODUCTION

America Ferrera

MY NAME IS AMERICA, and at nine years old, I hate my name. Not because I hate my country. No! In fact, at nine years old I love my country! When the national anthem plays, I cry into my Dodger Dog thinking about how lucky I am to live in the only nation in the world where someone like me will grow up to be the first girl to play for the Dodgers. I do hate the Pledge of Allegiance though, not because I don't believe in it. I believe every word of it, especially the "liberty and justice for all" part. I believe the Pledge of Allegiance to my bones. And at nine years old I feel honored, self-righteous, and quite smug that I was smart enough to be born in the one country in the whole world that stands for the things my little heart knows to be true: we are all the same and deserve an equal shot at life, liberty, and a place on the Dodgers' batting lineup. I hate the Pledge of Allegiance because for as long as I can remember there is always at least one smart-ass in class who turns to face me with his hand over his heart to recite it, you know, 'cause my name is America.

The first day of every school year is always hell. Teachers always make a big deal of my name in front of the whole class. They either think it's a typo and want to know what my real name is, or they want to know how to pronounce it (ridiculous, I know), and they always follow up with "America? You mean, like the country?"

"Yes, like the country," I say, with my eyes on my desk and my skin burning hot.

This is how I come to hate American History. Not because I don't love saying "the battle of Ticonderoga" (obviously, I do). But because no teacher has ever been more excited to meet a student named America than my first American History teacher.

He has been waiting all day to meet me, and so to commemorate this moment he wheels me around the classroom on his fancy teacher's chair, belting "God Bless America" while a small part of me dies inside.

His face reminds me of Eeyore's when I say, "Actually, I like to go by my middle name, Georgina, so could you please make a note of it on the roster-paper-thingy? Thanks." When he has the gall to ask me why, I say something like "It's just easier," instead of what I really want to say, which is "Because people like you make my name unbearably embarrassing! And another thing, I'm not actually named after the United States of America! I'm named after my mother, who was born and raised in Honduras. That's in *Central* America, in case you've never heard of it, also part of the Americas. And if you must know, she was born on an obscure holiday called Día de Las Américas, which not even people in Honduras know that much about, but my grandfather was a librarian and knew weird shit like that. This is a holiday that celebrates *all* the Americas—South, Central, and North, not just the United States of. So, my name has nothing to do with amber waves of grain, purple mountains, the US flag, or your very narrow definition of the word. It's my mother's name and a word that also relates to other countries, like the one my parents come from. So please refrain from limiting the meaning of my name, erasing my family's history, and making me the least popular kid in class all in one fell swoop. Just call me Georgina, please?" I don't say any of this, to anyone. Ever. It would be impolite, or worse, unpatriotic. And as I said before, I love my country in the most unironic and earnest way anyone can love anything.

I know just how lucky I am to be an American because every time I complain about too much homework my mother reminds me that in Honduras I'd be working to help support the family, so I'd better thank my lucky stars that she sacrificed everything she had so that my *malcriada** self and my five siblings could one day have too much homework. It's a perspective that has me embracing Little League baseball, the Fourth of July, and ABC's TGIF lineup of wholesome American family comedies with more fervor than most. I feel more American than Balki Bartokomous, the Winslows, and the Tanners combined, and I believe that one day I will grow up to look like Aunt Becky from *Full House* and then Frank Sinatra will ask me to rerecord "I've Got You Under My Skin" as a duet with him because I know all the words better than my siblings.

So I let it slide when people respond to my name with "Wow, your parents must be very patriotic. Where are they ACTUALLY from?" This is a refrain I hear often and one that will take me a couple of decades to unpack for all its implications and assumptions. I learn to go along with the casting of my parents as the poor immigrants yearning to breathe free, who made it to the promised land and decided to name their American daughter after the soil that would fulfill all their dreams. After all, it is a beautiful and endearing tale. Only later do I learn to bristle and push back against this incomplete narrative. A narrative which manages to erase my parents' history, true

---

*spoiled

experience, and claim to the name America long before they had a US-born child. Never mind that they'd already had a US-born child before me and named her Jennifer. Which is both a much more American name than mine and one I would kill to have on the first day of every school year.

But I am nine and I do not think too much about narratives and my parents' erased history. I think about my friends and getting to go over to their houses, where we play their brand-new Mall Madness board game and search Disney movies for the secret sex images you can see if you know where to pause the VHS. I think about how cool it would be if my mom ever let me actually sleep over at a friend's house and how that will never happen because she's convinced all sleepovers end in murder and sexual assault. I think about how cool it would be if my friend was allowed to sleep over at my house and how that will never happen because her parents, who are also immigrants, happen to agree with my mom about the murder and sexual assault thing. I think about how when I'm in junior high and look more like Aunt Becky I will have a locker and decorate it with mirrors and magazine cutouts like all the kids on *Saved By the Bell*. I think about how I will grow up to be a professional baseball player, actress, civil rights lawyer, and veterinarian who will let her kids go to sleepovers. And I think about boys. Well, I think about one boy. A lot.

Aside from having a challenging name, I feel just like all my friends. Even all the things that make my home life different from my friends' home lives seem to unify our experience. Sure, my parents speak Spanish at home, but Grace's parents speak Chinese, and Muhammad's parents speak another distinct language that I can't name, and Brianne's Filipino parents speak something that sounds a little like Spanish but isn't. My favorite part of going over to my friends' houses is hearing their parents yell at them in different languages and eating whatever their family considers an after-school snack.

Brianne and I consume an alarming amount of white rice soaked in soy sauce while we stretch in the dark, listening to her mom's Mariah Carey album.

Speaking Spanish at home, my mom's Saturday-morning-salsa-dance party in the kitchen, and eating tamales alongside apple pie at Christmas do not in any way seem at odds with my American identity. In fact, having parents with deep ties to another country and culture feels part and parcel of being an American. I am nine and I truly belong. By the time I reach ten, this all begins to change.

The first person to make me feel like a stranger in a strange land is the first boy I ever love. I am six years old when I fall in love with Sam Spencer.* And the full agony of loving him is bursting out of my tiny bones and pulsing through my tiny veins. He has very silky, soft brown hair that is almost entirely short except for the rat's tail that dangles down the nape of his neck. I sit behind Sam on the magic carpet at reading time, and I try to be sneaky about braiding his rat's tail. Whether we are making pizza bagels or building castles in the sandbox, all my little six-year-old mind can focus on during Ms. Wildestein's kindergarten class is braiding Sam's hair, talking to Sam, and sitting near Sam. With every passing year, new boys and girls are added to our class but my heart remains fully devoted to worshipping at the altar of Sam Spencer. By the time we are in third grade, I am aware that other girls also think Sam is one of the cute boys, but I am secure in the deep foundation we have built starting back in kindergarten. When I sit next to him at lunch, he does not tell me to go away, and that has to mean something. I don't need to tell him I love him or need him to declare his love for me. I just need to sit next to him on the reading carpet and stand as close to him in the lunch line as possible. I'm fulfilled with making him

---

*Name changed to avoid awkward Facebook interactions.

laugh from across the classroom by taking my long brown hair and turning it into a mustache and beard on my face. I think of him as mine, because my heart says he is. What more proof do I need? I never imagine that our relationship will ever need to be spoken about.

One day, we, the students of Ms. Kalicheck's third-grade class, are lined up after lunch. I am locking arms and stifling giggles with my girlfriends Jenna and Alison when Sam taps my shoulder. This is unusual. He is not often the initiator of our conversations. I turn to him very attentively and wait. He opens his mouth to say, "I like Jenna more than you. Do you want to know why?"

The masochist in me answers too quickly. "Why?"

He says, "Because she has blue eyes and lighter skin than you."

He turns around and rejoins his group of boys. I stand there frozen. Ice-cold. Learning how fast a heart beats the first time it is crushed by love, how quietly skin crawls the first time its color is mentioned, how wet eyes become when they realize for the first time that they are, in fact, not blue, like Jenna's, the color Sam likes better. I stand there wishing to return to the moment before Sam taps me on the shoulder, before I learn that it would be better to not look like me, at least if you want the first and only boy you've ever loved to love you back. Which I do.

Shortly after, I learn that it is also better not to look like me if you don't want to be singled out at school and questioned about your parents' immigration status.

It is 1994, and California just voted in favor of Proposition 187—an initiative to deny undocumented immigrants and their children public services, including access to public education for kindergarten through university. There is fear inside the immigrant community that their children will be harassed and questioned in their schools.

I am in third grade and do not know or understand any of this. Nonetheless, my mother pulls me aside one day when she is dropping me off at school and says, "You are American. You were born in this country. If anyone asks you questions, you don't need to feel ashamed or embarrassed. You've done nothing wrong."

I am so confused, but I take my mom's advice and feel the need to spread it. I mention to some of my friends that people might be asking them questions and that they shouldn't be afraid, they've done nothing wrong. They stare blankly at me and then go about their hopscotch. None of my friends seem to know what I'm talking about. I have the sneaking suspicion that their parents did not pull them aside to have the same talk. While I am grilling some more friends on the playground about whether they've been questioned about being American, a big kid I don't know interrupts me to say, "They don't care about *us*. It's just Americans like you." My mind short-circuits. Americans like me? What does that mean? I wasn't aware there were different kinds of Americans. American is American is American. All created equal. Liberty and justice for all. I manage to say something to the big kid, like, "Oh," and I never talk about it at school again. I never talk about it at home either. But I do spend some time wondering what the big kid means by "Americans like you."

Is it about my name? Is it the salsa music at home? Maybe this has something to do with my skin and my non-blue eyes again. That's ridiculous, we don't separate Americans by the color of their eyes. Do we? Are there different words for different kinds of Americans? Am I half American? Kind of American? Other American? I am nine years old, and suddenly I am wondering what do I call an American like me.

As I grew older, I got better at recognizing when someone was trying to tell me that I was not the norm and that I didn't really belong in a given place, which seemed to be just about everywhere. The Latina clique would call me "that wannabe white girl who hangs out with drama kids and does lame Shakespeare competitions" to my face because they thought I didn't understand Spanish. I let them believe that so I could keep eavesdropping. My AP English teacher would excuse my tardies because she assumed I was bused into the neighborhood like most of the other Latino kids. "Bus late again?" she would ask. I'd drop my eyes, take my seat quickly, and never really confirm or deny. The truth was I lived a few blocks from school but hated waking up early. Her assumption that a kid who looked like me didn't really belong in this neighborhood bought me a few extra hours of sleep a week, so I let that one slide.

I may have been a whitewashed gringa in Latino groups, but I was downright exotic to my white friends; especially to their parents, who were always treating me like a rare and precious zoo animal. They'd ooh and aah at my mother's courageous immigrant story, then wish out loud that my hardworking spirit would rub off on their children. They particularly loved having me around when they needed something translated to their housekeepers or gardeners. Seeing such a smart and articulate brown girl was like seeing a dog talk. They were easily impressed.

Even at home I walked a fine line between assimilating to American ways enough to make my mom proud, and adapting in ways that would disgrace and shame her. For instance, bringing home straight-A report cards was a good thing, but attending late-night coed study groups to achieve said A's was shameful and likely to turn me into a drug-addicted, pregnant high school dropout. Decoding people's expectations and then shape-shifting into the version of myself that pleased them the most became my superpower.

Shape-shifting was a useful skill to possess as an aspiring actress, but it didn't stop people from labeling and categorizing me. In fact, when people found out that my dream was to become an actress, they made it their duty to remind me of who I was . . . and who I wasn't.

Family members would say to me bluntly, the way families are prone to do, "Actresses don't look like you. You're brown, short, and chubby." Classmates would say, "You have to know someone to catch a break, and you don't have any connections to the industry." Teachers, hoping they could steer me toward a more sensible career path, would simply ask, "What's your backup plan?" But I wasn't sensible, I was an American, damn it! An American who wholeheartedly believed what she'd been taught her entire life: that in America no dream is impossible, even if you are a short, chubby Latina girl with no money or connections! What was wrong with these people? Didn't they know that in America fortune favored the dreamer willing to work hard? I mostly felt sorry for them and their lack of imagination, and went about working to make my dream come true.

I acted wherever anyone would let me—in school, the local community college, and free community theater programs. I spent one summer riding three buses to get from the Valley to Hollywood in order to play Fagan's Boy #4 in a community theater production of *Oliver!* I babysat kids, looked after my neighbors' pet pig, and waitressed to pay for acting workshops. It was impossible to know which opportunity would open a door to my career, especially in LA, "where there are so many scams designed to take aspiring actors' money," as my mom liked to warn me. But I threw myself and my hard-earned cash at every single opportunity that came my way. And to everyone's surprise, including my own, a few doors started opening for me when I was still only sixteen years old.

To nobody's surprise, except my own, Hollywood was not as ready for me as I imagined. I thought the hard part was getting through the door, and I was sure that as soon as Hollywood saw me in all my glory, passion, and optimism they'd roll out the red carpet and alert the press: America's new sweetheart has arrived!

Somehow the boxes I resisted being shoved into during my childhood were even tighter and more suffocating in Hollywood. The first audition I ever went on, the casting director asked me if I could "try to sound more Latina."

"Ummmm . . . do you want me to do it in Spanish?" I asked.

"No, no, do it in English, just sound like you're a Latina," she clarified.

"But I am Latina, soooo isn't this what a Latina sounds like?" I asked.

"Okay, never mind, honey. Thanks for coming in, byeeee," she said as she waved me toward the door. It took me far too long to understand she wanted me to speak in broken English. And instead of being sad that I didn't get the part, I was angry that she thought sounding Latina meant not speaking English well.

Even after I'd had some great successes with *Gotta Kick It Up!* and *Real Women Have Curves*, two movies that allowed me to play Latina characters who were not just broad stereotypes, I was constantly coming up against people who thought it was silly for me to expect to play a dynamic and complex Latina who was the main character in her own story. Even some of the people I paid to represent me did not believe in my vision for my career. When I was eighteen I told my manager that I was sick of going out for the role of Pregnant Chola #2 or the sassy Latina sidekick. I wanted him to send me out for roles that were grounded and well written. I wanted to play characters who were everyday people with relatable hopes and dreams. His response was "Someone needs to tell that girl she has unrealistic expectations of what she can accomplish in this industry." And the saddest part was that he wasn't wrong. I mean, I fired him, but he wasn't wrong.

After hustling for years to break down doors and working my hardest to prove my talent and grit, I had to admit that the stories I wanted to tell and the characters I wanted to play were virtually invisible from our cultural narrative. I have been supremely lucky to get the opportunities to play some wonderful, authentic, and deep characters, but if I look around at the vast image being painted about the American experience, I see that there are so many of us missing from the picture. Our experiences, our humor, our dramas, our hopes, our dreams, and our families are almost nonexistent in the stories that surround us. And while growing up that way might turn us into badass-Jedi-master-translators-of-culture who are able to imagine ourselves as heroes, villains, or ThunderCats, we deserve to be truly reflected in the world around us.

For seventeen years, I've had a front-row seat to the impact that representation has on people's lives. I've met people who've told me that *Real Women Have Curves* was the first time they ever saw themselves on-screen, and that my character, Ana, inspired them to pursue college, or to stop hating their bodies, or to mend broken relationships with a parent.

I've heard from countless young people who came out to their parents while watching *Ugly Betty*, and young girls who decided they could, in fact, become writers because Betty was a writer.

And, most common, I hear from all kinds of people that they gain confidence and self-esteem when they see themselves in the culture—a brown girl, a brace-face, an aspiring journalist, an underdog, an undocumented father, a gay teen accepted by his family, a gay adult rejected by his mother, a store clerk getting through the day with dignity and a sense of humor, a sisterhood of girls who love and support one another, and, yes, share magical pants—simple portrayals that say in resounding ways, you are here, you are seen, your experience matters.

I believe that culture shapes identity and defines possibility; that it teaches us who we are, what to believe, and how to dream. We should all be able to look at the world around us and see a reflection of our true lived experiences. Until then, the American story will never be complete.

This compilation of personal stories, written by people I deeply admire and fangirl out about on the regular, is my best answer to my nine-year-old self. My plan is to find a time machine and plop this book in her hands at the very moment she first thinks, *What do I call an American like me?* I'll tell her to read these stories and to know that she is not alone in her search for identity. That her feelings of being too much of this, or not enough of that, are shared by so many other creative, talented, vibrant, hardworking young people who will all grow up to transcend labels and become awesome people who do kick-ass things like win Olympic medals, and run for office, and write musicals, and make history that changes the country and the world. And it won't matter what people *called* them, because the missing pieces of the American narrative will be filled in and rewritten and redefined by Americans like her, Americans like you.

Americans like me.

Reshma Saujani is the founder and CEO of Girls Who Code, ran for Congress in 2010 as the first Indian-American woman to do so, and is the proud daughter of refugees. She is the author of *Women Who Don't Wait in Line* and the *New York Times* bestseller *Girls Who Code: Learn to Code and Change the World*.

Reshma Saujani

WHEN I ORDER THE grande chai latte at Starbucks, I almost always lie. It's a white lie, as innocent and airy as the foam on top of the drink, and it's been carefully constructed to make all our lives easier.

"Can I get your name, ma'am?"

"Maya," I say efficiently, pulling out my credit card.

The barista is a teenager with lavender-streaked hair and eyeliner so exquisite and precise, I wish for a fleeting moment I had chosen a more mysterious name, one that might impress her, as exactly nothing seems to do. She scrawls *Maya* on the side of the cup with her Sharpie and I think about Maya. The real Maya whose name I stole for my Starbucks order.

She happens to be my niece. She's a beautiful fifteen-year-old who has no idea I borrow her name regularly. But I do this because the baristas can spell and pronounce it correctly every single time.

————————

"Reshma, you won't find your name there," my mother tells me.

R-E-S-H-M-A. I whirl the squeaky cylinder kiosk around and around, searching for my name in the rows and rows of key chains. They are pink, pale blue, neon green, and black. Printed with gold lettering on each is what seems like every possible name that could be granted to a ten-year-old girl shopping for school supplies at a suburban-Chicago Kmart in 1985:

RACHAEL, RACHEL, RACHELLE, RAINBOW, RAMONA, REBECCA, REGINA, RENE, RHIANNA, RHONDA, RITA, ROBERTA, ROBIN, RORY, ROSANNE, ROSE, ROSEMARY, ROWENA, RUBY, RUTH . . .

The not-my-names dangle in front of me like shiny ornaments on a cruel Midwestern Christmas tree. Two different spellings of Rachel are offered, and to me, a young girl with a surprising sense of justice, this seems fair. There are at least two Rachels in my class at school, but I have never met a Rory or a Rowena, so it doesn't seem just that these names glitter past me on my search for *Reshma.* I am incredulous that somebody out there in America named their daughter Rainbow; enough somebodies, in fact, that each and every girl named Rainbow gets a key chain with her quirky, adorable name on it.

"In Bombay you would be able to find a Reshma key chain," my mother tries to console me.

Reshma, it turns out, is like *Rachel* in India. It is as common and standard a name as they come half a world away. But here in the United States, it is more acceptable to name your daughter Rainbow. My mother is right. There is no *Reshma* printed in gold, jangling on a hook for me. I check the boy-name section, just in case, but I do not find myself there either.

At this moment in time, there is no useless plastic object that could mean more to me. Seeing my name reflected on a cheap trinket would have changed my world. For years to come, I would grow used to this. I would never meet a Cabbage Patch doll with my name—though I did come across one named Rowena in my time. I never read a book about a brown-skinned girl named Reshma, and I never saw another mother wearing a sari and bindi in Kmart.

For a person like me who has run for public office twice and worked on several political campaigns, it is not advisable to admit to lying. But my Starbucks lie is just the first of many harmless assimilations I have perpetrated in my life. I have cultivated several everyday methods for making my name roll off someone else's tongue. At times, I can be jaded about hearing my name butchered over and over again, but I am pragmatic enough to know that you might not have seen my name before, and you might stumble when you try to spell it or pronounce it.

I grew up in Schaumburg, Illinois, a suburb connected to Chicago by a major interstate that brings people there to shop at one of the largest malls in America or happily disappear into a cavernous, endless IKEA. Schaumburg is close to the airport and populated with hotels, golf courses, and restaurants like P.F. Chang's, Outback Steakhouse, and Red Lobster. It wasn't a terrible place to grow up, but for a young brown girl, it was terribly lonely.

Ironically, when you are the only one of your kind, it is difficult to be authentic. You are unique. You don't blend in. This should make it easier to be the real you. Because there's no one like you. But, instead, this is isolating. You are so unique that they don't make a key chain for you. You will never blend in. You can't disappear into the crowd. I remember wanting to be white, wanting my key chain so I could unlock the secret to fitting in, having friends, and being happy. *My life would be better*, I thought, *if only I had blond hair and ate at McDonald's like everyone else.* But Hindus don't eat beef, so I was stuck with vegetable curry, which meant I was always scrubbing my hands and face. I was convinced my classmates could smell it on me (because they taunted me and told me all the time they could smell it on me). I brought white-girl food (bologna, cheese, and mustard on white bread) in my paper-bag lunches at school and kept my head down around Easter and Christmas. A lot of quiet effort went into ensuring that no one found out I didn't pray to Jesus. *White* wasn't necessarily *perfect* or *better* in my mind. But it was *normal.* It had a key chain, a presence, a home in Schaumburg, Illinois.

My parents came to Illinois from Uganda in 1972 after literally throwing a dart at a map of the United States to choose where to start over. The Ugandan dictator Idi Amin expelled them—and all other people of Indian descent—from the country. My parents were both born and raised in Africa. It was all they ever knew. They had engineering careers and a rich community of friends and family. And, suddenly, they were given ninety days to leave.

Before they threw the dart that landed on Illinois, they were denied access to several other countries. The United States was the only nation that would have them. My father immediately began looking for a job as a mechanical engineer and was promptly told by a recruiter that he should Americanize his name and lose the accent. My dad, Mukund, became *Mike.* My mother, Mrudula, became *Meena.* And a few years later, when he was working in a factory and she was working at a cosmetics counter, Mike and Meena had me.

And named me Reshma.

"Why didn't you guys give me a normal name?!" I remember asking this for the first time around the age of ten. I was reading Sweet Valley High books and contemplating how easily they could have made me an Elizabeth or a Jessica. Because even though my parents' name changes may have helped them get jobs, it didn't stop our house from getting regularly egged and TP'd by the kids at school. As we attempted to cover the spray-painted words *dot head go home* off the side of our house, I couldn't help but wonder if maybe they could change *my* name too.

I marveled at what it would feel like to wave your hand and transform everything. One day, *Mukund* was suddenly *Mike*. From that day forward his name was on a key chain. A person could simply authenticate himself as an American and enjoy the American-size horizon of possibilities that came with it. Why shouldn't I blink my eyes and reopen them as a Rebecca?

True to cultural form (at least if you're Indian), my parents didn't talk about personal decisions, emotional hardships, or the numerous dilemmas of safety and identity they must have faced in their young adult lives. They were political refugees with young children, living in a town where they were almost the only Indians. This could not have been easy. More than once, we were told to go back to our own country—a country I was not connected to at all but for my name.

And yet, my parents didn't push their culture on me. Of course I ate vegetarian with them in our house and accepted their pacifist ideals. But they never taught me their language. *Reshma* was my only connection to the fine, exotic, colorful fabric of a country I didn't understand. Even my parents grew up removed from India, the children of immigrants themselves, coming of age in Uganda, living as *Indians away from India.* Sometimes I pondered that they must have given me an Indian name out of loneliness. Maybe it was just nice to utter an Indian name every single day, to count one more Indian person living among them in Schaumburg.

Reshma, I have since learned, means *silken; she who has silky skin,* and I can't help but wonder if Mike and Meena were aware of this definition. Have they come to understand its irony like I have? Do they remember the moment *the girl with the silky skin* became *the girl with the thick skin*?

It was a schoolyard fight and her name was something like Melissa. I have changed it to protect her privacy, but names are important, so I use this one as a substitute. Melissa and her friends often called me names and made fun of the color of my skin. It happened all the time. I became very good at using the middle school tactic of pretending to laugh and be in on the joke. I would ignore how much it hurt and allow them to make fun of me more. *Be a good girl, like your parents taught you. Hindus are pacifists. Don't fight back.* Better to deny myself my anger. Easier to focus on my extreme desire to *just be white.* But when Melissa told me to meet her in the back of the school for a real fight that day, an impulse awakened in me to fight back.

Maybe my sudden chutzpah came from the fact that it was the last day of eighth grade. Summer had finally arrived, and high school was looming. I could start over there. This was my opportunity to stop hiding from them—and myself. To stop wishing to be white, and to start being me.

I arrived at the designated spot behind the school and was met by Melissa, a tennis racket, and a plastic bag full of shaving cream. And also almost every member of the eighth-grade class. Before I could even set down my backpack, they were coming at me. Knuckles crashing into my eye, I blacked out almost immediately.

A few days later, I walked across the stage in my eighth-grade graduation ceremony sporting a black eye and a new attitude. I wasn't going to try to be white anymore. I was brown. And for the first time, I was ready to embrace it.

When I started my freshman year at Schaumburg High School a few months later, I volunteered to start a diversity club. I knew I was going to have to be an active member of the community to defend myself—to *find* myself. So I created Schaumburg High's PRISM, the Prejudice Reduction

Interested Students Movement. Names matter, and I wasn't kidding around when I came up with that one. My confidence was still a little shaky, and I was still struggling to find a way to be proud of what made me different (or "diverse," as the kind, liberal, white teachers in suburban Chicago liked to call it then). Yet I somehow knew that activism was my avenue to fighting prejudice and finding a way to be brave about being me.

One of PRISM's first big events was an assembly where the students of color stood onstage in front of the whole school while the rest of the mostly white students sat in the audience, invited to ask us questions. This was purely my idea. To make a zoo animal of myself and all the other "diverse" kids. There we stood in front of the microphones, Schaumburg High's Indian, black, Latino, and Asian kids, ready to take questions about our identities, our parents' cultures, our souls. Looking back, it seems like this could have been a traumatizing event for a ninth grader, but it was my way of stepping out. I was determined to open a dialogue. I was ready to stand in front of a very white room and shine a spotlight on my very brown face. The questions poured in like bullets from a firing squad:

"Were you born with a dot on your head?"

"Are there terrorists in your home country?"

"Are you an American citizen?"

"How many Hindu gods are there?"

"Do you bathe in curry?"

Despite the vaguely racist questioning, I was proud of what I had organized. I wanted to "reduce prejudice," and the sometimes-insensitive curiosity hurled at me that day was a starting place. And it changed my thinking. It positioned me as the Indian girl who wasn't ashamed. In fact, it actually created a framework for how I discussed my culture with white people for the rest of my life ("Ask me questions," I still tell them). And for the first time, I was publicly expressing some pride in who I was. And I managed to assemble an entire community of fellow kids without key chains.

I was beginning to learn that bravery is like a muscle, and once you flex it, you can't stop. And being authentic requires a lot of bravery. We closed out the PRISM assembly doing a step dance to Aretha Franklin on the loudspeakers, singing the lyrics "Pride, a deeper love! Pride, a deeper love!" This dance was fundamental to everything in my future. I was no longer going through the motions of trying to fit in. I was literally parading my true self right there for all the white kids to see. Pride and bravery were magical feelings, and I wanted more of them.

Years later, when I ran for political office for the first time, I was exercising my bravery again. I had enjoyed several years of a lucrative career at a Wall Street law firm but longed to make my life more about helping to build communities and improving the future of this country. I wanted to push myself. And much like barging into Schaumburg High to start a diversity club, the idea of running for public office felt good—like I was flexing that bravery muscle again. So I bravely quit my job. I bravely ran for Congress. And I bravely lost by a landslide.

But I did it authentically, as myself, as *Reshma*. In the early stages of campaigning, I was told to change my name to Rita, given the advice that people are more likely to vote for you if they can pronounce your name. But my bravery had brought me this far. I wasn't going to stop now. I could never turn my back on Reshma to become a Key-Chain Rita. And losing authentically allowed me to articulate something I was passionate about. I wanted to find a way to address the fact that American girls are often raised to value perfection over bravery. They want to be Sweet Valley Jessicas instead of Schaumburg Reshmas. So I ran my campaign on a platform of bringing computer science into every classroom and making sure girls were given equal access to learning coding. I focused on this because the process of learning to code—building something from the ground up, using trial and error, failing and starting over—allows you to see for yourself that perfection is pretty pointless. And bravery leads to wonderful things.

I should know. After the election loss, I had the gall to start a national nonprofit called Girls Who Code, and I don't even know how to code, myself.

But thanks to my childhood, growing up with two very brave immigrants as parents—who just like me were children of immigrants in Uganda—I now know it is more important than ever to be brave and proud of my identity, to own my role in changing the world, one election loss at a time.

Yes, I did run for office again a few years later. And yes, I lost again. But bravery is contagious.

On election day, I was running around in the rain shaking voters' hands up to the very last minute. I met a woman—I did not catch her name—who was rushing to the polls. As she passed by me, I smiled and said, "Who are you voting for today?"

She hesitated, flustered but kind. Embarrassed she couldn't pronounce it correctly, she fumbled out an *uhh* as she frantically pulled one of my fliers from her bag.

"This woman," she said as she pointed at my name on the piece of paper.

Even though she needed a cheat sheet to remember who she was voting for, I couldn't help but swell with pride that I had an Indian name. I couldn't help but think of my parents. When they chose to name me Reshma, did they dream of a world where it would be unthinkable to go by Rita instead? I had spent years assimilating as a child, and for the first time, I thought I knew why my parents named me Reshma.

Maybe they didn't want me to blend in as much as I thought. They blended in *so I wouldn't have to.* They paid the ultimate price for my authenticity. They gave up their community, their careers, their language, their own *names.* These were the steep taxes they paid to make a better life for me. Assimilating in the ways my parents did can invite accusations. Changing your name and hiding your accent could be seen as passive or fearful gestures. But my parents' immigrant experience reveals the great reserves of bravery and pride they had in order to survive in a new country with no familiar community of support. I think my parents are the bravest people I know. They traded in their names for the freedom and privilege I experience every day. Because of them, I have the platform to be brave. They built the stage I stood on at the PRISM assembly. They laid the groundwork for a little girl named Reshma to grow up and become the first Indian-American woman to run for Congress.

They changed their names so I wouldn't have to.

And while I plastered campaign signs all over my district in New York with bold block letters reading RESHMA, they were still signing "Mike" and "Meena" at the bottom of birthday cards and letters. Even though they had initially Americanized their names purely for their résumés, *Mike* and *Meena* eventually took a very strong hold—as names have a tendency to do. And now even their closest friends and family members call them by their American names. My husband, Nihal, who is of Indian descent himself, calls them Mike and Meena.

Sometimes Nihal and I watch Bollywood movies with our two-year-old son, Shaan, in the hopes he will learn some of the language. I want him to delight in the music and color, and somehow absorb the culture I did not grow up in. He watches with bright wide eyes, and I consider how he will never see my parents as the struggling refugees walking the fine line of sacrifice and assimilation. To Shaan, they are not Mike and Meena. They are the people with loving arms who bring him red lollipops and soccer balls, who light up his whole face every time he sees them.

To Shaan, Mike and Meena are Granddad and Nana.

But to me, they will always be the people who made it possible for a girl named Reshma to grow up in America and name her son Shaan—the Sanskrit word for *pride*.

Best known as the senior Latino correspondent on *The Daily Show with Jon Stewart*, **Al Madrigal** has made a name for himself in both stand-up comedy and acting. He stars in the movie *Night School* and is a series regular and writer on Showtime's *I'm Dying Up Here*. His latest hour special, *Shrimpin' Ain't Easy*, premiered on Showtime in 2017. He is also the cofounder of the All Things Comedy podcast network.

Al Madrigal

IT'S TOUGH TO ADMIT but . . . I'm frugal. I love a deal . . . because I'm cheap. Madrigal men, as far back as I can find, have always been cheap. It's in our DNA. Our family crest has a knight shoving Tapatío packets into his sheath metal. Most likely our thriftiness comes from the fact that my Mexican grandfather, Liborio Madrigal, came here with nothing. Many immigrants come to this country with nothing. But Liborio had less than that. The only thing he had on him when he entered the state of Texas was a stab wound.

The story is—and I just learned this at a family reunion—my grandfather, a successful rancher in El Chante, Mexico, near Guadalajara, was in his house in the middle of the night. Somebody pounds on his door. My grandfather answers the door; guy stabs him twice in the side. Apparently, this was pre-peephole. I have a difficult time opening the door for Girl Scouts holding *my* cookies, so I'm definitely not going to open up for someone who's stab-ready. The backstory is that my grandfather was in love with this guy's wife and the guy wasn't taking it so well. So he decided to employ some 1920s Guadalajaran revenge tactics. Couple of stabs.

So my grandfather says, "Not here, not here. Let's go to the outskirts of town where all the murdering is done." They get out there. The guy takes out his knife. My grandfather takes out his machete. *Rock, paper, scissors* . . . Machete beats knife. The guy is dead in one blow. My grandfather knows the guy is a nephew of an infamous Mexican general, so he gets the hell out of there, rides his horse *No Country for Old Men*–style into Texas, where he works with the Chinese building the railroad. If you've ever taken a train, you're welcome. Then he makes his way up to San Francisco, where he meets my grandmother. Long story short, that's why I'm sitting here now writing about the roots of my thriftiness.

I'm not suggesting that all Mexicans are penny-pinchers or that all immigrants are cheap, only that we have to do the most with what little we have—and Madrigals are no different. My dad, like a true Madrigal, loved nothing more than negotiating with people and getting a great deal. He passed that on to me and I certainly have passed that on to my kids. Dad had a taste for the finer things in life. He just didn't want to pay full price for them.

So here are some guidelines that I learned from my father. Not because he formally laid anything out but just my own list I compiled through watching him operate.

Number 1: Prey on the new guy. You think you want the veteran salesperson. You're wrong. That guy already has a Jacuzzi. You ideally want the person who doesn't really know what they're doing. You're looking for the weak in the herd. My father would call up car dealers and manipulate his way into getting the new guy on the phone. He'd say, "I was just talking to the new guy . . . What's his name again?" You wanna show up at the end of the month when he has to meet his quota and they want to give those guys some wins.

Number 2: Show very little interest. As a matter of fact, go a step further and *insult* the thing you want. "Gray interior? I really had my heart set on tan." If it looks like you want it, they know they got you. And everybody's gotta be down with the plan. You can't have your spouse there saying, "Honey, you don't love tan! Remember?! You hate the tan. Remember how you said you spit on tan? It was either gray or you'd rather take the bus! Remember when you said that?"

Number 3: Get deep into the process. Then walk away. If you don't walk away at least once from the thing you want to buy and the person who's trying to sell you that thing, you're not even trying. And tell them exactly where you're going. "I'm gonna go check out another place in—[*insert shithole city right here.*]" If they know you're willing to drive to Van Nuys or Rancho Cucamonga or Stockton, they know you mean business. What you're saying is, there are better deals out there, and if you don't give us a better price, we're going to go consider them. You've got to be the fish that got away.

Number 4: Whenever possible, have cash. Your cash needs to be organized. Your cash needs to be ready to go at a moment's notice, 'cause you're gonna show 'em that cash. And you want the person that you're dealing with to be convinced they're getting all the cash you have. "This amount in my hand, that you're seeing, is all I've got. . . . And it could be yours . . . If you would just take it . . . and give me that vintage mid-century lamp."

When I was twelve, I remember my father running into the house and saying, "I found it, I found it. And I need cash now!"

My mother had no idea what was going on. "What?! You found what?!"

"The Mercedes. Boz Scaggs is getting a divorce, and it's ugly! He's having a fire sale before his wife can get her hands on any of the money!"

So we went to the bank to get cash, and then we drove over to Boz Scaggs's Russian Hill apartment as a family. And that day, my dad drove away with his 1972 dark champagne 450SEL. And that car, that was sold to him out of spite, couldn't have made him any happier. Please imagine my little five-foot-six dad wearing driving gloves and humming "Lido Shuffle." We got a taste for the finer things in life, but we didn't want to pay anywhere close to full price for them.

So Boz Scaggs's messy divorce leads me to my fifth and final guideline: Where there is deep sorrow, there are deep savings. That Mercedes wasn't the only time a celebrity's troubled life allowed my father to practically steal a luxury item. No, that car just whet his appetite. Now, I'm not going to say the boxer's name. Let's just say it rhymes with Oscar De La Oya. That boxer may or may not have gotten in trouble with the *Federales*, who told him to never return to Cabo San Lucas. To this day we are the proud owners of his bodyguard's condominium. Not his! His bodyguard's. Now, why does a boxer need a bodyguard? I don't know. But what I do know is it's on the sand, has a full ocean view, and currently appraises for 600 percent of its purchase price. Boom!

Remember: Deep sorrow, deep savings. Now don't get me wrong, I'm not gonna buy a murder house, but a messy divorce? I'll take that flat-screen off your hands. To this day, when I drive by an estate sale, something tingles inside me. You see a dead grandma; I see a cabinet full of jadeite bowls. Am I right?

Having internalized the Madrigalean methods and techniques, I have proudly passed these lessons along to my children. I found the perfect opportunity with my son when he was just eight years old. The two of us were walking our dog in Eagle Rock and we stumbled upon a garage sale. Not just any garage sale. Divorced dad and his two young product-of-divorce sons. Deep sorrow? Check! On display was an entire table dedicated to kids' toys. The tit-for-tat one-upmanship of their broken relationship on full display. Me and my son made our way over to the toy table and he noticed hundreds of Pokémon cards.

To this day, I don't know how the game works. All I do know is that from eight to nine years old, kids love Pokémon. At exactly the age of nine, they fall out of favor, and you're left with hundreds of unwanted cards. I knew he wanted the cards, mainly because his eyes lit up, and he started shaking, which I quickly shut down. I told him to go look at the puzzles so we could come up with a plan.

Rule number two, don't show any interest. The two sales kids were even more excited that someone was showing interest in something on their table. And then their dad came over to supervise the possible transaction. So I asked the kids, "How much for these puzzles?"

"Fifty cents for the puzzles."

I said, "Okay, and what are these? Pokémon cards?"

The dad then quickly explained that they weren't just any Pokémon cards. The Pokémon cards had been divided into three categories. Category one: a shoebox full of loose, run-of-the-mill, lower-end cards. Category two: a binder filled with your better, midrange cards organized neatly in protective sleeves. And category three: a small, hardcover leather-bound Pokémon book with only the highest-quality, rare Pokémon cards. The kind only a true Pokémon aficionado or a sad divorced dad, willing to throw money at his kids' affection, would dare to buy. The father confirmed that the book did not contain just *any* cards, and that his boys didn't just *casually* play Pokémon at school. He had spent hundreds of dollars on these cards. They went to tournaments and, with the contents of this book, fucked up some other divorced dads and their kids. I acknowledged that they were something. I could see how proud he was of them.

It was time for rule number three. We walked away. My son couldn't understand what was happening. Those were the best cards he'd ever seen. I produced a ten-dollar bill and explained the plan. "We're going to go back to those Pokémon cards and we're going to listen to everything that they have to say without saying a word. The dad's going to talk about the tournaments again. Which I will never do by the way. I don't care how good these cards are. He's going to talk about how much money they spent on the cards. And how rare they are. He's gonna try and sell you some of the cards from the shoebox. Maybe some from the binder. But when they're done talking I want you to take this ten-dollar bill out of your pocket. Show it to the younger of the two kids. The shorter one with the sad eyes. And say, 'All I have is this ten dollars. And I want the book.'"

And as that boy snatched the ten dollars out of my son's hand, the dad looked at me as if to say, "You motherfucker. I know what you did. You preyed on the new guy." But I was too busy holding my son's hand, walking away, humming "Lido Shuffle."

Watching my son execute that deal was one of the proudest moments I've had as a father. Sure, I was happy he'd gotten his Pokémon cards, as short-lived as his interest in them would be. But I was happier that he'd learned this skill. He was now a true Madrigal man. I knew I had passed on a lesson that would serve him well for the rest of his life. Only suckers pay full price, and Madrigals are no suckers.

I realized something else that day. We're not actually cheap. It's not about frugality; it's about resourcefulness. Just like my grandfather talked his enemy into changing locations so he could win the great stabbing battle of El Chante, my father had employed his own resourcefulness and passed it on to me. And then I passed it on to my son, who used it to score some badass Pokémon cards. Sure, the stakes in those two stories aren't the same, but the lesson is: *do what you can with what you have*. If my grandfather hadn't known this lesson, I wouldn't be here today to share this story with my own son. Knowing where I came from made all the difference.

Someday, my own grandson might be hearing a story about his father and me while he learns how to strike a deal of his own. I hope so, and I hope he remembers to prey on the new guy.

PHOTO BY JENNY ZHANG'S MOM

Jenny Zhang is the author of the poetry collection *Dear Jenny, We Are All Find* and the story collection *Sour Heart*, which won the 2018 PEN/Robert W. Bingham Prize. She was born in Shanghai and grew up in Queens.

Jenny Zhang

SIZZLER WAS WHERE WE went to have steak and salad, not to mention one of the rare instances when my family used forks and knives (we had exactly two forks in the house growing up and some butter knives my grandfather scavenged from a literal dumpster) instead of chopsticks (we ate everything with chopsticks—fried eggs; pork chops; tiny, little green peas—nothing was too big or too small). It was also one of the few times I was permitted to order a soft drink (normally ordering a beverage at a restaurant was seen by my parents as a colossal waste, as it didn't require any significant human labor or ingenuity to pour liquid into a glass, and, on top of that, it was cheaper to buy soda in bulk at the supermarket). The rationale behind allowing it at Sizzler was because dinner was so cheap that it made my parents feel rich. It was the highest order of indulgence, and I loved it. Fruit punch was my potion of choice. It came with free refills and tasted like bubble gum, the latter of which, in my estimation, was double magic, how the flavor of one thing could conjure up the chewy gumminess of another. Sizzler was where I became a budding synesthete.

At home, my parents mercilessly mocked American habits of eating: steak was nothing more than "a slab of rubbery meat without any seasoning," salad was a pathetic assortment of bottom-shelf reject vegetables like iceberg lettuce, soggy cucumbers, soapy shreds of carrots, thrown together—"you can hardly call that cooking!" By contrast, in our culinary lives, we were used to food with *flavor, depth, complexity*—sautéed strips of beef with asparagus seasoned with oyster sauce; hand-folded dumplings plump with ginger, pork, and chives; massive hot pots crammed full of fresh crab; fish balls stuffed with minced meat, shrimp, vermicelli noodles, daikon radish, tofu sheets, six different types of mushrooms, eight different types of green, leafy vegetables that didn't even have English names. We dined like royalty while living like vermin, often four or five families crammed into a single-family house, everyone sleeping and sitting and eating off furniture found on the sidewalk on garbage days. It was a strange kind of poetry how my family managed to eat so decadently on a fraction of the income our white counterparts raked in. Even stranger were the things white people were willing to shell out money for: a dry slice of turkey, a pile of steamed vegetables. *These people are mad!* I would often overhear my father saying to my mother.

During our early years in America, my family, like all "good" immigrants, made many attempts to blend in. Food was the most accessible avenue, and so we went down it . . . or at least tried to, but the so-called American dream of assimilation tasted terrible. The worst was the time when we saved up for months to treat ourselves to fresh lobsters from Maine and realized Americans *boiled* their lobster. *Boiled!!!* we cried in astonishment to each other. To Chinese people, boiling your food was about as impressive as pouring water into a glass. It was something a child could do blindfolded. It was what you did if you were ever in the position to serve dinner to your enemy. It was like kicking dirt into the air and saying, *Here you go, enjoy.*

But we made an exception for Sizzler. This was the early nineties, during Sizzler's heyday, when it aired commercials targeted at the segment of the population who wanted to have three-course meals but could only afford Cup Noodles, a.k.a. people like my family. Sizzler embodied the very essence of America—that even the poor could be greedy, overstuffed even, as they filled themselves on endless plates of food. At Sizzler, flavor and skill were beside the point, as the point was to eat as much food as possible. For my parents—who were born into a decade-long famine that killed somewhere between thirty-six and forty-five million people, who were so malnourished as children that they would sometimes eat expired plain flour fried in oil that had been reused dozens of times for sustenance, and who were unable to grow hair on their arms and legs even after the famine ended—for them, the phrase "all you can eat" was intoxicating. It was like being told: anyone could win the lottery! The concept was unheard-of for people like my parents who grew up in China, where there was never enough to eat. My father was the first to try it after being taken there by some colleagues from work. The next weekend, he took my mother and me to try it, and from that point on, we were hooked.

It was $5.99 for the all-you-can-eat salad bar and $7.99 for a steak dinner, and because I was so small I qualified for the even more reduced children-ten-and-under pricing. At those prices, and with the buffet selection, which included an ice-cream-sundae bar, we could tolerate any amount of underseasoning or oversteaming. My father would always order the steak dinner, and my mother and I would get the salad bar buffet, the scam being that, in the end, there was nothing stopping all three of us eating from the salad bar. As long as my father kept his plate of steak at the table, we felt free to bring plate after plate back, heaping with chicken wings, french fries, rubbery filets of unidentifiable white fish covered in a mustardy, buttery sauce, spaghetti and meatballs, macaroni and cheese, every permutation of raw veg-etables and salad dressing, ice-cream sundaes with whipped cream, fudge, car-amel, sprinkles, and chocolate chips. It was at the Sizzler salad bar and buffet that I was finally permitted to try Jell-O and realized, to my great disappoint-ment, that it was horrible. It was at the Sizzler salad bar and buffet that I be-came addicted to shrimp scampi, a dish that bore no affinity to the flavor or texture of the fresh shrimp I was used to having in Chinese restaurants and at home. This kind of shrimp was merely a vessel for butter and parsley. It was at Sizzler that my father developed a taste for sirloin steak, medium rare, and my mother discovered she liked ranch dressing. Sometimes the two of them would hover by the salad bar and wait for the next batch of king crab legs, a hot commodity that lasted exactly a minute before it was all scooped up. My parents were hell-bent on eating as much king crab legs as possible. Anything that expensive, we'd eat. Whether it tasted good or not didn't matter; all that mattered was that we ate double, triple, and quadruple what we paid for. We'd eat until our bellies were distended, until even the last notch on our belt was too constrictive. We'd walk laps around the salad bar for ten minutes to speed up digestion so we could eat more. Once, when my grandparents from Shanghai were living with us for six months, we took them to Sizzler, and my grandfather, so overwhelmed and giddy at being presented with the concept of all-you-can-eat, ate until he had to vomit, then came back and proudly de-clared, "Now I can eat more!" It was a marathon sport for us, it made us feel like we had beat the system. "We've earned it all back," my mother would say, beaming after polishing off her *tenth* plate of food.

In our early years, the kind of American food that was accessible to my family, who had come over to New York by way of Shanghai in the late eight-ies and struggled at the edge of the poverty line, was fast food and the occa-sional TGI Fridays–type establishment where the cost of a meal would have been exorbitant if it weren't for a family friend or two who moonlit as waiters and slid us free appetizers and drinks. Neither were worthy competitors against the Chinese food my parents cooked at home. Sizzler, however, was the exception. It appealed to my parents' thriftiness, and it appealed to their desire to embrace the American fantasy that there was plenty to go around for everyone!

As my family started to become upwardly mobile, our trips to Sizzler became less and less frequent. It was no longer satisfying to eat until we wanted to puke; it no longer felt like we were robbing the restaurant of its profits; it felt instead like we were robbing ourselves of health, comfort, taste. Like all things too good to be true in our consumer-capitalist society, the quality of food went down as the prices went up. Eventually, in 1996, Sizzler went bankrupt and closed a ton of restaurants. Around the same time, my family moved out of the mostly Asian and Central American immigrant enclave in Queens to a far wealthier, majority-white suburb on Long Island, where there weren't any Chinese supermarkets or restaurants serving the kind of Chinese food we knew and loved. The white kids in my school mocked me whenever I brought Chinese food in for lunch. Just as my family placed American food on the lowest of rungs, the white kids I encountered did the same with Chinese food—it was too oily; it produced the kind of flatulence that shook heaven and earth; it had primitive flavor profiles; it was unhealthy. Everything we thought about American food was mirrored back to us with regards to our food. The Chinese food I grew up eating was so abundant, varied, fresh, light, bursting with flavor, and yet somehow always cheaper than American food. This is what I knew, but at my new school, I had no allies to back me up on my claims. My classmates mostly ate greasy Chinese take-out that had no resemblance to the Chinese food we ate at home or in restaurants. Whenever my family went to Chinese restaurants in our mostly white neighborhood, the Chinese restaurant owners would apologize profusely in advance for catering to American tastes. "That's how they like it," the owner would say, shaking his head while we waited for our order—"slathered in flour, drowning in MSG, and deep-fried. That's what these people want."

Over time my parents eventually developed a gag reflex against "American" food. The sight of a chicken breast made my father queasy, whereas my mother became unilaterally opposed to white food, as in food that was literally the color white. With the exception of white rice, my mother could no longer tolerate any and all white-colored foods—mashed potatoes, cream of broccoli soup, Alfredo sauce, even her once-favorite ranch dressing was now repulsive. As for me, I still craved, from time to time, that garlicky, buttery shrimp scampi, picking it out of the linguine, since carbs had to be avoided at all costs when partaking in a Sizzler's buffet (they filled you up too quickly and were a waste of money). Even more, I continued to dream of drinking fruit punch that tasted like bubble gum—two things that were so all-American, whereas I was so not. Constantly, I was reminded of how not all-American I was. From the way my eyelids looked, to the way my last name sounded, to the way the back of my head sloped, to the dances I wasn't allowed to go to, to the homes of my classmates that I wasn't permitted to hang out in—and even if my parents had let me, no one was inviting me anyway. I was a lonely, strange teen who lived mostly in the past and the future, as both were more romantic than the present.

The loneliness of being different turned out to be more than bearable, it spurred an interest in wanting to learn about the deep roots of racism and xenophobia in this country, and anyway, adolescence ultimately did not scar me, but fortified me. Though there wasn't much that could penetrate my teen angst during those years, I do remember one particularly low evening, when I couldn't wait for time to go any faster, when all I wanted was to skip forward in time, when I was in the back seat of my parents' car, driving through Queens, and we drove past the Sizzler on Northern Boulevard, abandoned and lifeless, but still with the old sign intact. Seeing it again, the part of my brain that felt pleasure and joy lit up like crazy, remembering how when we pulled into the parking lot, the three of us would become ebullient, knowing that we were about to have the most special of nights—a night when we could eat like a bunch of sloppy Americans and come home, happy and in pain, vowing to never do it again, knowing we would surely do it again.

Bambadjan Bamba is an actor, filmmaker, and immigrant activist. He is the proud son of Ivorian immigrants.

Bambadjan Bamba

WHEN I WAS TEN years old, in the winter of 1992, my family moved to the South Bronx from Côte d'Ivoire in West Africa. For my family, moving to America meant falling from upper-middle class to poverty. Back then, my pops was a high-level banker and we were "balling." We lived in the best neighborhood in Abidjan, we attended posh French private schools and spent Christmas Eve at the Hotel Ivoire ice-skating rink. Yep, ice skating in Africa. Imagine that! When I landed in the cold concrete jungle that is the South Bronx, nothing could have prepared me for the brutal culture shock I was about to experience. We lived about a mile away from Yankee Stadium. Right off the 167th Street stop on the 4 train. It was the hood but a step above the projects. It was a predominantly Puerto Rican, Dominican, African-American, and African community. This was pre-Giuliani era, so you could get robbed for your sneakers and MetroCard just walking down the block. Not speaking a lick of English and having a name like Bambadjan Bamba definitely didn't help.

My first day of school at James McCune Smith P.S. 200 was probably the worst day of my life. The only advice or warning I was given by my pops was "*Il ne faut pas te battre sinon tu va en prison.*" Translation: "Don't get into a fight or else you will go to jail." It was the first week of January in 1993, right after the winter break. I was three weeks shy of my eleventh birthday, which meant I belonged in the fifth grade, but I ended up in the fourth—probably because my parents didn't speak English either. But that one little mistake made me lie about my age throughout all of grade school. I didn't want my friends to think that I was left back a grade and therefore I was stupid. I was the biggest people pleaser in the world, but we will get to that later.

If getting left back wasn't bad enough, I was thrown in a Spanish ESL class because that was all there was for someone like me. The school was primarily African-American, Puerto Rican, and Dominican kids. The only other French-speaking person in the entire school was a kid named Alpha, who was from another African country. The teacher called him from his class and asked him to hang with me the entire day to show me the ropes. When I met him, he seemed thrown off by my excitement, but I was hyped because I wasn't the only African kid anymore. Alpha was going to help me figure this whole thing out. I started asking him mad questions. When I spoke French to him, he responded in monosyllables as if he wasn't proud of speaking French. I'd say, "Why are the kids in class coloring and not learning multiplication tables?" He just shrugged. I kept the questions coming. "Why are there police officers in the school?" And "Where the heck are all the white kids?" He just shrugged again and said, "*Je sais pas.*" Translation: "I don't know." Then I asked him how to ask the teacher to go to the bathroom. He told me to raise my hand and say, "Kiss my ass." Not only did I raise my hand, but I also stood up like we did in Côte d'Ivoire and said, with the thickest African accent you can imagine "Kiss. My. Ass." The entire class was on the floor rolling, including Alpha, who couldn't contain himself. The teacher got a bit stern with him and the entire class and said, "Bambadjan needs everybody's help to adjust." Yeah right! Then, the bell rang and all the kids jetted out of class, just like in *Saved By the Bell*. The teacher told Alpha to escort me to the bathroom and then to the cafeteria for lunch.

Of course he tried to lead me to the girls' bathroom, but I didn't fall for that one, because I saw the pictures on the doors. He was having the time of his life misleading the FOB (fresh off the boat) African kid. What he didn't know was that I had a reputation for being a trickster in Abidjan, but since I promised my parents I wouldn't get into a fight and I didn't want to go to jail, I played it cool. As we headed to the cafeteria I was so excited to have American food. Until then, all I had in Abidjan was our version of overmarinated French-style pizzas and hamburgers. The cafeteria looked and smelled like a hospital. There was nothing appetizing about the way the food was presented either. The food looked like it had been in the freezer forever. I chose lasagna, because it looked like spaghetti. I also got the cup of mixed fruit. For drinks, the only options were small red and brown cartons. I asked Alpha which one was sweet, and he told me the red carton. When we sat down to eat, I almost puked! The food had no taste at all. The lasagna was dry as hell, and the cheese inside smelled disgusting. The mixed fruit was slimy. How can people eat this? Alpha was laughing so hard he was almost crying. The straw that broke the camel's back was the unsweetened, cold white milk. First of all, I couldn't get the carton open! After trying a few times I just ripped it. Now, mind you, in Abidjan milk has to be warmed and sweetened before you drink it. As soon as the nasty cold milk hit my tongue I spit it out. It was almost like a gag reflex. Alpha was laughing out loud by now with tears in his eyes. That was it. I grabbed the chocolate milk off his tray, ripped it open, and tried it. It was sweet. I guzzled it down quickly. Alpha wasn't laughing anymore. He took his tray and jetted outside in a fit of anger. I was actually smiling now, because I had finally given him a taste of his own medicine.

I didn't see Alpha again until the final bell rang when school was letting out. When I got outside to the playground, kids were coming up to me telling me something about Alpha. I didn't understand anything other than the word *Alpha*. I felt kind of bad and wanted to talk to him. Before I got to the exit I saw him with a group of kids behind him. *"Alpha il y a quoi?"* Translation: "What's going on?" I tried to talk to him in French, but he pushed me back and started swinging. I was completely caught off guard, because I never imagined that he would go from zero to one hundred over chocolate milk. He kept swinging at me, and I kept backing up, trying to talk some sense into him. He wasn't hearing it. We were surrounded by a crowd egging him on. I wasn't used to boxing, because in Abidjan we would wrestle. I grabbed him and tried to hold him close, but he broke free and clocked me with a couple of good ones to the chin. My temper started to rise, but I couldn't allow myself to fight back and get arrested. An officer stopped the fight, Alpha said a few things, and they let him go home, but I ended up in the principal's office. I was upset because I couldn't express myself, and I was scared because I thought I was going to end up in jail. Plus it was guaranteed that my pops was going to tear my ass up when we got home.

When my pops showed up, he was visibly angry. I did the one and only thing he told me not to do. I tried to explain to him how I didn't fight back because he told me not to. He yelled in the most disappointed tone you could imagine. *"La ferme!"* Translation: "Shut up." *"Quand j'avais ton age, je ne laissais pas mes amis me frapper."* Translation: "When I was your age, I never let my friends beat me up." That statement broke my heart. He disregarded the fact that I kept my word to him in the face of being ridiculed in front of the entire school. I guess he, too, was trying to teach me what he had to learn the hard way. In America, he didn't have any family around, or a family village as a plan B in case it didn't work out in the city. He went from traveling the world and making huge financial deals for the bank to driving people in a gypsy taxicab. He was alone in a new country with new rules and he was doing his best to provide for his family. He had enough on his mind and didn't have time for any additional unnecessary nonsense. Even Alpha was probably trying to take some heat off his back too. Now that I was here, he wasn't the only African kid anymore. They say hindsight is twenty-twenty but in my ten-year-old mind I didn't understand any of this. All I felt was betrayal from my pops and that I needed to teach Alpha a lesson.

The next couple of weeks in school were like breaking out of jail every day. After the final bell rang I had to run as fast as I could to catch the train because a mob was after me to jump me. I had become the punk African kid who didn't fight back. They called me African booty scratcher and Kunta Kinte. They asked me if people wore clothes in Africa and if we slept in trees with monkeys. The jokes were never ending. I kept trying to figure out why it was mostly African-American kids I had the most beef with. I finally caught up with Alpha and actually kicked his behind, but beating Alpha down didn't help me much because I was still African. Back then, being African made you a target. We didn't have Akon, Idris Elba, or Black Panther. All people knew of Africa in the hood was *Roots* (the TV miniseries, not the band!), African safari programs on the Discovery channel, and charity ads about starving kids. Those ridiculous stereotypes about Africa were perpetuated everywhere you turned on television and in the movies. The way that dehumanization manifested in the minds of kids was that since Africa equals war, disease, and poverty, then being African made you an easy target for bullying.

My new MO was that if I was to survive in this new world, I had to learn English and be as American as possible. My solution was to watch a lot of television. I would not miss an episode of *Teenage Mutant Ninja Turtles*, *Gargoyles*, *The Fresh Prince of Bel-Air*, *Family Matters*, and *Martin*. Those television shows were instrumental in the beginning—especially for learning what was cool in America and what wasn't. For example, being smart made you a dork. I couldn't understand the logic. Dumb guys were popular and got all the girls. It was the complete opposite in Abidjan. There, it was a ranking system, and if you were last in class you were humiliated.

Within a couple of months I was fluent in English, but I was still being bullied for being African because I didn't have the fly gear and my pops was not going to buy me anything above Payless knockoffs. I had to figure out how to make money. I started bagging groceries at the corner Dominican store, and people gave me their change. I remember the day I saved enough money to buy my first pair of white-and-blue Grant Hill I shoes. The smell of brand-new sneakers was heavenly; the fly designs with the big *F* and Fila on the base that continued into a wave of white on the side of the sneakers was immaculate. The first time I stepped out in them, I didn't want to walk too fast because I didn't want to put a crease or a stain on them. Fly sneakers in the hood earned you respect! And that day, I was respected. People were blown away. How the hell was this poor African kid able to afford these dope sneakers? It all started to come together once I started wearing fly gear, but it wasn't until I discovered hip-hop that it all clicked. The Fugees, Snoop Dogg, Tupac, Jay-Z, and Wu-Tang literally raised me. I knew side A of Ma$e's tape *Harlem World* by heart, from beginning to end. There's cool and then there's hip-hop cool.

Fast-forward two years. I had completely lost my accent and I was down with hip-hop, doing everything possible to hide the fact that I was African. I spent most of my time hanging with a neighborhood crew. We got into a lot of trouble, but we had each other's backs. No one could mess with me anymore. No one said my real name ever—my friends called me BJ. I was finally "cool." But deep down I was a fraud, desperately trying to be someone I wasn't, which was so obvious to everyone else except me. Eventually my boys asked: "What's up with you? We know that you're African. Why don't you ever represent where you're from?" That was a huge question for me to answer. While I was trying so hard to become American, I internalized all the pain and anger. It wasn't until that moment that I realized that I was ashamed of being African.

That realization made me do some serious soul-searching over the next couple of years. It is said, "When you submit your will to other people's opinion, a part of you dies." Well, I was dying inside, because I was a people pleaser. I spent most of my time trying to be something I wasn't just so I could survive and fit in with my peers. I was trying to be my idea of cool. It wasn't until I started studying acting in college that I allowed myself to emotionally explore how this internalized resentment affected my life. As an actor you have to draw from your own personal emotional bank to breathe life into characters. I did not have the capacity of being my authentic self. I usually said things for the sole purpose of having a desired effect on people. I had become a master manipulator. It was hard as hell to acknowledge it and be that vulnerable with others, but it was the most important self-improvement journey of my life. I started keeping a personal "emotional bank" journal as a way of training myself to express my true feelings. Over and over again, I would force myself to confront how I really felt about circumstances in my daily life that may have previously inspired me to default to people-pleasing or manipulating. Telling people what they wanted to hear was disempowering. Truly understanding the deep effects that this self-hatred was having on my soul was liberating.

I started doing some research to find African role models that I could look up to. I had a mirror in my room, and I put pictures of my African heroes all around its edges, so when I looked at myself, I saw them too. From Thomas Sankara, the revolutionary Burkinabe president who's considered the African Che, to Kwame Nkrumah, the first president of Ghana, who started the Pan-African movement toward independence. I fell in love with the prime minister of Congo Patrice Lumumba, who was assassinated by the CIA. Marcus Garvey, Bob Marley, Martin Luther King Jr., and Malcolm X. Reading about these powerful black leaders and understanding the history and lasting effects of slavery, colonialism, and imperialism helped me understand the African struggle. I started to value the age-old traditions and saw the wisdom in them. I saw the beauty in respecting my elders. I learned to accept that my parents' way of saying "I love you" was by praying for me and blessing me. Hip-hop played a big role in my journey. Lauryn Hill's *Unplugged* album, Kanye's *The College Dropout*, and Blitz the Ambassador's *Soul Rebel* became the soundtrack to my search for authenticity.

I was curious and interested in connecting with the African community in NYC and sought to hang out with other Africans like me who grew up here but still honored their culture. It gave me a sense of purpose, belonging, and pride in being African. It was around that time that my acting career started taking off. As an artist, being authentic and having a distinct voice has been one of my greatest assets. I still have a lot of work to do, but I've made a lot of progress.

My past experiences have helped me define what it means to be American. It has nothing to do with speaking perfect English, trying to be the American version of cool, or fitting into a mold. It's about celebrating the diverse cultures and heritage that enrich this country. It's about playing your part to help make it a better one.

Becoming the best version of you is hard as hell—and it takes time. But as long as I'm doing that, I'm cool.

Padma Lakshmi is a *New York Times* bestselling author, the host and an executive producer of Bravo's *Top Chef*, and an ambassador for immigration/women's reproductive health for the ACLU. She lives in New York with her daughter.

Padma Lakshmi

I HAVE NEVER BEEN a very religious person. My sweet mother would beg to differ. Seeking the best education America could provide her Indian Hindu child, she enrolled me in Catholic elementary school in Queens, New York. One day, while she was putting me to bed, I confessed that I was terrified because I ate some cookies without permission and thought Baby Jesus was going to be mad and send me straight to hell.

The next day she marched right into the principal's office at drop-off to explain that it was the math and reading she was really paying for and that they were to exempt me from as much of the biblical religiosity as possible without offending their beliefs or other students. And so, from then on, and well into first grade, I was relegated to sitting in "Siberia"—at the back of the church—as my classmates rehearsed for their First Communion. I looked on longingly as they planned for their big day, replete with frills, shiny patent Mary Janes, and lacy white veils.

Catholicism seemed so much more glamorous and manageable to me than my own strange Hindu religion, rife with literally thousands of gods, goddesses, demigods, and semidemons, who could be good, bad, or just weird depending on what boons had been granted through a complicated series of Sanskrit-laden penances. Catholicism was straightforward. You did what Jesus said, or you went to hell—period and end of story. None of this attaining atman, dharma, or nirvana through years of penance or karma, and then only if you were in the right caste, horoscope, et cetera, et cetera. No "life is cyclical"; no "there are all these realms." No layers of reincarnation before you even could entertain what the heck heaven was or meant.

Catholicism was pure, usually practiced in hushed tones with whispered prayers, and just one book to carry. There was only one serene-looking benevolent lady they called the Virgin, in a light blue veil, who always seemed to have her hands free and outstretched for holding the hands of children and shepherds, or clasped in prayer as she looked inexplicably, sheepishly, calmly off to the side (never mind the near-naked guy who liked to hang out on a cross with a really uncomfortable-looking crown who was supposed to be her son). The Catholic Church was peaceful, soothingly dark, and had order to it. Everyone seemed to know their place, their row or pew, and in what order to line up for their snack, given for being good until the end of mass, by the fully clothed and beautifully robed priest.

Hinduism, on the other hand, had several books and was cacophonous, loud, the chanting incessant, with no seeming beginning or end to its procedures, like mass, and no order ruling its patrons during any of these rituals. While, in truth, our blessed snacks or *prasadams* at the end were much more varied, and did taste far better, one could never tell what was real food and what was "blessed" food and therefore was required, mandatory eating. Add to this fact that our priests were scantily clad in white loincloths and it wasn't enough to kneel and say brief prayers at bedtime and go to church before brunch on Sundays. No, you had to actually wake up at five each morning as my mom did, to bathe, light the oil lamp and incense, and sit on the floor uncomfortably cross-legged and read scriptures from the Ramayana and chant prayers a hundred and eight times before you got to get up. I would take ten Hail Marys any day.

My well-meaning, immigrant mother, trying mightily to preserve my heritage and spiritual culture in spite of our American surroundings, sent me to India every summer for three months as soon as school got out in June, to help me retain my all-important *Indianness*. When I returned from India for second grade, my mother was delighted to take me to the newly consecrated Hindu temple in Flushing. This, at the time, consisted of only one big plain room that had a modest deity in it, with no architectural flourish whatsoever. Where were the church bells in a tower; the ominous-sounding organ, or, at the very least, the large imposing stone carved structures with *gandharvas*; or voluptuous women figurines, like in the cone-shaped temples I had just left in South India? My mom would definitely have to try harder if I was going to forsake Jesus. I couldn't believe this is what my mother thought would seduce me away from the cult of Mary and the Holy Ghost (whoever that was).

I knew enough even back then not to openly ridicule her though. My mother's piousness ran deep, and this was indicated to me whenever I came to her with a problem that invariably originated from some culture clash or other. My mother, while thinking she could really help, simply said that I should pray to Ganesh for guidance. (We were more like the Catholics than she knew!) In truth, my mother found it hard to navigate the straits of American culture with her young daughter. She was more liberal than most mothers and certainly most Indians, but she held tight to those aspects of our heritage that gave her comfort, religion being the strongest.

So she often took me to the temple against my will. I begrudgingly uttered some scant prayers I could not help but absorb through sheer repetition of exposure and counted the minutes before we went home so I could watch the hours and hours of television I relished as my right as a "typical (Indian) American kid." She, on the other hand, flourished at the temple. She reveled in knowing all the prayers, bowed at exactly the right time, and put the second-tier priests who were forced to slum it in America to shame. She didn't particularly like hanging out with other Indian immigrants—she found them too clannish—but she was fine rubbing elbows with them while they all prostrated themselves, my mother always being the one with the deepest bow. It was this performance that reassured my mother's own insecurity that she had abandoned all righteous connections to our culture in order to have the freedom and happiness she craved in America, away from her abusive marriage, away from judgment, except of course, that of her own guilty conscience. In truth, my mom had nothing to worry about. She was living out her own American dream of self-reliance, financial independence, and liberated freedom. Which is why I was so baffled by her shackle-like connection to our arcane belief in an elephant-headed God who could grant wishes and good luck on school exams.

After elementary school, we moved to the West Coast and I was spared these temple visits due to the fact that the nearest Hindu temple was in Malibu, some fifty miles from our home in San Gabriel Valley, in Southern California. And while my Indian mother became more Americanized, long opting for pants and dresses instead of cumbersome saris, she still rose at 5:00 a.m. daily. To this day the wafting smell of incense and toast makes me think I am late for school.

Then one day, in the first semester of my freshman year of high school, I became gravely ill. What started out as the common flu quickly progressed to a serious and rare form of Stevens-Johnson syndrome. At first, no one could figure out what was wrong with me, and my fever was dangerously high, with no sign of going down. My mother, after taking me to one hospital and finding no answers, moved me within days to a research center called City of Hope, where she worked as a nurse. I developed lesions in my mouth, eyes, and nose that were so severe, I had to sleep sitting up so that I could breathe and wouldn't choke on my own saliva. I was blind and mute at the same time for three weeks. But the doctors there gave me amazing care, and in short order treated my symptoms. While I had lost an enormous amount of weight and was quite frail, I began to be well enough to go home. I left the hospital in her arms. This was on a Friday.

My distraught, worried mother had mentally promised her Hindu gods that if she could finally bring her little girl home from the hospital, she would immediately do penance, by driving to the temple and making an offering in gratitude. My mother was big on ritual at the best of times, so she was taking her promise to God very seriously. Forty-eight hours after I came home, bundled in blankets and with Band-Aids still covering my IV pockmarks, my mother and I piled into the front seat of our red Ford Mercury with my stepdad, who drove, and headed to Malibu on the Hollywood Freeway.

I was still too sick to even exit the car. Sick enough that my folks thought it best to wedge me between them in the long couch version of the front seat that cars of the time had. This way my mom could tend to me. I stayed there in the car while they both exited and did their praying and prostrating at the temple. I heard the chants of the priests and the tinny sound of brass bells shaken by hand. I smelled the incense and camphor that by now was as familiar to me as lentils and rice at dinnertime. Eventually, my mother returned with a Styrofoam plate with some yellow lemon rice, and other foods that had been part of the sacred offering during the pujas, or ritual prayers. These *prasadams* I knew I could never refuse. Never mind that it hurt to eat, that I still had lesions in my mouth, which the food stuck to. I began to gingerly take small bites as my parents reentered the car, vermillion powder and holy ash smeared on their foreheads.

Traffic was heavy on that Sunday. And it was about to be even heavier. On the way back from the temple, our car would be rear-ended so hard, that it careened down an embankment. It would be twelve hours after the accident before I found out both my parents had survived and were indeed alive. They had taken me to one hospital, while airlifting my folks to another with a trauma center where a helicopter could land.

The months after the car accident involved many surgeries and so many weekly hours of physical therapy for all of us. The season would change and the school year would be over before we finally said goodbye to all the home-health nurses who lived with us around the clock. It would be years before my mom ever drove on the freeway again, even though she hadn't been the one driving that fateful Sunday. And it would be decades before I would ever enter a temple again.

What kind of God would allow an innocent sick girl and her family to be involved in such an accident after all the suffering we had already gone through with my unknown illness? While I had long let go of my fascination with Catholicism as a means to fit in with my American peers, I now saw no reason to entertain my mother's illogical attachment to our, né her Hindu religion. I became a teenage atheist. And I somehow lumped all the aspects of my Indian culture into the basket I was now throwing out in disillusion and disgust. I had no faith, not in God or saris or samosas. No need for the most vital aspect of my identity because to my adolescent reasoning, it had only brought me strife, teasing, isolation, and otherness. It had set me apart, and not in any good or positive way I could discern.

I couldn't wait to get away. Years passed as I waited for my future to begin. Lonely yet never alone. I applied only to colleges on the other coast, far away from the aroma of curry and the limitations of my Indian home life. After college, I moved to Europe and spent my twenties there before returning to America and marrying an atheist, albeit an Indian one. My family would have to wrap their heads around the fact that there was to be no mention of God at my wedding, because my husband and I did not want to feel hypocritical.

I would divorce the atheist for reasons altogether unspiritual and start life over. It was during this period in my late thirties that I got a call one day from my cousin who had moved to the States in the intervening years from India, to meet her at the temple. She lured me there saying she didn't have time to meet me in Manhattan, but that the temple had a canteen in the basement and she thought I would enjoy lunch there with her and her husband. I didn't know it at the time, but she was pregnant with my first nephew and had wanted to do an offering there to bless her pregnancy. Rajni and I had grown up like sisters, and on all those summer trips back home to India, we had bonded over things large and small but seldom shared the ritual of going to temple together. Still I was happy we were reconnecting as adults now that she had joined me on the East Coast, so I could not refuse her request.

I arrived to find a big gray-blue structure nestled between row houses. There were some parts of the building that were still under construction, but it was easy to spot the high-carved conical peak sprouting above the residential housing. Rajni was not overly pious herself, and, in truth, our whole extended family tends to be quite secular, so I knew something was up when I saw how tenderly her husband, Ananth, marked her forehead with vermillion and holy ash, as they walked circles around the huge Ganesh deity that sat in the middle of the temple. Around the deity in the great hall were other gods and goddesses, each with his or her own corner, adorned with flowers, silk fabric, and jewels. The priest rang the big brass bell that hung by a rope in front of the Ganesh figure and as it echoed through us, I took mental note of this sweet gesture. We then went down to check out the supposedly amazing food in the basement.

As we found a free table to park our orange plastic cafeteria trays, groaning with foods such as folded crispy, savory crepes called *dosas*, stuffed with potato and drenched in soupy lentils called *sambar*, and pillowy, soft round rice dumplings with bright green coconut chutney, I began to realize that this edifice was indeed my old childhood temple, only much larger and much more delicious. Like me, the temple had moved up in the world. On the same grounds as that one-room humble structure, another more elaborate building had been built. I scooched into the table as my metal folding chair squealed, scraping against the linoleum, and asked Rajni if I was right. She simply shrugged her shoulders and said there were many Hindu temples nowadays.

That night I went home and verified my suspicions on the phone with my mother in California. "Yaas, it sounds as if it's at the same address, Paddy," my mother lilted in her still-remaining-strong Indian accent. "But does it re-a-lly matter? What matters is that you've found your way back, *kanna.*" I irately told her I was just there for the food. "Whatever helps you, *kanna.* God is always there." I quietly decided to ignore my mother. I feared missing out, due to my allergy to religion, on what were definitely the best *dosas* and *sambar* this side of the Indian Ocean.

So much would happen between that visit to the temple with Rajni and the next couple of years that is hard to explain, but suffice it to say that I found myself there often. I'm not sure why. Maybe it was the food. My family had certainly noticed a rise in my piousness since the opening of the basement canteen. Through my own pregnancy, a lover's terminal illness, a lawsuit, and much more, it comforted me to have that place to go to across a bridge or tunnel where the familiar sounds and smells of my childhood calmed my senses enough to allow me to think or reflect outside my usual daily life.

As my own toddler child began to grow and ask questions I wondered how much of my already-watered-down Indian heritage I could pass down to her, a biracial kid in New York City. While I spoke Tamil and Hindi and still spent time each year in India, what was it other than the food that signified my Indian background in my daily life? What could I give my child that I had not in some way shunned myself over the years? Luckily it didn't matter.

My daughter, Krishna, loved all the sights and sounds. She relished the self-service, haphazard chaotic temple, where no one had a pew to sit in and everyone talked during the rituals. She loved the humid smell of ripped flower petals, the deity festooned with brightly colored saris and heaped with glinting jewelry. She jumped high over and over, trying to reach the brass bell as she circled the Ganesh statue, walking as fast as her young legs would take her. She wanted to break her own coconuts, though she could barely lift the brown fibrous orbs with her soft little hands. She reveled in wearing shiny bindis each day on her forehead, and dozens of clinking bangles on her wrist, although sadly this phase would pass, along with "pink and purple everything."

Every fall, we now celebrate Divali—the most important Hindu holiday— at home with lots of food, flowers, live music, and prayers chanted by her great-aunt in Sanskrit. While we are still unsure of what God actually looks like, whether he is a guy on a cross, a woman with a veil, a goddess with many arms, or a chubby man with the head of an elephant, or even if such a thing does exist, we savor the celebration of being together and the act of remembering who we are.

Randall Park is an American actor, comedian, writer, and director. He was born in Los Angeles to Korean parents. He has appeared in numerous films and television projects.

Randall Park

WHEN AMERICA ASKED IF I'd be interested in contributing to this collection, my first thought was probably not. Writing about my parents and their immigrant experience would be too tough a task. It's not that I don't love my mom and dad. Of course I do. Their struggles and sacrifices are the reason why I am who I am today. They are, more than anyone in this world, my heroes.

But here's the thing: I barely know them.

Now that might sound strange to some of you. But for me, and for many American-born kids of Korean immigrants, it's not that uncommon. The parents of my non-Asian friends growing up would talk openly about their childhood, past relationships, their struggles. Some would even talk about their sex lives (which to this day I find very weird). My folks, on the other hand, were never an open book. If anything, they were more like an instruction manual: there for setting up and for troubleshooting, but not the most riveting when it comes to story.

I don't mean to make them sound cold or emotionally unavailable. They were great parents. But they were never like the Keatons, the Seavers, the Huxtables or any of the other parents I grew up with on TV. My parents' way of saying "I love you" was to work *really* hard, to always have food on the table, to make sure that their sons prioritized education and stayed away from doing stupid things, like drugs, or one day becoming a professional actor. I guess in some ways, they succeeded, and in other ways they didn't. But I never once questioned their love for me.

I did, however, wonder why they rarely ever shared their personal stories with me. Sure, I'd get bits and pieces here and there, but they'd never go into much detail. I wondered if elements of their past might have been too painful. Or maybe they felt that the cultural chasm between them and their American-born sons was too wide a distance to pass along something so delicate, so personal. Or perhaps, they're just very private people, even when it comes to their own kids. I don't know.

But as I've gotten older, I've become obsessed with learning more about them. Simple things like what their life was like in Korea, why they decided to come to America, and what those early years in this new country were like. (I'm okay with not knowing about their sex life though.) I guess something inside of me just wanted to connect with them on a more human level, and I wanted to do it before it was too late. Now that I have a wife and a daughter of my own, I've come to the startling realization that all parents are in fact *human beings*. With feeling and emotions. And, unfortunately, an expiration date.

So over the past several years, I'd ask them questions. I'd inelegantly slip them into random conversations and sometimes I'd bring them up, out of nowhere, like a pop quiz: "What was your childhood like in Korea?" "Why did you decide to come to America?" "When you got here, were you scared?" Invariably, my folks would respond with annoyance. "Why are you asking me this? Stop it!" my mom would yell from the other side of the bathroom door. "Don't talk to me when I'm on the toilet!" I'd come to the conclusion that maybe I would never learn these stories.

Then, America called and asked if I'd be interested in contributing to her book. And it got me thinking . . . What if I used this as an excuse to sit down with my parents and ask them everything I've wanted to know? If it's for a book, then it's kind of academic, which means they'll be more likely to say yes, right? Also, I know for a fact that my parents were fans of *Ugly Betty*, and quite frankly, who doesn't love America Ferrera?

So I strategized. I decided to ask my mom, since she's always been the more communicative of my parents and thus more likely to agree to do something like this. My mom was always the artist in our family. She's a painter, so I grew up with easels, tubes of oil paints, and canvases leaning up against the walls of our home. My dad, on the other hand, is practical, hardworking, humble, and not one to waste words. He'd for sure have no interest in being interviewed for this book. But if I went through my mom, there would be a chance.

I called her up and I asked if maybe I could take her and Dad out to breakfast to interview them for this collection of essays.

My mom casually responded, "Sure, why not?" I couldn't believe it. It worked.

The next Saturday morning, I set out to meet my mom and dad at Factor's Famous Deli on Pico Boulevard in Los Angeles. I grew up having breakfast at Jewish delis with my family, so I figured the familiarity would help ease the process. I'd record them on my phone, background noises and all, and I'd keep my list of questions short and simple, because I wanted it to be as painless as possible. For example, I started off with:

Me: So where were you born?

Mom: In Korea. Taegu, Korea.

Dad: Southern part. Near Pusan.

Mom: It's the third largest city. Taegu, Korea. 1947.

Dad: Me, same thing. Taegu.

Mom: 1939, right?

Dad: 1939.

Wow. With one question, I got a plethora of information. Even a statistical fact! And within minutes, the floodgates had opened. As expected, my mom did most of the talking. But my dad would chime in every now and then, sometimes at surprising moments. And in one sitting, I learned more about my parents' pasts than I had in my entire life.

I learned about their childhoods, growing up in Taegu. We touched upon their college years at Yonsei University and Ewha Womens University in Seoul. I learned about my dad's move to San Francisco in 1964, where he studied economics while working as a busboy in a French restaurant in Sausalito, California. And how that experience somehow led him to study French at Sorbonne University in Paris. I never figured my practical, no-nonsense dad as one to give in to wanderlust, but there it was.

Apparently, my parents met when my dad went back for a visit to Korea. He was thirty, and all his friends were getting married. Their families, who had known each other in Taegu, essentially set them up. My mom pretty much summed it up as an "arranged" situation. I was a little bummed to learn that their story wasn't more romantic, like the way my wife and I met. (We were both sitting in an audition waiting room going up for the same part.

Neither of us booked the part, but we ended up booking each other!) According to my parents, in those times, things were generally more "practical."

Still, my mom, in her early twenties at the time, was excited to come to this country that had been romanticized in all the Hollywood movies she had seen growing up.

> **Mom:** But when I got here, I was really disappointed. Full of disappointment. Because in reality, your dad was poor. And as a young girl at twenty, twenty-one, I thought that when I'd come here, I would have some sort of standard of living. Like in the movies. But we didn't. We struggled.

This theme of "struggle" seemed to permeate throughout the entire interview. Despite having almost idyllic childhoods in Taegu, things seemed to change for my parents once in America. And despite the fact that these struggles were often shielded from my brother and me, they would play a major role in our upbringing.

For example, I always wondered why, unlike most Korean parents I know, my folks were never that adamant about their kids maintaining a strong sense of cultural identity. For most Korean families, holding on to Korean traditions and language and pride is essential. Yet for my brother and me, this wasn't the case. My parents spoke to us mostly in English. We rarely ever went to community events or the Korean church. The only consistent Korean thing in our home (aside from ourselves) was the food. There was even a time during my teenage years when I resented them for this. But I finally got a sense of why this was:

> **Mom:** That was my fault. When I first came to this country, your dad was working all the time. I had two kids, and no family or friends, no

help from anyone. At the same time, I was struggling to learn the language, the culture here. When your brother was born, I had a lot of complications. They gave me a shot in the back that gave me back problems for years. It was really difficult. I actually got depressed. That's why I never focused on that stuff with my kids. I didn't have the luxury. Every day, I was just focused on making this place my home. Our home.

Picturing my mom, in her early twenties, in a completely foreign country, sitting alone in a tiny apartment with two kids, while also in severe pain, gave me a newfound respect for her. And a deeper understanding of my own upbringing.

She would eventually learn English from watching television shows like *Gomer Pyle: U.S.M.C.* and *Gilligan's Island.* And once my brother and I started school, she would find an accounting job, where she'd work for the next thirty years. Meanwhile, when my dad found out the company he had been working for was relocating, he decided to stay in Los Angeles for the family. He ended up working several jobs, eventually opening up his own one-hour-photo store in Santa Monica, which would die with the dawn of the digital age. Ever the workhorse, he continues to work till this day. I could safely say that I got my work ethic from both of my parents.

One of the biggest struggles I experienced with my folks was when I told them that I wanted to pursue a career as a professional actor. I was already into my midtwenties, and having worked a string of office jobs, I was ready to take the leap and follow my dreams. But my fanciful "dreams" of success in entertainment wasn't a concept that my parents were interested in:

Mom: The way I was brought up, actors and show business meant a life of struggle. And I didn't want you to go through that. We already went through that.

Dad: In Korea, we admired the scientists, professors, doctors . . .

Mom: I remember one of your teachers at Hamilton High School said, "Randy's a very smart guy. I can see him going into science." And I never forgot that. We thought you'd become a scientist.

Me: Mom, I never once thought I'd become a scientist.

Dad: We thought, as an Oriental guy, to succeed as an actor in this country would be very difficult. That's why we worried. But you did a good job for yourself. We're proud of you. . . . Are we done yet?

Yes, there were times when my dad got antsy. And yes, he does call Asians "Oriental." I've given up on trying to correct him. But overall, the experience was incredibly rewarding for all of us. I was especially moved by how openly proud my parents are of me today. They expressed a keen understanding of how difficult it is to succeed in my industry, especially for Asian-Americans. Still, I came away with an even better understanding of why they would've wanted their son to take an easier, more traditional route to success.

During the course of our interview, I not only got closer to my parents, but I also got closer to myself. Despite being born and raised in the United States, there was always a part of me that felt like an outsider. At the same time, I always felt like I was never quite Korean enough. But upon hearing these stories, I began to feel more anchored to both sides of me. Getting more familiar with the details of my lineage fills me with a better sense of what got me here, to where I am today, and how my story is directly connected to theirs. These stories remind me that I am a person who is here, in this country, for a reason.

And the best thing about it all is that this was just a beginning. At the end of our interview, I asked my parents if we could sit down and do this again.

My mom casually responded, "Anytime," as my dad nodded while finishing the rest of his hash browns. Good enough for me. Maybe next time I'll ask them: Why now? Why, after all these years are they willing to be so open? Is it because I have a family of my own now? Is it because I paid for breakfast? Is it because of their undying love for *The Sisterhood of the Traveling Pants*? I'll get back to you on that.

My original plan was to publish the entire interview, but now I kind of feel weird about doing that. For now, I want to hold on to this experience for myself. Besides, this interview will be more meaningful to me than to any of you. To you, I say, collect your own stories from your parents, your grandparents, your guardians, and your mentors. Then pass those stories down to your kids, your grandkids, and anyone who can really benefit from them. And if you're having trouble getting to those stories, try making an event out of it. Take Grandma to her favorite restaurant, sit down with her, and make a meal out of it. Show her that these stories are important to you. It may feel weird at first, but see it through. It'll be worth it. Oh, and also, make sure to do it somewhere meaningful and not while she's on the toilet.

Roxane Gay is the author of the books *Ayiti*, *An Untamed State*, the *New York Times* bestselling *Bad Feminist*, the nationally bestselling *Difficult Women*, and the *New York Times* bestselling *Hunger: A Memoir of (My) Body*. She is also the author of *World of Wakanda* for Marvel and the editor of *Best American Short Stories 2018*. She is a contributing opinion writer for the *New York Times* and a 2018 recipient of a Guggenheim fellowship.

Roxane Gay

I WAS EXPLAINING TO my therapist that Haitian parents don't believe in boundaries, and he did not quite believe me. The week before that conversation, while my parents were visiting me in Los Angeles, I was telling them about therapy and how I was working on establishing and maintaining better boundaries both personally and professionally. My mother laughed, genially, and said, "Boundaries? There is no such thing with your family." I smiled and bit my tongue and understood that boundaries do exist, no matter how willfully some people try to ignore them. I also understood that, for my mother, and in our culture, boundaries do not really exist. Or perhaps, more accurately, boundaries exist but they are ignored and trespassed at will with, generally, the best of intentions.

As the daughter of Haitian immigrants, I've always had to hold on to multiple truths. I've had to live with multiple identities. Most first-generation kids are familiar with the negotiations of who we are at home and who we are in the wider world. On the whole, I'm the better for it. I am better for the benefit of enjoying diverse cultural experiences and knowing exactly where I come from.

It's a familiar story—growing up, I was Haitian at home and American at school and out in the world. There were different rules for each world I moved through, and I had to learn those rules quickly. I knew nothing about boundaries or other such *American* things. My American classmates rarely understood the rules I lived by at home, and my parents were bewildered by the permissiveness of those classmates' parents. This was particularly true where privacy was concerned. There were no closed doors in our household. A closed door meant we were probably up to no good. A closed door meant we were trying to shut our parents out of our lives when they wanted nothing more than to have their lives wholly entwined with ours.

My parents were then, as they remain now, deeply invested in the lives of me and my brothers. This investment rarely felt overbearing, but the older I got, the more I realized that they loved and nurtured us in a very specific way. My parents loved us with their whole hearts. They wanted the best for us and expected the best from us—at school with our grades and how we behaved in the classroom, at home with how we treated them and each other, at church as we practiced our faith. All of this expectation was intense, but I know no other way of being part of a family, of being loved. And it wasn't just my parents, both of whom come from big families. My aunts and uncles and grandmothers were and are just as intense in their love. Now that we're all adults, my brothers and cousins and I have largely adopted our parents' ways of loving and looking after each other and our children. The only thing really separating us from one another is our skin, and even that is incidental.

Sometimes, when I think of how I am loved, I am overwhelmed. I can hardly breathe. I can't wrap my mind around people caring that much about me. Even when I rejected my parents, they were there; they were steadfast in their devotion and determination to love a child who did not want to be loved by them, by anyone. They loved me through the worst things I've endured and the worst ways I've behaved toward them. They loved me through my tumultuous tweens and twenties. In my thirties, as my life started coming together, they became my friends. Now in my forties, we talk daily. They generally use FaceTime because they don't just want to hear my voice, they want to *see* me so they can determine, for themselves, how I am doing. They continue to parent, because Haitian parenting does not end when their children turn eighteen. We do not ever really leave home, even when we eventually leave home. Haitian parents parent forever and do so unapologetically.

A few months ago, my mom texted me about my propensity for profanity, particularly on Twitter. "Clean it up; it's time," she said. I had no idea what she was talking about, so I asked and she elaborated, chiding me about "the four-letter word you overuse." I could only respond, "OMG. Stop stalking me," to which she quickly replied, "I will not." That stubborn refusal to let me be a fully grown adult who can make decisions about how she speaks sums up our relationship. That she will not stop caring about who I am and how I am in the world is her way of loving me, my boundaries be damned.

My father also stalks my Twitter account for extra information about me. He knows more about my travels and publications than I do. He is the keeper of my archive. He reads the comments on nearly anything I write, even though I consistently warn him not to, knowing the cruel nature of online discourse, and then he gets furious and righteous on my behalf. Both of my parents attend my events when they can, beaming proudly as I talk about my latest book. They are often flanked by my aunts and uncles, cousins and their children. I don't just have a family, I have an army. They are omnipresent and overbearing and confident that their way of loving is the right way, the only way.

The older I get, the more I understand why my family loves the way they do. I understand what it took for my parents and their siblings to come to the

United States. They had no money. They did not speak the language. They had no guarantee that the American dream would extend to them. All they had was each other. All they had was a fierce kind of love to see them through. When I consider what they sacrificed, what they went through as they made this country their own, and how they never let go of where they came from, it makes perfect sense that they would love without boundaries. They are people who have spent the whole of their lives crossing borders that were, often, unfriendly and unwilling to welcome them. They could not, I imagine, tolerate inhospitable borders within their own family, so they loved us in a wild, irrepressible, boundless way. They taught us to love that way in return, and so we do.

Carmen Perez is the executive director of The Gathering for Justice and has dedicated twenty years to advocating for many of today's important civil rights issues, including gender equity, violence prevention, racial healing, community policing, and ending mass incarceration.

Carmen Perez

IT HAPPENED ON MY seventeenth birthday—that was the day I decided I was going to change the world. I walked into the church in front of all my family and friends. There was a cake with candles and a dozen bright balloons. HAPPY BIRTHDAY, CARMEN AND PATRICIA, read the colorful cake that was placed right beside my sister's open casket.

Patricia and I had experienced everything in life together. We weren't twins—just sisters with exactly 366 days between us. But our whole lives, we lived like twins and best friends, sharing a bedroom, birthday parties, friends, and all the hardships of our childhood. When she died in a car accident, I had to start a new life without her. And that's when it happened—when I decided I was going to fight to make the world a better place. I'd had it in me for a long time, but Patricia's loss made it real—and urgent.

"What do you want to be when you grow up?" I remember my other sister, Leti, asking me several years earlier, when I was still very little. Leti was twelve years older than me, and she probably didn't expect my answer to be: "I am going to change the world!"

"Oh, okay, Carmen!" She laughed skeptically as she dressed me for ballet practice.

Patricia and I were always listening to music, thinking we could dance and sing our lives away. As kids, we took ballet and as I got older, I did modern jazz and hip-hop. In my mind, I was a professional hip-hop dancer, but I also loved Selena. Although we didn't speak Spanish or understand it, Patricia and I would both sing along to Selena, pretending to be her. Because she looked like us, with her black hair, high cheekbones, and slanted dark brown eyes, it was a lot easier to imagine we really *were* her when we sang passionately to our reflections in the mirror.

As we got older, our big brothers (who were older than us by six and fourteen years) introduced us to NWA. I didn't understand the lyrics any better than Selena's Spanish, but I knew right off the bat, this music was for me. I was beginning to form my own identity and loved Snoop, Dr. Dre, and DJ Quik. I joined a dance crew called Something Too Sweet that performed at our junior high school and at the local Boys & Girls Club. As a crew, we were about as sweet as Eazy-E himself. Which means we were *not* sweet. We were hard. At least that's how we liked to act. I was always the tomboy, with Eazy's Jheri curl, and I dressed, acted, and walked around like I was in a rap group. I remember being in junior high school when our dance crew performed "We're All in the Same Gang" by West Coast All-Stars. I wore a black Sacramento Kings hat, a black bomber jacket with Nike Cortez shoes and black Dickies. I rapped the lyrics of the various artists in the song, trying to convey the message to all the other kids in the audience—we were all impacted by gang violence.

Thank God for hip-hop and music in general. Nothing else besides basketball made me so happy at that age. Nothing saved me from the difficult day-to-day in my hood like rapping, playing ball, dancing, and putting on a front of hardness. Hardness with so much joy underneath because I was with my girls.

My dance crew in those days was as diverse as the neighborhood we lived in—made up of the same girls on my basketball team: Mexicans, Chicanas, African-Americans, Samoans, Koreans, and Filipinas. My neighborhood in Oxnard, California, was home to gang violence, drugs, alcohol, poverty, and a whole lot of racial and cultural diversity. There were three naval bases and a lot of migrant workers living side by side—most people surviving on small incomes. Ironically, I look back on it as a wonderful little bubble where I could be whoever I wanted to be. I am the youngest of five kids, the daughter of an American-born Chicano father and a Mexican immigrant mother. My favorite food growing up was the *lumpias* and *pancit* made by the Filipina moms in my neighborhood, and one of my nicknames was "Little Samoan." This was not a dig but a celebration of my kinky hair and facial features. Somehow I resembled my Samoan friends as much as my own parents. I could say "I love you" in several different languages—would yell it to my girl-friends when saying goodbye—but I didn't speak Spanish—my mother's only language.

I used a lot of slang with my friends, saying things like "Whazzz sup?"

"*¿Por qué hablas así?*" ("Why do you talk like that?") my mom used to ask me, her eyes wide with concern, love, and confusion.

She was a Mexican immigrant who was mostly monolingual and ex-tremely monolithic in her love for the Catholic Church. She left her family in Mexico to marry my father in California, after they fell in love on a dance floor in Jerez, Zacatecas, when he was on a road trip with his cousin. Once in California, my young, strong parents worked the fields, but by the time I was born—their fifth child over the span of fourteen years—my father was work-ing as a forklift driver and my mom packed frozen food at a plant. She worked very long hours but still made time for her side gig: praying hard for the community. There was not one incarcerated family member, drug-addicted friend, or gang member on the streets who didn't receive her prayers. On the daily. Even though she married a Chicano man from California with a good twenty years on her, she was a proper, God-fearing woman who never *dreamed* her own daughter would dress like a rapper and play ball like the boys. She did her best to raise her five children, but the long hours she and my father worked meant leaving Patricia and me to be raised by our older siblings.

Unlike our mother, Patricia and I were not monolithically anything, especially not monolithically Mexican. Our three older siblings were bilingual—the bridge between my Spanish-speaking parents and me—and they brought me and Patricia up to speak English—and only English. I was not part of the protective Mexican family you hear about who lights candles and goes to church. Our older siblings made sure we played sports and were out in the community. On holidays, we'd exchange food with the Wilsons, a black family across the street. They gave us pecan pies and we provided them with tamales. We loved growing up in a neighborhood with so many different cultures. I was never uncomfortable speaking with someone else about their background or their home life. I gladly tasted their foods, listened to their music, and drank in all our differences. I was culturally fluid and happy and not tightly connected to just being Mexican.

If anything was first and foremost about my identity, it was that I danced hip-hop and played basketball.

Since Patricia was older than me, we usually played on different basketball teams, but we shared the same coach, who was often like a dad to many of us. Pat Bell was a brave black man stepping into a diverse community that was very much not his own. Our parents relied on Pat to keep us safe and off the streets. He was hope for them. They knew that if we were with Pat, we were going to be okay. Pat was a man who demanded respect. He was dark-brown-skinned, five feet eleven inches tall, and had a nineties flattop. He spoke assertively, and he himself could do anything he asked of us on the court. Thinking back now, Pat only spoke English, but somehow he knew how to communicate with our parents. Pat's family came from the South, and he was rooted in Southern traditions, raised playing the guitar in his Baptist church. He would often make us attend church with him to keep an eye on us, and, believe me, there was no dispute coming from our parents, even though they were devout Catholics. As long as we were praising God and off the streets, they were content.

Coach Pat had so much confidence in us, and he was the first adult in my life who told me through his actions that *I had power in me* and *he would help me find it*. On his court, I sometimes felt that I really would change the world. He was not concerned with what language you spoke at home, how little you saw your parents at home, or what kind of hardships you dealt with behind closed doors. He just knew you needed a home away from home to clean the slate and keep you safe.

"Run it off, Perez!" he used to say when I would arrive at practice visibly shaken, tired, or angry about one of the many hardships of my life. I was the best at suicide drills, running off the pain so fast on the court that he got me into track and softball too, which he also coached. He offered me a place to be, where the best part of myself was awakened, relevant, *necessary*. Sports were my salvation, and Coach Bell was our home base throughout our entire childhood—even when my sister Patricia and I would fight. He would show up to pick me up from my home and take me to his house for dinner or to the court to shoot around.

There was comfort on the court, in the drills and regimens, in getting so sweaty and loud with your best friends every day. At every single practice and game, Coach made us repeat his five values:

1) Never give up

2) Dedication

3) Determination

4) Confidence

5) Family

Every girl on the team could repeat these backward and forward. The team looked something like this: Vanessa (who we called Vern) was Mexican. Charleen was a light-skinned Mexican girl whose family was super Chicano— her brothers would all drive nice old cars. Then there was Korina, who we called Popcorn because she used to pop up to get the rebound and then pop up to put the ball right back in. She was from a household with monolingual Spanish-speaking parents and was very culturally Mexican, but she knew how to navigate both worlds. Trish was Korean but adopted and raised by a white mom. We rubbed our skinned knees together to become blood sisters in fifth grade, and we are still best friends to this day. Shawanda, who was black, was the Michael Jordan of our basketball team. She had hops! And Louisa was Samoan. As kids, we were curious and loved listening to Louisa's parents speak. In fact, we learned how to address all our teammates' parents with respect, calling them *mom* or *dad* in their native languages.

Our lineup may sound more diverse than your typical girls basketball team, but in Oxnard, it wasn't that unusual for Latinas to hang with black girls, or Korean girls to hang with Samoan girls. Our overlapping struggles both on and off the court made us more alike than different. But when we left our neighborhood for traveling games we encountered racism right and left. People couldn't believe that Samoan and Chicana girls could play ball. It was outside their expectations and just plain threatening. Especially given how confident and spirited we were rolling into a gym together. The best possible reaction to the sight of us was usually a raised eyebrow, and the worst was a crowbar to our taillights and windshield.

There were many times when we were underestimated, and that just made us more determined to show the other teams where we came from. We would dust them up by thirty, forty, and sometimes fifty points, which didn't make them too happy. We caught a lot of aggressive shoves in the lineup after the game when you're supposed to slap hands and say "good game." One time, the shoves led to an actual fight, so we were kept inside, handed a box full of all our trophies, and finally excused—only to find that our van had been vandalized.

Getting our car smashed in by rival teams was nothing. As we got older, we were waking up to the world outside our bubble of sisterhood, and that world included all kinds of violence and racism. We watched on TV while Rodney King was beaten by the police and saw Los Angeles go up in flames less than an hour away. One time on the drive home from one of my games, my brother got pulled over. Patricia and I were in the back seat, and my teammates were in the bed of the truck—all of us still in our uniforms, sweaty and ready to go home and shower. I'll never forget the police officers making my brother get out of the car with his hands up and then throwing him to the ground, hog-tying him at gunpoint right in front of me and all my teammates. Then the police made all of us put up our hands, and we were escorted to sit on the curb at gunpoint. As I watched my brother's face being pushed into the pavement, I wished the police could see my brother the way I saw him. The way my Samoan, Korean, Filipina, Chicana, black, and white sisters all saw each other: as family.

Coach always taught us that you can't get the ball in the basket if you have drama with your teammates. You won't communicate well *on* the court if you don't legit hang out with each other *off* the court. And unless you truly see each other as sisters, you cannot protect each other and you cannot win games.

I think Coach knew we would need each other well beyond the basketball court. And he was right—we would need each other our whole lives. When each and every one of us went through personal hardships, we always had each other's backs. It was a blessing that I was never on the same team as Patricia, because it allowed me to form a sisterhood with other girls, who I would need after Patricia passed. We were all there for each other. Throw anything at us, and the friendship of our crazy little circle would get us through.

And when Patricia died, I survived because of them. It was through their prayers and visits that I felt Patricia near. Having this sisterhood helped me understand it was one of the greatest strengths in my life. There was so much violence and hardship around us, and if anything was ever going to change, we would have to stick together. After losing Patricia, I wanted to fight all the wrongs I saw in the world. My sister wasn't going to be able to speak anymore, so I would have to speak for the both of us.

After the funeral, my mother took me to Mexico to visit her family for the first time. It was a part of how she mourned her daughter. To go home— the place of her birth, where she hadn't been for so many years. It was strange to grieve for Patricia in a place she herself had never even been. I felt her absence strongly in that new place. I was lonely, sad, and for the first time in my life, I felt very foreign. I felt out of place—among people who were *my family.* I was shocked to find that my cousins there all spoke English, which they had learned at school—no big deal. They wondered why I hadn't learned to speak Spanish at school—or at home with my own parents. I recognized an internal hidden sadness that I was not connected to this Mexican part of myself. I wondered if I had grown up too disconnected from what I was supposed to be. Was I missing something by not knowing more about my roots? Was it wrong to feel more urban, more basketball, more hip-hop than Mexican?

"Why didn't you teach me to speak Spanish? Why didn't you ever bring me to this place?" I asked my mother.

"You have always been so American and had sports, Carmen. I didn't want to confuse you or take you away from your responsibilities," was her reply.

But the confusion only grew when I became the only kid in my family to attend college. At the time, I felt applying to college was my only way to start fresh. But this didn't come easy. My parents had just finished paying for a funeral and couldn't afford to pay my tuition. I had to work while in college to cover the cost—all while feeling homesick and grieving my sister. And the confusion didn't stop when the school kept pushing papers in my face asking me to check the box every single time: *Hispanic*—a term I have never identified with.

College was supposed to be where you open your heart and mind to new experiences. But in some ways, that first semester, I felt my world becoming shrunken and confined. Someone in the leadership of MEChA* on campus informed me I *wasn't* really Mexican after all, because I couldn't speak Spanish. And I kept learning new terms and labels that were applied to me and my experiences in a way that made me feel like an alien. Besides *Mexican*, I was a *person of color* who had grown up a *latchkey kid*. And I even learned there was a term for what used to happen with my brothers getting hog-tied at gunpoint by the cops: *racial profiling*.

---

*Movimiento Estudiantil Chicanx de Aztlán

There was also a word to describe me and my girls back home. Apparently, our overlap of cultures, races, and "social disadvantages" had an academic title: *intersectionality.* It's a big word that sounds as made up as it does heavy. But I didn't want to run from it. I wanted to embrace it, because it felt like a word for something I'd lived my whole life. It sparked a new feeling of pride in me for myself, Patricia, and the relationship we had with our extended neighborhood family. Far beyond a textbook word used by academics, my friends and I were a living, breathing collective of people who experienced a magical level of togetherness in our multicultural neighborhood. We were unified for life. We weren't just a bunch of separate ethnic groups that correspond to boxes you check on an admissions form. We weren't just Mexican, Korean, Pacific Islander, or African-American. We were intersectional. We were the kids who didn't know we were supposed to be labeled and divided, who instead *collided*—and generated our own power.

And even though people always tell you that collaborating with people from other walks of life is complicated—a pipe-dream even—for us, in Oxnard, California, coming together was easy, natural, and real.

This, I realized, was my gift. To take my pain, my knowledge, and my unique experience of intersectionality and to figure out a way to help people with it. *This was how I could change the world.* I was one of the lucky ones who made it to college and had encouraging mentors. I had the self-motivation and inspiration to live for my sister when she couldn't, to speak for my mother when she couldn't, to bring what I knew to the movement and make it stronger.

So even though I had considered going back to Southern California after college and coaching with Pat Bell, I decided to take my place in the movement for social justice. And because I grew up side by side with people from so many backgrounds, races, and religions, my heart was already in it. I already spoke the language. My first meaningful cultural exchanges had happened long ago, when I was a little kid and didn't know any different. So I fit right in with the community of people working intersectionally to fight for social justice. I'd been organizing my entire life. I already feel so connected and parallel to marginalized communities. I don't need to be black to care about Black Lives Matter. I don't have to be locked up to care about incarcerated people. My intersectionality and empathy became my power, and Coach Pat's five values are still my secret weapon.

He always taught us that having heart wins games. Grit, determination, and family will get us through. He was right. My diverse family of basketball teammates has always gotten me through. I am still close with most of those girls. They mourned with me a few years ago when Coach Bell died on the basketball court at the age of forty-four. And because of them, I have never forgotten where I came from. They continue to remember Patricia with me. They continue to remind me that out of tragedy and hardship can come blessings and change. They remind me of our shared humanity, no matter our backgrounds or differences. They help me understand that our liberation is bound together.

They were my strength on my seventeenth birthday at Patricia's funeral, and they were my strength exactly twenty-three years later—to the day— on my fortieth birthday in Washington, DC, when I took the stage at the Women's March and asked five million people to help me change the world.

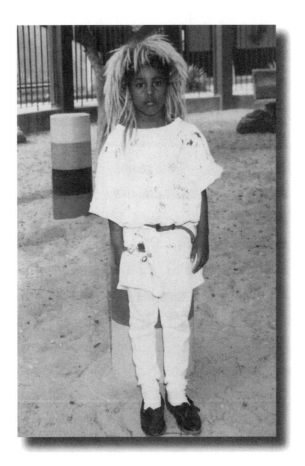

With her own unique flare and infectious sense of humor, **Issa Rae**'s content has garnered millions of views online and two Golden Globe nominations for Best Actress for her hit show, HBO's *Insecure*. Issa's web series, *The Misadventures of Awkward Black Girl*, was the recipient of the coveted Shorty Award for Best Web Show and her first book, a collection of essays, is a *New York Times* bestseller.

Issa Rae

WHEN I WAS SEVENTEEN, I decided to celebrate Ramadan for the first time. After a lifetime of telling my Muslim dad and extended family, "I love y'all, but I'm not fasting," I finally decided to celebrate it too. And by "celebrate," I mean starving during daylight hours for a full month. Good times.

Except not. I decided to do Ramadan, and I did Ramadan wrong.

My whole life I had lived in fear of it. Not because it was foreign to me. My dad is from Senegal—where almost everyone is Muslim. I grew up visiting Senegal and even lived there for a short period of time as a very young child. It's more that I just don't like being hungry or checking off a list of things I can't do. And when it comes to Ramadan, you can't eat, drink, have sex, or even think ungenerous thoughts for an entire month. You also have to pray a lot. Which I didn't do, outside of "I pray they don't serve Domino's for lunch, Lord Allah, because I may be tempted." Ramadan is a beautiful tradition, but I had not grown up developing the strength or discipline to properly celebrate it the way so many of my family members had.

When I gave it a shot, I really truly wanted to feel like I was putting my whole being into it (for reasons I'll get to later). My initial failings were due to straight laziness for the most part. I had trouble waking up in advance of the sunrise, which is when you are supposed to get out of bed so you can have your food and water for the long day ahead. Then once the sun was up I acted nasty and hangry all damn day till the sun set, at which point I would grossly overeat to make up for lost time and calories. Which isn't really the point of the fast. The idea is to focus on what you can sacrifice and give, not what you wish you had more of. And I'm pretty sure you're not supposed to turn your thoughts to how to sneak boys into the house and get them to go down on you, but that's what I did the whole damn thirty days. Because that shit is hard. And I have deep respect for Muslims who see it through every single time. I remember I kept telling myself, "Damn Jo-Issa, your ten-year-old cousins are doing this, so your seventeen-year-old ass can do it too." I think the first week, I was drinking water during the day because I didn't know you weren't supposed to because what kind of dehydrating shit is that? And then my Muslim classmate was like, "What are you doing? You know you're not supposed to drink water, right?" And I was like, "Girl, I know. I was just rinsing my mouth out. Chill." I presented it to my friends all wrong too, like I was tackling a new diet, as opposed to being connected with my Senegalese side. They were mildly impressed: "If you're not eating during the day, can I get your lunch tickets?"

Looking back, I am not proud of how I did Ramadan wrong. I am not telling this story to make light of Ramadan or to pat myself on my weak-ass back. It was not my finest moment. But it was a rare moment in my life where I was seeking religion. My mom is from New Orleans, and she won the "debate" about which religion me and my four siblings would be raised in. So even though my dad never let us forget that we were Senegalese, we grew up attending Christian churches. Despite being raised Catholic herself, my mother was heavily involved in the church and made sure we were too. I never wanted to be there on Sunday mornings. Most kids and teenagers don't. It was not fun. And I wouldn't call myself religious today. Of course, looking back I can see how the church rooted my family and gave us community. It also gave "younger me" an audience. My mom's church is where I put on my first play. Church is where I was standing the first time I said something into a mic that I had written myself. It's where I found my creative roots. That meant a lot to me. Plus, they don't make you fast, so . . .

Spending time in Dakar, Senegal, growing up, sometimes my visit overlapped with Ramadan. It's a monthlong holiday that is based on the lunar calendar, so it doesn't happen in the exact same month every year. One year it might fall in June and another year it's in April, so sometimes it would creep up on me. And I was always disappointed if my time in Dakar was shadowed by Ramadan. I know that sounds selfish or disrespectful, but I was a kid—away from her regular home and school life—in a place where I got to have fun. All the rules were different there. The age limit at the clubs was only sixteen, which felt too good to be true. But during Ramadan everything would shut down. You couldn't go out dancing. You couldn't even go to restaurants. It was so irritating. Those teenage summers were supposed to be all about *me* living my best adult life—and then Ramadan had to get in the way. And my cousins did *not* play when it came to maintaining it—which I couldn't really be mad at. As a culture, everyone was united in being hungry and bored together. Even if you weren't celebrating it, you had to respect it.

But then when it's over, you get to wild out. Imagine that almost a quarter of *all the people on the entire planet* are on their best, foodless behavior for an entire month. They've all been celibate, quietly fasting and focusing on spiritual matters and now they get to feast (and *feast*, o-kay?!). It has a real exuberant vibe. There's food and gifts and music and parties. In Senegal, they wait a little while after Ramadan has ended to kick off the holiday called Tabaski.

People get dressed up, do their hair, and, for weeks, you see them fattening up the goat or sheep they're going to feast on for the big day. It's a celebration honoring Ibrahim's willingness to sacrifice his son Ishmael to God. As the story goes, at the last minute, God provided a sheep instead of asking Ibrahim to take his son's life. People at my mom's church were also all over that biblical story (except Christians call them Abraham and Isaac), but they didn't actually reenact the slaughter/eat/party part the way they do in Senegal.

I still remember my first Tabaski experience. I was about five years old, but the memory is pretty vivid. You don't soon forget the sight of a live goat's throat being slit. It played like a horror movie. Except everyone was watching and cheering. Just gathered around while the poor goat lay there bleeding his little goat life out. That goat had been hanging around for the month prior, just chilling with us. To five-year-old me, he was our pet. We named him Martin le Mouton and everything (RIP Martin). After they had finished butchering the goat to prepare it to be cooked, my older cousins, who smelled my fear, would come at me with a severed goat leg and chase me around the yard. I had nightmares about the whole thing, and in following years, actively decided not to watch the killing go down. And every damn year, I would get too close to that goat. I'd give it yet another name and allow myself to get attached while fully knowing our time together would be brief. Pretty soon his head was going to be floating in a soup that I was supposed to get excited about eating.

So I got a rough start with Tabaski, but it didn't take too long for me to look forward to it. My dad's very favorite thing was to take us to Senegal, and my mother was just as enthusiastic about it. She was already fluent in French by the time she met my dad in college, and over the years she learned to speak Wolof and even learned how to cook Senegalese food, thanks to my dad's sisters. The food in Senegal (pet goats notwithstanding) is 100 percent my favorite thing to eat. They used to try to teach me to cook there too, and I skirted that responsibility/privilege for a long time.

"Oh, y'all make it so perfect, you don't want me messing it up!" I'd say, and backward tiptoe out of the kitchen.

I remember my aunt saying, "Oh, Issa, you will have to learn to cook for your man. Get in here!"

The gender roles are real there. And yet, my mother never felt so respected and regarded as she did in Senegal. She was born in New Orleans in the fifties, and my grandparents moved her and my aunt to LA when she was four. But her parents had been brought up in the time when you had to slip under the radar if you were black. They were afraid for my mom when she would speak her mind in any way. Even though they lived in the more liberal California, they still didn't want her to wear her hair in an Afro, much less discuss civil rights. I'm sure my mom has all kinds of stories about being a black woman of her generation and all the obstacles that came with that. But both of our experiences in Senegal were loving, warm, and welcomed respect for black women—all women really. It's a culture that has gender roles but feels to me that it pays due respect to all the roles. I can understand why my mother was very attracted to it.

I have so many good memories of being there and feeling connected to something that I couldn't fully explain—it just felt right. And it was also hella fun. Not like the kind of fun you expected to have in the United States as a kid in the nineties—here in America we're always on a phone or a computer. Kids spend their time playing video games and going to the mall to buy shit. But in Senegal, most of what we did, even as kids, was sit around and . . .

talk. There was never anything good on TV there (when the TV actually worked). I remember when they first got Wi-Fi at my aunt's house in Dakar because it was a pretty momentous day—not that it really changed things for us. The internet only worked in my aunt's bedroom and it was hot as fuck in there, so you had to ask yourself, *Do you want to be hot on the internet or catch a breeze and talk to Grandpa?* When I would make the mistake of asking what we were doing today, I got blank looks because my cousins were basically like, "That's on you, bruh." Boredom was not a thing to complain about there. Parents weren't always scrambling around figuring out how to entertain us. It was just *Go play*, or *Go sit outside and talk*. So we played a *lot* of games and did a *lot* of talking.

We would make up games to entertain ourselves. There were always so many kids, babies, and toddlers around that you had to kind of invent an activity that would be good for all ages. I excelled at this (probably my need to entertain, or just my inherent geekiness). There was the game "questions in a hat," where we'd rip up small pieces of paper and write anonymous, naughty questions for each of us to pull out of a hat and answer (I've since turned it into a drinking game with my friends). We made up dances to show off in the club. We'd play characters and perform skits for one another. We were all the entertainment we had and it was glorious.

You'd think as I got older, this environment wouldn't hold as much appeal for me. But Dakar was so dope, and I felt like a queen. I'm not trying to be conceited, but I was beautiful there. The first time I ever got catcalled in my life was on a street in Dakar. I was so excited that I turned around and answered the guy. It wasn't a clapback either. "Hey, girl, where you going?" *Wherever you'd like to go, boy.* "Oh . . . uh . . . never mind." My older brothers, who were so used to me being completely safe from any sort of sexual interest from men on the streets of Los Angeles, had not learned to be protective of me in any way, shape, or form. They were not wrong to assume that no one would ever sexually harass their sister. But in Senegal, there was a new girl in town, and she was fly.

One of my Senegalese cousins had to pull me aside and say in a very gentle way that it was not a good idea to respond to random men who yelled things about my body out in public. "*Tu es trop façile*," he told me, frustrated, which meant I was too easy. He told me that I should have more respect for myself because I deserved better. I wanted to cry happy tears. I was so touched, because not only did men here think I was hot enough to whistle at, they also thought I deserved respect.

This was a very empowering and exciting feeling as a teenager. By this time, I had become a well-established awkward black girl back in America—a progression that had come to light at the beginning of middle school. When I was in sixth grade, I moved across the country from a mostly white, gifted school in Maryland, where I was one of the only black girls, to a predominantly black middle school in Los Angeles, where I was berated for "acting white." Being a young adolescent is hard enough. Being black is hard enough. But I had awkwardness in the mix too. Yet somehow in Senegal this awkwardness got lost in translation.

I had this amazing currency there because I knew more about pop culture and I lived thirty minutes from Hollywood in America. By the time I was a teenager, I started bringing over VHS tapes and CDs to show my cousins all the latest American TV shows, music videos, and songs. One of the few American shows they already had over there was *Beverly Hills, 90210* and we'd all watch it together, and then I would field questions about all the cast members.

"Have you ever run into Dylan, walking around on the street, Issa?"

"Oh yeah, yeah, me and Dylan have crossed paths," I'd say without missing a beat.

"Whoaaa. What about Donna and Kelly?" (I love that they knew exactly what was up and didn't care about wack-ass Brenda either.)

"As a matter of fact, I was just at Kelly's house last week."

They totally bought it. I was a hero. I was cool.

But back home, I would regularly embarrass myself with my lack of coolness. When Tupac was shot, which was a huge event in LA, all the kids were talking about it at school. My nerdy self had no idea who Tupac was, which I blame on my older brothers, who usually would have introduced me to stuff like that, but they had all gone off to college at this point. So I didn't know a damn thing about Tupac. I remember kind of edging into someone's conversation at school one day trying to fit in, mimicking their hushed melodramatic tones.

"Yeah, I heard Two-Pack died." I nodded my head slowly like I was so devastated. "That's so sad. What did he sing?"

People rolled their eyes and walked away. It was humiliating. I was chubby (something my Senegalese aunts thought was lucky and healthy), and always in love with boys who wouldn't give my tomboy-looking self the time of day. Meanwhile, all the girls would make fun of my "Valley girl accent" and natural hair. It all got to be pretty exhausting.

It was so much easier to be myself in Senegal. And it was so much clearer that I belonged. I looked like regular women you'd see walking around there. I had so many cousins and aunts and uncles. I could have written my grandfather's biography. I was a dignified cultural ambassador. They thought it was cool that I wanted to write plays and TV shows. My dance floor movements registered as actual "dance." No matter how confused I was about myself, my identity, or my family—in Senegal I always found a feeling of home.

I remember going back just after my parents divorced, when I was sixteen. It was a really difficult time for me because I was angry at both of my parents in different ways. And yet, it was impossible to hate on my dad in his homeland. He was never the most present in my life, but his presence was so strongly felt there. He was a hero—one of seven kids, who became a successful doctor and helped so many people from his family and community. Whoever he was—which was mostly a mystery to me as a girl—translated better in Senegal. People always had huge smiles on their faces when they talked about him. It was an honor to be his daughter. I felt closer to him.

As for my mom, being there without her was deeply sad. My relationship with her was suffering as a result of the divorce, but I still missed her presence in Dakar. I knew she loved that place just as much as I did. Even though she wasn't Senegalese per se, she held on to it like I did. She had raised her kids in that culture and built her whole life around it. She loved my dad's family as much as her own. And now she was going to lose it all.

I remember having some long talks about Islam with my seventeen-year-old cousin Malick Seine during that trip. He was very religious, but also the bad boy of the family who smoked and drank and reveled in being the black sheep. He used to take pride in the fact that he was an excellent liar who could con anyone out of money, and he bragged about all the creative places he found to have sex with girls around the neighborhood. A picture of morality. Yet he could casually quote the Quran, and he clearly found strength and comfort in the role his religion played in his life.

It really inspired me, because I was just awkward and pessimistic about everything.

Hence my attempt to observe Ramadan when I got back home—which I already explained wasn't my most graceful gesture. I still give myself an A for effort. My Muslim family members in America were beside themselves with excitement. They used to tease me that I was too good to fast, so this was surprising news for them. My cousins were asking if I planned on keeping it up year after year. My dad would call to check in on me to see how I was doing, like a Weight Watchers buddy. He was proud of me. I was—mostly—proud of myself.

And PS, I would like to formally ask forgiveness from the religion of Islam as a whole for humoring me. I wasn't trying to become a devout, disciplined Muslim. I just missed my family and my dad. And I don't know if I learned anything deeper about myself, but it did allow me to pause for a moment at a troubling time of my life and collect myself. Connect myself. It wasn't a deeply religious gesture, but I can see now that in its own awkward and reluctant way, it was a spiritual one.

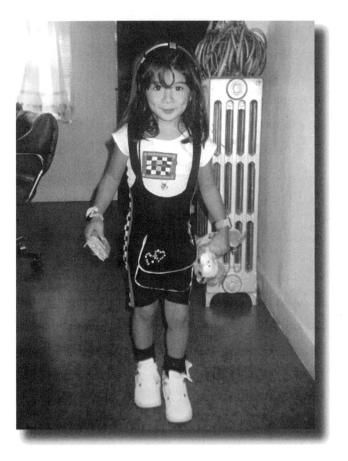

Diane Guerrero is an actress, activist, and author known for her roles on *Orange Is the New Black*, *Jane the Virgin*, and *Superior Donuts*. Her memoir, *In the Country We Love*, details her life as a citizen daughter of undocumented parents and highlights the consequences of our broken immigration system.

Diane Guerrero

WHEN I WAS A kid, my dad gave me the Mattel mini Cabbage Patch doll named Norma Jean for Christmas. She had peachy skin and long blond hair that she wore in pigtails that stuck straight out of her head and defied gravity. She had the typical Cabbage Patch doll freckles, fat rosy cheeks, and that sweet overbite. She also had these thick Harry Potter–style glasses that magnified her baby-blue eyes and made her look intentionally shy and a bit geeky. She was dressed in red, white, and blue—a little gingham dress with flowers on it.

I loved Norma Jean. She represented the American dream to me—a kid living the childhood idealized on TV. She represented clubhouses, talent shows, and the Fourth of July. She represented white picket fences, water balloon fights, and apple pie à la mode. I imagined all the Cabbage Patch Kids lived next door to one another and would play in their backyards and have slumber parties with flashlights and matching pajama sets. I imagined they had beautiful bedrooms where they would talk on the phone with each other to discuss boys or weekend plans. I never had my own room, much less a room with a phone in it, but the combination of these two things seemed like *the life* to me. I would holler at my mom in the kitchen that I was going to go talk on the phone in my room, and take a toy phone into *her* bedroom, pretending it was all mine.

I had a deep passion for pretending as a little girl—I would make up stories and songs and tell them to just about whoever would listen. I could stretch my imagination far enough to pretend I was Norma Jean in a squeaky-clean suburb with her own phone in her own bedroom. I could imagine that I, too, was named after America's most famous icon of beauty, Marilyn Monroe. Norma the doll looked nothing like Marilyn . . . or did she? Maybe Marilyn did look like Normie when she was her age. Either way, neither one of them looked anything like me. Or like anyone in my family. I look like my parents, who both have dark eyes, dark hair, and olive skin. My parents are good-looking people who always carried themselves like they were proud of who they were.

Both born in the same small town in Colombia—a country where nearly a third of the residents are born in poverty—they never had anything easy. Both came from very large families with parents who died too young. My dad worked the bean fields as a child and had to quit school to work full-time and support his siblings after his parents died. But he was always fit and charming, and my mother fell in love with him at a salsa party she was hosting when they were both in their late teens. Even though I always saw them working tough jobs, doing physical labor, busy from sunup to sundown, they always looked almost glamorous to me. And when you think about it, it's kind of funny that these two hardworking, self-respecting beautiful Colombians came all the way to America, where they worked their fingers to the bone so they could buy their daughter (me) this nerdy white doll.

My childhood was filled with dolls, toys, and characters from TV and movies whose lives weren't much like mine. But it didn't matter that Ariel and

Belle lived in another time and place or that they looked nothing like me. I related to their dreams, their passion, their long flowing locks, and their need to share their feelings in song. I loved to imagine I was a tragically beautiful fish out of water just like Ariel—wanting to belong on land and kiss that dreamboat Eric. *There must be more than this provincial life.* Yes, Belle, I hear you, girl. I feel you and I always have.

I wanted escape and excitement too—to be part of the grown-up world of love and adventure just like they did! The only difference was the fact that I dreamed those dreams from my urban concrete stoop instead of a charming French village. Instead of clapboard cottages, I lived in a funky house that was sort of falling apart. On my block, we'd sit outside with neighbors and listen to Puerto Rican freestyle like Stevie B or Lil Suzy and eat our mother's empanadas—or if I was at my friend's stoop, it was *pastelitos.* Sometimes we'd run through sprinklers in the public park, and buy all the twenty-five-cent popsicles, chips, and *limber* (flavored ice) we could get at the corner bodegas. The closest thing you got to seeing my childhood on TV was *Sesame Street,* but Grover never said anything to me about my life.

My parents struggled all the time—holding several jobs to pay the bills, trying so hard to give their kids a better life than the one they had growing up. Because they worked long hours, my obsession with singing solos to myself in the bathroom mirror was pretty convenient. I was born to be a storyteller, and there was no better way to pass the lonely time as a kid than to watch TV. I would disappear into shows like *The Wonder Years* or carefully study the movements and expressions of Kelly Kapowski on *Saved By the Bell* so I could pretend to be just like her. I was also taken with Nick at Nite and the old sixties and seventies reruns they aired on kids' networks for some reason. They were mostly shows about grown-ups from another time. It felt like learning American history—an America that was way out of my parents' reach but strangely within my grasp (at least in my own imagination). My favorite was the *The Mary Tyler Moore Show*. Mary was fly! I sensed what was rebellious about her, how she was different than the Cleavers or even the scandalously divorced Bradys. She was smart and broke the mold—all while looking amazing. Kind of like Miss Piggy, another leading lady I adored. When Mary threw her hat in the air in the opening credits, I pictured myself as her one day, feeling as happy as she did because I too was making it in my dream job.

I always wanted to be a performer. That's all I did as a kid. Not professionally of course. But I did think about it all the time, even though it seemed impossible. How could I make it as a performer when I never saw kids like me—or stories even remotely close to my life—on television? Sometimes I'd watch telenovelas, but I couldn't really relate to them either. I didn't have an evil twin sister, and I didn't fight with young girls in wheelchairs like on *Maldita Lisiada*. My life wasn't that melodramatic and I wasn't Itatí Cantoral. I was American, and I identified more with the American story. So even though there never seemed to be roles for girls like me, the arts did make me happy and they kept me out of trouble. They also stimulated me in a way nothing in school could. I realized this was a safe outlet for me, so I stuck with it. I always participated in any extra activity I could and took it one step further when I auditioned for the Boston Arts Academy for high school.

When I got accepted into BAA in ninth grade, it felt like a game changer for me and my family. A good public school I could attend—and a free one—where I could truly be my passionate, artistic self. I had teachers who encouraged me to sing and find my voice. It was suddenly *my homework* to devour the songs and stories of characters in great American musicals like *Miss Saigon*, *Rent*, *Jesus Christ Superstar*, *The Sound of Music*, and *Chicago*. I was introduced to American jazz singers like Nina Simone and Sarah Vaughan—who I wanted to embody. They were full of sorrow and yearning and loneliness, but they were still devastatingly beautiful and badass. They had something to tell me about pain, strength, and *me*, and I was all ears. Singing in school made me feel like I had a voice, like I was on my way to being something—maybe just myself—in a loud and proud way.

I was always paying attention to what might inspire me—ever sensitive to the music, TV, and movies around me. Just like when I was a little girl, except now it felt like my job. My calling. I felt everything. All the time. That's why it was such a big deal the day my best friend Stephanie and I were flipping through the channels and saw the preview for a movie called *Real Women Have Curves* starring America Ferrera and a lot of other real Latina women. Just the trailer alone was thrilling. Just the sight of all these Latina women having regular relationships, showing their bodies, expressing their hopes and dreams. Just seeing Latina actresses in bit parts would have been exciting, but in this one, they were the *main* characters—and they were being funny, loud, and genuine. Stephanie and I were dying to know when and where we could watch the whole movie. The day we finally got to see it, we were at her house flipping through the TV guide and saw that it was coming up next. We were over the moon excited, and we were jumping up and down going crazy. Stephanie's mom came into the living room to see what the commotion was. We said, "*Real Women Have Curves* is on! *Real Women Have Curves* is on . . . and it's a Latina cast!!" Her mother, who often just let us do our own thing, took the opportunity to sit down with us and watch the movie. It meant so much to me. I couldn't stop crying. It reminded me I was alive. It was such a special moment in my life to feel revived by these women on a screen—women who I didn't even know. September Eleventh had just happened, and attitudes had very rapidly become negative toward immigrants in America.

Every day on the news, you saw brown people villainized and treated like outsiders and enemies. But something about that movie made me feel safe, alive, loved, and lovable.

Around the same time is also when my friend Grisel and I discovered John Leguizamo and his one-man show special on HBO called *Sexaholics*. It was riveting and exciting. It felt like a miracle to see a Latino on TV talking about issues that mattered to us. We nearly memorized every word of that special. He talked about growing up as a Latino in New York, and I loved the fact that he was Colombian. That was really relatable to me. At school there was a constant fight with the Puerto Rican kids who would try to claim him. (It was before we could get that much information from the internet.) They would argue that he was Puerto Rican, but Grisel and I just couldn't let them have this. Not this. We knew the truth—he was ours. We'd watch the special over and over. He talked about sex, of course, and love, but he also made hilarious jokes about the fact that no one knows the history of Latinos in this country. I still remember him saying not even the Discovery channel knows our story. And no offense to current-day Discovery channel, which I kick back and watch from time to time, but I think it was one of the most rebellious expressions we'd ever heard. It was as if he was saying, *America has no idea who we really are, and we're about to change all that!*

It's pretty telling that anytime I saw a brown person on TV, I acted like I'd won the lottery. Like I was seeing a rare extinct animal in the wild. But I was growing up and realizing that my girlish dreams were kind of unlikely. There just weren't a lot of people like me on TV. And this did not make my pursuits in high school and college easy. Not only was it a very impractical career choice for a girl like me who had no money, I also struggled greatly with just allowing myself to believe I was worth such an impossible dream. I'd had a lifetime of pretending to be other people whose lives were *very* different from mine—and idolizing other characters who looked nothing like me. It sometimes felt like too much just to stay grounded, work enough to pay my way through college, and hang on to that lofty vision that I was gonna make it after alllllll.

Somehow—through dedication and even more struggle—I made it. But also, I'm just getting started. Because even though I have been so lucky to get to tell the stories of characters on shows like *Orange Is the New Black*, where diverse women from all walks of life are humanized and celebrated, and *Jane the Virgin*, where a multigenerational Venezuelan family gets to live the American dream, these shows are still fairly rare on television. My latest role was a smart young business owner who sells health-conscious food on the CBS comedy *Superior Donuts*. These are the kinds of characters that I want to portray—conscious women. These are the kinds of women that my community needs to see.

I think about the people who crave these kinds of stories. And I think about the kind of kids who turn on a TV every day, looking for a story that expresses their dreams or reflects their reality. And I want more for those kids.

So now I'm doing whatever I can. I wrote a book about my life and did a middle grade version of it so younger kids can read it. I visit colleges and schools and talk to young people about loving themselves and being proud of where they came from—even if it doesn't look like what they see on TV. I want them to feel worthy of their own dreams. My immigrant parents taught me to believe in the American dream. And immigration is part of the American fabric. Our stories matter. I still remember what it feels like to be that young teenager, flipping out to see *Real Women Have Curves*—and wanting to help John Leguizamo teach this country about Latino history. So now I'm helping with efforts to advocate for a Latin American Museum of History. Because the story of Latinos and Latinas *is* the history of our nation. It's a beautiful American story that all kids deserve to see.

Sometimes I imagine myself as a little girl again, walking the halls of a museum where my heritage is celebrated, where I learn about the great Latino heroes in American history. Or I imagine playing with Norma Jean again—only this time she looks a little more like me. Curling up on the couch, watching a TV show for kids, and laughing in recognition at what I see on the screen—a little girl with struggles and dreams like mine, with parents like mine—in a culture that tells beautiful, diverse stories.

Joy Cho

Joy Cho is the founder and creative director of Oh Joy!—a lifestyle brand focused on injecting happiness into every day through joyful products and creative editorial content. She is a first-generation Thai-American living the American dream. She lives with her husband and two daughters in Los Angeles.

My parents came to America from Thailand in 1975 with just
$600 and big dreams to study at an American university.

When they got pregnant with me a few years later, they decided to
stay in America for a better life
for their daughter . . . for me.

Despite having other first-generation friends
in the small town outside Philadelphia where I grew up,
I still spent much of my childhood and adolescence
wanting to look like the "norm"
(blond or brown hair with blue eyes).

I wanted to be American SO bad.
I knew I was American in theory, but I wanted to be *American* American.

I made it my job to teach my parents everything
they needed to know about
how to be "American parents."

For dinner, I instructed them to make classic American foods like mac and cheese, meat loaf, and mashed potatoes, *not* noodles with fish balls or roasted duck that they bought hanging in some window.

I totally love eating with *chopsticks,* but sometimes I wanted them to let me eat with *a fork and knife* too.

When we would go out to restaurants, I asked them not to order a side of white rice to go with everything and made them throw away the to-go containers at home instead of using them over and over again.

On Easter, I explained how to buy an Easter-egg dyeing kit from the store, boil the eggs, and dip them in food coloring so they could hide them in the backyard. It seemed weird to them to do anything with an egg other than fry it and put it over rice, *but I promised them we'd have fun!*

I begged them to pack a turkey sandwich in my school lunch instead of leftover Thai curry so I didn't have to hear all the kids ask, *"What's that smell?"*

On Halloween, I asked if they could give normal store-bought candy to the trick-or-treaters instead of White Rabbit candy from the Asian grocery store or homemade desserts like dried mango or sticky rice.

On Christmas, I thanked them for always working so hard to provide for us, but told them *they still had to give Santa credit for all the toys they bought us.*

On Thanksgiving, I said, "I know you want to eat Thai food for Thanksgiving 'cause it's the best food. *But can we please make a turkey with all the fixings just this one time?"*

When school was closed for the holidays, I explained that none of the other kids were doing extra tutoring sessions or bonus homework.

I must have said a million times, *"An A minus is still really good, I promise!"*

When my friends came over, I gently guided my parents into understanding that they aren't being nosy if they *ask my friends about themselves and their families.* But I never expected them to remember all my friends' American names!

I begged them to relax their *"no sleepovers before the age of fifteen" rule.* I promised I'd be good and that my friends' parents would always be watching us.

I convinced them that playing sports would be good for us, that we wouldn't get hurt, and *we needed to exercise more than just our brains.*

I agreed to go to Thai school on the weekends, but informed them *I would not be meeting my Thai husband there!*

But the older I got, *the less I "parented" my parents*
about how to be an American.

I found myself less embarrassed about my love of Thai food and even
wanted to share it with my friends.

I realized I had a *strong desire* to learn my parents' language better—
and not because they made me.

I realized the *best part of ME* is how I stood out from the crowd.

I no longer wanted to be like everyone else.

I wanted to be my Thai-American self, who stood out
because of my parents and what they gave me—
an incredible work ethic, and an amazing culture, rich in stories and
traditions that *NO ONE ELSE* will have in the exact same way ever.

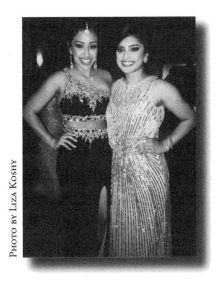

Liza Koshy, actress and entertainer, is most well-known for creating comedy skits and characters within her social network of more than forty million fans. She is the star of the YouTube original *Liza on Demand*, Hulu's *Freakish*, and host of MTV's reboot of *TRL*. Raised in Houston, Texas, as the youngest of three daughters, Liza is a dedicated sister, daughter, friend, and advocate for mental health.

Liza Koshy

SOMETIMES WHEN I TELL certain circles of people that I grew up in Houston, Texas, they get a pitying look on their face and say, "Ohhh, wowww, so you must have had to deal with a *lot* of racism growing up. . . ."

They give me those sad, knowing eyes, crinkling up their noses in a concern-troll kinda way, like they *really* feel for me and my brown skin. Then they keep going.

"I mean, you know, since you're . . ." They pause, considering my ethnicity, realizing they've just backed themselves into a corner. Because they have no idea what I am.

"Since you're . . . well . . . Wait, what are you? Where are your parents from? Are you Mexican?"

I am brown. And people have no idea why. It must be very stressful for them. But I like being racially ambiguous. Forever the ethnically mysterious little brown girl. People have mistaken me for being Polynesian, Puerto Rican, Mexican, Brazilian . . . the list goes on and on. And people aren't wrong to be confused. I mean, I do look a little bit like I'm from . . . *the whole entire world.*

My own hair doesn't know what I am. It is dark and curly and sometimes I wake up with a morning Afro. And even though my skin is mostly brown, it is also very, very white in all the places where the sun doesn't shine. My father immigrated here from Kerala, India, when he was sixteen. And my mother is a white lady from Virginia. He is dark chocolate, she is white chocolate, and I am their smooth milk chocolate. I am biracial, but growing up in the humble Houston suburb of South Braeswood made me so much more.

I consider myself extremely fortunate because South Braeswood was one of the most racially integrated places I've ever experienced. I grew up around equal numbers of Mexican kids, African-American kids, white-blond Baptist kids, white dark-haired Jewish kids, Asian kids, and, yes, even Indian kids. And we were all friends.

It was a place where people like my parents could thrive. Their love wasn't forbidden or difficult. No Romeo and Juliet drama for them. They got together and had three biracial kids—and they didn't struggle to equally share their white and Indian cultures with us. Even though my mother's church was Mennonite, which I'm thinking is about as white as they come, she was also a yoga teacher with Asian and Latino best friends. She loved Indian food and made our home into a baroque sanctuary of Indian culture with Indian carpets and artifacts from my dad's background. She raised me to appreciate a good white-dad joke, and we regularly ate both corn on the cob *and* curry. But she didn't push anything on me either. She never insisted that I share in her obsession with the ancient Indian yoga practice, but rather, let me twerk at dance practice. She was visionary enough to let me come to the realization on my own that I can't twerk. Because, as I learned, there's a big difference between having a "butt" and a "booty." And I have neither.

Anyway, as much as it may surprise some non-Texans, my friends and I didn't struggle with our ethnic identity as much as we had fun with it.

Every now and then, a well-meaning person on the street would ask my mother if I was adopted from Mexico. Because she and I don't look much alike. My parents thought this assumption was funny and called me their adopted Mexican daughter. My whole life.

Then they doubled down on their Mexican-child joke and sent me to a Spanish-immersion school where I learned to speak fluent Spanish as a child. That's a proud Texan right there. I can speak it better than some of my Texas-born Hispanic friends. My parents used to take the whole family to Mexican restaurants, where the waiters and cooks were from Mexican backgrounds, and insisted that I order for everyone in Spanish. You might assume my dad would have pushed me to learn his native tongue, Malayalam, so I could understand more about him and his upbringing, but instead he poured all his resources into looking like a baller when ordering enchiladas.

I wasn't the only butt of my parents' jokes. One of my sisters looks more Indian than the rest of us, so my parents gave her the most Indian-ass name they could think of. Rahel. But me and my other sister are named Elizabeth and Olivia. Way to be discreet, Mom. Rahel looks a lot like one of my Indian aunties, so my parents always used to joke that Rahel actually belonged to my aunt and they were just borrowing her. My other sister, Olivia, looks Polynesian, so naturally when we were on vacation in Hawaii, my parents kept joking that we were only there to look for Olivia's real parents.

My parents aren't cruel or weird. They're just funny. And a little bit weird, I guess. But we all looked different enough from one another that we had to have a sense of humor about it. Even my white grandfather used to call me his coffee-colored grandchild. There was such a mix of colors and cultures in my life, none of this seemed odd. As a kid, my two best friends were (1) a half-

French, half-Thai kid named Francois, and (2) a half-Jewish, half-Argentinian friend name Bessita. In the school lunchroom I was just as likely to be found eating with the white kids (who ate PB&Js and Slim Jims with handwritten notes from their moms on their napkins) as I was to be found eating with the Indian kids (who used their hands to shove last night's chicken curry down their throats). But most of the time I was eating with the Hispanic kids, who were eating collard greens, or the black kids, who were eating tamales. We did a lot of food trades.

My parents, with all their jokes and quirks, set the best possible example for me, making me comfortable with people of all backgrounds. In our little corner of Texas, culture and race felt fluid, natural, and fun. I experienced so many different religions, races, and cultures as part of my everyday life. It truly wasn't ever too stressful or confusing. Except when I had to fill out the forms and figure out which box to check.

Caucasian? Not entirely.

Asian? Hmmm. Well, India is in Asia.

Where was the box for "mixed"? Where was the box for me? Probably in the same place as that box my real parents shipped me in from Mexico.

See, *even I* can't get too serious about it.

I've usually been able to shrug off any identity confusion, because I had such chill parents and was surrounded by so many accepting families of different backgrounds. Sometimes my friends and I would casually reference each other's heritage in a way that people in other times and places might even think of as racist. For example, one of my really close white friends used to give me spices for Christmas. In another time and place, people might have thought this was a stereotypical gift to give an Indian—to the point of being reductive, rude, and racist. But to me, I was just psyched to get my hands on some fresh turmeric. One year, I was lucky enough to get curry powder.

Another time, I was showing some of my girlfriends pictures of my cousin's wedding. She was a spectacular, gorgeous Indian bride, complete with flowing red sari, bangin' beadwork, henna tattoos for days, flawless eyeliner, and a stunning, sparkling *tikka* draped around her head that dangled a beautiful string of gems down the center of her forehead.

We were talking specifically about the *tikka* and one of my friends said, "Yo, that ding-a-ling looks dope!"

I didn't even think twice about the *tikka* being called a ding-a-ling. Nothing offensive about that to me. Seriously. I didn't really know the proper name for the ding-a-ling either. I just had to google it right now for this essay. We never felt that we had to say stiff things like "I appreciate your cultural attire." We felt free to compliment it in our own way, with our own words. We were a generation of mixed-race kids who felt comfortable being curious. We always brought respect and love to our conversations.

As a teenager, I spent every Friday for four years straight with my dance team. Just like my neighborhood and my school, there were girls of every color and background on our squad, and I was the captain. The team was fifty shades of brown, and beautiful. Before every football game, we'd spend hours together doing our hair and makeup so we looked as fly as possible on the bus ride to the game. The time spent getting ready was the best. We'd trade off whose music we'd listen to, and which kind of dance we'd do to impress one another. Sometimes it was pure rap. The utmost ratchetry going down. We'd throw on a beat and make our own awful raps or throw ass to Drake. Other nights it was emo rock, lip-synching to Fall Out Boy. Then we'd eat tacos while listening to Tim McGraw country music—or grab Mexican-sushi fusion at our favorite restaurant, Japaneiro's. Our music and our food choices were just like us. *Mixed!* Everyone was always introducing their favorite music and foods to the rest of the team, and everyone loved what everyone else was sharing.

I know I am making it sound like we were one big beautiful rainbow with butterflies and candy sprinkles. But we kinda actually were. I had it pretty good. I know not everyone out there has the experience I had. But it wasn't all unicorns and cookie poops. There was that one angsty moment in my teenage years when I felt a little confusion and disappointment in my heritage. It happened when all my friends started having their special "becoming a woman" ceremonies, and I realized my culture had no such thing. I was envious as hell.

First there were the bat mitzvahs when my Jewish friends started turning thirteen. These kids *ball out* for their thirteenth birthdays. DJs. Magicians. Buffets and buffets and buffets of food. Chocolate fountains. Not just one. But maybe three per party. Ice sculptures in the likeness of the birthday girl's face. I've yet to ever have a party that good in my entire damn life. For a minute, I was pretty jealous of my friend Zoey Katz and was strongly considering becoming Jewish.

And then, as we got a little older, all my Hispanic friends were having their *quinceañera* celebrations for their fifteenth birthdays. I wanted one so badly for myself. I was usually the most excited guest at the party. When Alondra, Yadira, and Yajaira turned fifteen, I would *turn up*. I wanted that big sparkly ball gown and tiara. I wanted the satiny shoes, the shiny ribbons, and the delicate princess pillows they kneeled on while they prayed. I was thrilled when I got to be on Alondra's court of honor. I presented her the ring at the ceremony and watched with misty eyes as they gave her the *muneca*—a ceremonial doll symbolizing the transition into womanhood. Basically, they were giving her permission to stop playing with dolls and start wilin' out with an entourage of her closest friends right behind her. What could be better than that? Your whole community giving you the pass into the good life?! I was always the last one to leave the dance floor at the reception, salsa dancing and singing in Spanish with someone's uncle. All told, I attended over a dozen *quinceañeras* in my life. I even performed a dance at one. It was the closest I ever got to being celebrated like I thought I deserved.

I wanted to be a part of these ceremonies. Where was my symbolic doll, my chocolate fountain, my womanhood?

There was nothing my Mennonite-n-Curry family was going to do to help me out, so I decided I was just going to have to figure it out for myself. I would throw my own party. I got real creative one day after watching another rerun of MTV's *My Super Sweet 16* and decided my ceremony would be called My Spicy 16. You know. Spicy. Because I'm Indian. And Indian girls get to celebrate their womanhood too!

I went crazy with the theme. I decided that when I became a lady, it was going to involve mad coconuts. Which aren't spicy, I know. But they are very prominent in Indian food, and I happen to love them. My mother made coconut curry, and my white grandmother found a recipe for a delicious coconut cake. We had coconut macaroons, and I even wore a coconut bra. Because nothing says "I'm a woman now" like having tropical fruit shells hold up your lady biscuits. I'm sure the rabbis and priests at my friends' bat mitzvahs and *quinceañeras* would have gasped at my outfit. Alondra looked like a princess on her big day, and Zoey looked like a proper little lady. I just looked like a low-rent Moana. But I never felt more excited to share my big moment in a culturally fun way with my friends.

Because I kind of sprung this on my parents, we didn't have an all-out rager like my friends got to have. It was a modest festival of coconuts, held at my house, and I invited just a few of my closest friends. There was one white girl, one Hispanic girl, one mixed girl, and an Asian guy. They were all there to celebrate my womanhood, to raise me up as a beautiful graceful Indian adult. I imagined them gathering around me to admire my coconut bikini, and congratulate me for my new attitude as a spicy young lady. They were such good friends. All of them would be by my side and would cheer me on, ready to get coco*nuts*.

Except, as it turns out, three of the four of them were allergic to coconut.

And I had no idea of their allergies until they showed up and saw that literally nothing on the menu was coconut-free. It was a complete fail. One of them sneezed on my coconut boobs. My mom had to order pizza, and I ate the coconut cake all by myself. It wasn't glamorous or chocolate-fountain-like. There was even some talk of my coconut bra being a potential hazard to the white girl whose coconut allergy was especially fierce. So I had to remove my costume and just changed into my sad unisex pants that wouldn't offend anyone's food sensitivities. For a minute, I thought I was doomed to welcome my womanhood with very little fanfare. I was so sad.

Until I remembered. Prom was coming up! Perfect! What better place than prom to have a second chance at spiciness? I would have my Indian-woman moment after all.

In case you've been living under a rock, prom in Texas is as serious as a heart attack at a BBQ. This rite of passage is as extra as it gets. Extra glamorous, extra ridiculous, extra big, extra everything. This is the one day when the sixteen- to eighteen-year-olds who aren't really allowed to publicly party can get crazy. And in Houston, girls wear tiaras and crowns. Guys ask girls to prom with elaborate proposals that are fancier than their actual marriage proposals later on in life. The month before prom at a Texas high school is like being on an episode of *The Bachelor*, roses and balloons and flash-mob-type productions left and right as kids arrange their dates to prom. And girls spend all their bat mitzvah / *quinceañera* / sweet sixteen cash to ensure they show up to the big night dressed like a queen.

This would be the perfect place for me to have my coming-out party. My debutante ball. And this time it wouldn't involve coconut boobs.

I decided my prom dress was going to be half Indian and half white. Like me. I started looking for a dress by shopping at the pronounceable Caucasian stores. Indian dresses are so elaborate that you can't really take one and make it more white. But I figured I could always make a white dress more Indian. Much like my white mother—a Caucasian dress would be much more customizable and versatile. I ended up finding the perfect bright blue two-piece dress that resembled an Indian sari. It had the high-waisted fitted floor-length mermaid-style skirt and a separate top so my stomach was exposed. The top was like a halter top that only had one shoulder strap. It was extremely uncomfortable, so it checked off all the Indian boxes. It was very wildly bedazzled. You could say it was jewel-encrusted. For a white person, the level of sparkle was over the top. But for an Indian it did not even register as blingy. It basically looked like a sari without the drapey long piece of fabric wrapped around it. I will let you google exactly what that piece is called, but you can probably picture what I'm talking about. You know, that long beautiful cape-over-the-shoulder thing that hangs down the side or back? Sometimes it's sheer or lacy or covered in jewels. Anyway, I wasn't having that thing, because I can't twerk in a shawl. Even though we've already established I can't twerk in anything.

I topped it off with some very large, dangly, spectacular earrings that were so bright they created solar flares in all the photos, and of course I also wore the traditional Indian ding-a-ling on my forehead, a.k.a. my *tikka*, a.k.a. my very own brown-girl Texas tiara. I sparkled like Bollywood incarnate and I was ready to shake and grind as much as my tight dress would allow.

And my friends and I tore it up that night. The crowns, the gowns, the ratchet mermaids all around. It was a night to remember. I can still see us all in our big messy cluster on the dance floor. My white friends, my Mexican friends, my black friends. We all looked different, but we threw booty in unison. Our beautiful, booty-full world in Houston, Texas.

People talk about the diversity of American culture as being this big magical "melting pot." Which is a term that grosses me out. It makes me think of cheese. And all the cheese I eat, even though I'm lactose intolerant. And how gross and sad that is for anyone around me. But anyway, I don't think my friends and I melted together into one cheesy goo. We weren't a melting pot who forgot our differences. We recognized them loud and clear. We pointed them out to each other all the time. They were pretty obvious, and we had a lot of fun with them. Some people use the term *mosaic* instead of *melting pot*. And I guess that works a little better, but it also sounds like a word for stuffy, fancy people who go to museums and don't know how to twerk. I think I prefer the term *salad bowl* instead. Yes, it's a thing. Google it. You still have your browser open.

I never thought I'd be using salad metaphors, because I am more of a cheese-loving-lactose-intolerant girl—and a Texas one at that—but it works. We were a salad bowl. A bunch of different ingredients all tossed haphazardly in a way that came together as something delicious. No matter what color we were, we all saw each other as part of the same bowl. We each belonged and provided our own special flavor or texture. Am I the tomato? Cute and juicy and round? Wait, no, I don't have a booty. Maybe I'm the corn, because I'm hard to digest. . . . Either way, we had a little spice, a little sour, a little sweet, a little crunch. Cucumbers, carrots, chickpeas, olives, croutons coexisting in one place, and bringing out one another's complementary flavors. With a cozy blanket of salad dressing (ranch dressing, because it's Texas, y'all) tying us all together.

Thank God I'm a mixed kid from a Texas-salad-bowl world. I wouldn't have it any other way. I never had to be ashamed of my Indianness. Or my whiteness. No one called me out for speaking Spanish or twerking poorly. I was welcomed with open arms to drink from the fountain of liquid milk chocolate—and got to grow up just being me.

Oscar-nominated **Kumail Nanjiani** is an actor and writer.

Kumail Nanjiani

I REMEMBER THE DAY I first started learning English in Karachi, Pakistan. The first grade had just started for me. I was still trying to get acclimated to being away from home every day with all these kids and this stale chalk smell that, unbeknownst to me at the time, would be a massive part of my life for the next twelve years. We were a week in when the teacher pointed to a drawing of a tiger and said, "Tiger." I remember being annoyed. I already know how to say tiger. *Sher*. Why did I need another whole new way of saying it? *Now I will have to choose whether to use the Urdu word or the English word the next time I see a tiger.* I was six years old. I couldn't handle that kind of choice and the effort that came with it. I felt frustrated and angry. This first-grade scam was a real waste of my time. By the time we got to the word for rainbow, I had had enough. I threw the book down on the ground and pouted "Now this is getting ridiculous." In Urdu, of course.

I was eighteen years old when I moved to America from Pakistan. I moved, on my own, to Iowa for college. Not just Iowa, but a small town in Iowa called Grinnell with a population of fewer than ten thousand. When I tell people that, they get a quizzical look on their face. "Why Iowa?" And I always tell them the same thing: I truly had no idea how big America was. I wasn't yet aware of the great overabundance of choices one has in this country. It's so big and contains so many completely different terrains, cities, towns, and villages. I had known America from movies and TV shows (*Ghostbusters* and *Teenage Mutant Ninja Turtles* and *Gremlins 2*), so I assumed all of America was New York or LA. I landed in Des Moines, Iowa, and said, out loud to myself, "Where are all the buildings?" Then I was driven to Grinnell, and I said, this time under my breath, "Where are *any* buildings?" This was not the America I was shown in Pakistan. Karachi is a bustling metropolis too, and a rural area was so outside my reality.

My first two weeks in America were an extension of my first days learning English as a child. My jaw hurt from speaking a new language all day. I knew how to speak English (I'd learned how to say *rainbow*, *tiger*, and a whole host of other words), but I think my mouth wasn't used to making those English sounds all the time. I remember thinking that I should have never left Pakistan.

I didn't belong here. They didn't have any of my favorite foods, but they did have a lot of Rice Krispies. The other thing that struck me was just how many different brands of the same thing America has. In Pakistan, we had two brands of sliced bread, with wheat and white variations, for a grand total of four different types of bread. In the entire store. Occupying one portion of one shelf. Easy. The first time I walked into a grocery store here I remember seeing just rows and rows of bread. A sea of bread. Potato bread. Rye bread. Pumpernickel. No wonder everyone in America is always stressed out. Picking out bread is a massive undertaking each time! Oh, and peanut butter. We didn't have peanut butter. Here? Peanut butter on everything. Crunchy and smooth and kinda smooth and kinda crunchy. Peanut butter was a weird concept to me: Butter from a peanut? Listen to how that sounds. I'll stick to cow butter (or butter butter), thanks. But I couldn't say I didn't like peanut butter! To Americans, it seemed as if not liking peanut butter was akin to burning the flag. Even though you had a million choices for which kind of peanut butter you preferred, you did not get to choose to dislike it altogether.

Little things heightened the sense of strangeness of being in a new country. The average height in America is two inches taller than in Pakistan. In Pakistan I was one of the taller people. I would walk into a room and see the tops of people's heads. And now suddenly I was shorter than most people. It wasn't like I was in a land of giants, because it's only two inches. It was more like I was standing in a ditch . . . that moved with me.

My dorm room freshman year was tiny, just large enough to hold a chest of drawers and a bunk bed. My roommate had the top bunk; I had the bottom. Every night I looked at the metal bars of the bed on top of me and they looked like prison bars. And that's how I felt. Like I was in prison. Trapped. My prison bars would be the first thing I would see every morning. It didn't make sense. I would lie there and think, *This is the first time I'm out on my own, away from my family, out in the world. I should feel free*—but I felt trapped. Trapped in this land of overwhelming options and choices.

But there were some good things too.

I saw snow for the first time. The first time you see snow, it is beautiful and terrifying. I was standing outside in a cornfield, watching it fall slowly from the sky. I had never seen anything fall slowly from the sky before. I had seen rain and I had even seen hail, but those fall fast. And here I was, watching these beautiful white flakes fall slowly from the sky, and it seemed like the whole world was in slow motion, except me. That I was moving at a different speed from everything around me. And I could focus on the whole, or just

pick one snowflake and watch it sway to the bottom, as if there was no gravity, as if each flake was deciding where it wanted to land.

Then I shook hands with a girl for the first time. I don't want to overstate
things, so I'll just say I felt alive for the first time. In Pakistan I'd only ever
touched females I was related to.

I started making friends from all over the world. And the culture at our
school was so accepting that people went out of their way to make me feel
welcomed, even if they didn't understand that English made my mouth hurt.
I had gotten obsessed with Bruce Springsteen at the age of sixteen in Pakistan.
Something about the yearning in his music really connected with me. So
much of his work is about hopping into a car and driving away, every lyric
tinged with excitement, romance, sadness. "Well, the night's busting open,
these two lanes will take us anywhere." I felt the bigness of the world, but I
hadn't seen any of it yet. Perhaps that's why his lyrics spoke to me. Maybe
that's why Iowa was an accidentally fitting place for me. He sings about people in small towns as if they are heroes destined for adventure. Whenever I
mention to people I love Bruce, they go, "Isn't that ironic? 'Cause of 'Born in
the USA.' "

I always smile and go, "I don't understand." I make them explain it to me.
(By the way, I was the only kid in all of Pakistan obsessed with Springsteen. I
would make my friends listen to his songs and they'd go, "Why do you listen
to country music?")

One of my first weeks in America, my new college friends got together to
go and steal road signs. I'm not proud of it, but that's what we did. Not stop
signs or anything real like that. The DRUG-FREE ZONE sign was real popular. As
we ran around in the dark, hiding from campus security, I realized that America is just like the one that Bruce Springsteen sang about, with people trying
to find adventure in the dark, trying to find their way through the American

dream. I'm realizing that the American dream means choice, or rather, the promise of choice. Choice in where you want to drive to, choice in what kind of bread you want, choice in what kind of peanut butter you want to spread on that bread, choice in what kind of life you want to live. You can choose to locate yourself wherever you want among so many cities; you can listen to any kind of music, eat any cuisine, worship whomever you want—or no one at all. You can even marry whomever you want. Most people here have a handful of ethnicities that make up their DNA, and they can choose to identify with whichever one they feel most akin to. You can be born into a poor family and grow up to be American royalty. You can speak any language, raise any flag. Do what you want! You can be whatever you want to be! Now, what are you going to do? Who do you want to be?! *Choose!*

It's a lot of pressure! There is tremendous opportunity, but with that comes tremendous room for failure. And, of course, these choices are not available to everyone, even though that is the promise of America. And most Americans choose to believe in this promise, despite piles of evidence to the contrary.

As the years have passed, I have become more acquainted with American choices, and all the paradoxes that follow. I have become more comfortable with the luxury of decision making, and my jaw is no longer in perpetual pain. I am no longer dazzled and puzzled by bread choices as far as the eye can see. I enjoy a wide variety of carbohydrates regularly, and I even named my own cat Bagel. I can now confidently say I don't like peanut butter without fear of people going, "*You don't like peanut butter?!*" I understand that access to opportunity is not available to everyone, and that I've been very lucky in that regard. I mean, I got to choose the career where you stand in front of crowds of people, telling jokes into a microphone. It is a viable career option in this country. It is even a viable career option here to sit in your living room all by yourself with a microphone and record podcasts. The options truly are endless. And I've been fortunate enough to be able to enjoy this culture of choice, to build a wonderful life with my wife, a life neither of us could have dreamed of ten years ago. And now I live an existence full of daily options. Just yesterday, I got to choose from a dizzying assortment of fifteen different sauces for my chicken sandwich. Fifteen!

Despite the glaring disparities of choice that still exist in this country, I still think it's a great place. I can look past the bizarre confederacy of peanut butter eaters and still be extremely grateful to America.

I wouldn't choose anywhere else.

Michelle Kwan is the most decorated figure skater in US history. She is a two-time Olympic medalist, a five-time world champion, and a nine-time US champion. She is a former senior adviser/envoy for the US Department of State and serves on the board of directors of Special Olympics International.

Michelle Kwan

FIGURE SKATERS CAN LOOK so perfect. Gliding across the ice, beautiful costumes flowing in the wind, music swirling, graceful leaping, precise twisting . . . it can look impossible and magical.

But behind the scenes is a different story. It can get ugly.

Learning to skate means falling down over and over and over again. It means working on the same jump repeatedly for hours and falling painfully every single time. There is no grace or magic. Just skating, jumping, falling. Twisting, turning, falling. It is literally like banging your head against the wall repeatedly. Sometimes it's more like a car crash.

My coach Frank used to yell "*Stop*, Michelle! You've hit a wall. Let's take off your skates and call it a day." I was ten years old and relentless. I would want to skate longer, jump more, and fall again—until I finally got it. I was determined to keep working, to take more crazy, difficult leaps in the air. I inherited this from my parents. Taking risks and chances is their story too.

My mom and dad immigrated to America from Hong Kong and Guangzhou before I was born. They were in their early twenties and did not complete their education. They spoke almost no English and literally used all their money to buy the plane tickets to get here. They took this leap because they knew there was more opportunity for them and their future children here. They knew they had to be bold to achieve the American dream.

For my family, the American dream wasn't just a fairy-tale notion or a meaningless phrase. It has always been real and extremely motivating. It was the idea that if you work hard and take big risks for what you believe in, you can accomplish anything. My parents didn't feel like they had this chance where they grew up, so they brought themselves and their extreme determination to America.

This was a huge risk but still not the most daring choice they made. It's a far crazier decision to support your two daughters in ice skating than it is to come to a foreign country with no money in your pocket. Paying for kids to skate is like having negative money in your pocket.

My dad started out in America working in a Chinese restaurant and then later bought one when he'd saved enough money—and shared expenses with his parents, who had come to California along with him. My mom worked in the restaurant, and we ate a lot of our meals there too. At the age of seven—just a few years after I tried ice-skating at the local mall for the first time—I already had my sights set on becoming an Olympic skater. My parents thought this would just be a hobby for their rambunctious daughters, but suddenly they were on the hook for skates, costumes, rink fees, and—by the time I was age nine—a professional skating coach. My parents worked so hard to keep it all going. They both had to work multiple jobs to cover our costs. Everything was sacrificed for their children's dreams.

My parents didn't do all this with the Olympics in mind. They just wanted me to have the opportunities they never had. They hoped I would be strong and healthy and have a good childhood. My dad used to worry that I felt pressured to skate, because I was so intense about it. He'd hand me the amount of cash I needed to get into the rink and say, "Here's five dollars and seventy-five cents, Michelle. Use it for whatever you want. You can go skate, or you could also go buy some candy!" In some part, I think that it was a reminder to us of how much money they were spending in order for us to continue our hobby. Of course, I would always choose ice time over candy. Even when he was convinced the motivation was all internal on my part, he still never pushed me. I think the best-case scenario in his mind was that I'd get an athletic scholarship one day, because my parents had no idea how they were going to put three kids through college.

Just stepping into an ice rink costs money—not to mention buying the clothing and gear and paying coaches, choreographers, dance teachers, and physical trainers. Just the skates alone are pricey. If you don't replace them as soon as you start to outgrow them, you risk breaking an ankle. Even *used* skates can cost $500, plus $750 more for the blades. I always had holes in my tights and gloves, and I wore hand-me-down costumes. Paying for everything was a constant struggle. One time my dad brought home a pair of new skates, and I could see how proud he was to have been able to provide them. He said they were custom-made, but I knew this wasn't possible, since I hadn't been fitted for a mold—not to mention the girl's name written on the bottom of the shoe that my father had done his best to scratch out with a thick black marker. At the 1993 national championships, my parents borrowed a costume for me from another competitor. Even at the point that I was skating on the national level, our family had to rely on donated gear. I was very fortunate because I received a travel and training grant from the Women's Sports Foundation, which helped my parents out a lot. Looking back, there were so many times that I almost had to quit skating because of our financial situation.

At one point, my parents literally sold their house and moved us into a smaller one so there was more money for me to skate. We saved money like crazy in my house. We had a five-gallon jug where we squirreled away change and we'd use it to buy groceries. My parents never had nice things for themselves. My dad drove an old beat-up blue Pinto that my sister and I were embarrassed of at school drop-offs. We gave up things like new clothes, vacations, and Christmas presents so my sister and I could compete.

One year my sister and I were determined to have a Christmas tree. We begged our parents, but there was no money for it. "*Skating* is your Christmas," my dad said. But as luck would have it, there was a competition going on at school that year. Whoever could string the longest popcorn garland in the shortest amount of time would win a fully decorated miniature Christmas tree (as tall as my waist) to take home. I saw an opportunity, and I seized it. I threaded that Jiffy Pop on the needle so fast my fingers could have bled. I was determined to get that tree. When I want something, I don't give up. Later that day, my dad picked me up from school and helped us load my winnings into the back of the Pinto. My siblings and I laughed all the way home and used our meager savings to buy a few presents to put under the tree.

My parents gave us whatever Christmas or Chinese New Year they could. They worked and earned as much as they could to support my skating dreams, but their greatest sacrifice might have been their time. Neither one of them slept more than five hours per night for a good fifteen years. Free time was utterly nonexistent for them.

There were a couple of years when we'd have to wake up at three forty-five in the morning so we could skate a few hours before going to school. My sister and I would go to bed the night before wearing our tights so we'd have one less thing to do in the morning. Later in my athletic career we trained at a special ice rink for serious skaters competing at the highest level. This facility was two hours away from our home, and during those years my dad would commute four to five hours at the wheel every single day to support us. It makes me shudder to think how much of his life was spent working and driving. I remember seeing my mom up in the middle of the night painstakingly sewing teeny-tiny beads onto my costume. She is not a seamstress by any means, but she wanted me to have good costumes like everyone else, and the tedious work of gluing on every little crystal did not deter her. If we couldn't afford to buy something in my family, we'd borrow it or make it ourselves. If we didn't know how to make it, we'd learn how. This kind of grit was expressed in everything my parents did—so I learned from the best. It's not surprising I won the Christmas tree contest or often skated through injuries and illness.

I remember overhearing quiet conversations between my parents when they were stressing about money. It was always difficult to figure out which corners to cut, and how much more they could spend on a skating expense. When things would get especially tough and my dad would need to lean on my grandparents for financial help, he was sometimes met with scrutiny and questioning. Shouldn't skating be the first thing to go if bills couldn't be paid?

As far as my grandparents were concerned, we had a great life in America—we had a roof over our heads, clean water to drink, food to eat, and most of all, each other. My grandparents' lives had been unspeakably hard. When my grandfather was a child in China he was given to a local farmer to help tend to the crops and animals. His parents couldn't afford to take care of him—something that was not uncommon in the desperate economy he grew up in. So for my grandparents, living in America with their son, running a family restaurant together, enjoying their grandchildren—this was the life they had always dreamed of.

And rest assured it was a dream for my father too. He risked everything to come here, after all. But he wasn't going to stop there. He wanted his children to have it even better, no matter how crazy that may have seemed to his parents or his friends. It's remarkable how much my grandparents endured, and how much my parents sacrificed and worked. The least I could do is be scrappy on the ice. I came from a long line of hardy people, and it wasn't going to stop with me. The only difference was that I was lucky enough to be born into a place where hard work could actually yield extraordinary results—something the previous generation would have never dreamed possible.

In addition to learning to be extremely hardworking, my home life made me very resilient and self-sufficient. I put myself to bed when I was tired and chose to eat healthy foods for my training regimen when everyone else my age was eating whatever they wanted. Because of my training schedule I didn't have much time to hang out with friends or go to movies, but I never felt like I missed out, because skating was an incredible outlet where I could be creative and expressive. It also kept me from boredom or the kind of teenage rebellion a lot of kids go through. I was too focused on making it to the Olympics—and I would do whatever I could to fast-forward to my goal.

Competitive skating has several levels that you have to test into—and you can't qualify for the Olympics until you reach the highest level, senior. As I started competing seriously, I decided I was going to get to senior level as fast as I could. It was 1992, I was eleven years old, and I wanted to be a part of the 1994 Olympics. It was a very ambitious goal, especially considering I was still several levels away from senior and it takes most skaters at least a year to advance through each level. But I was a beast, mastering all the jumps and moves I needed to pass each test, and by the time I was twelve, I was at the junior level. I only needed to advance one more level, but my coach Frank didn't think I was ready for the senior test because I'd only placed ninth at the national junior competition. I was young and unrefined, bold and . . . well, twelve.

So one week when Frank was out of town, I told my dad to take me for my test, and I led him to believe that Frank was okay with it. I was nervous going behind my coach's back, but I felt very strongly that I shouldn't play it so safe or conservative. I didn't want to rise slowly in the rankings as he was advising. I wanted to be a shooting star—and the youngest in the senior level by many years. It was a huge risk, but once I made up my mind, I had to go for it. It was like my parents coming to America, carrying out what was maybe not the most ideal plan but definitely *the right thing to do*. My mom and dad have demonstrated time and again that you don't have to plan perfect transitions in life. You don't have to land flawlessly. You just have to take the leap.

I passed the test and confessed to Frank when he got back to town.

It was (and still is) viewed in the skating world as an act of unconventional defiance and rebellion. But it got me into competitions where I was skating against my idols, and it ultimately landed me a spot as an alternate on the 1994 Olympic team at the age of thirteen. I went on to compete in the 1998 and 2002 Olympic Games and win several national and world titles, becoming the most decorated skater in US history. I owe this to the fact that I skated at the senior level for more than a decade and I worked really, really hard all along the way. But most of all, I owe this to my parents, who were willing to set aside their lives for my dream. My whole childhood, my dad didn't sit down for a meal, much less sit on any chance to help his children. There's not enough time in my life to express my gratitude to my parents. I always felt their confidence in me no matter how well I was performing or how much it cost them.

The American dream is a ladder of opportunity. It's not just for the rich to climb. It's not just for those whose great-great-great-great-grandparents were born here. It's for anyone, including people like my parents, who are willing to take a leap, work hard, fall even harder, and get back up again.

Geena Rocero, born and raised in Manila, Philippines, is a model, host, producer, and trans rights advocate. On March 31, 2014, in honor of International Transgender Day of Visibility, Rocero came out as transgender at the annual TED Conference. Her viral talk has since been viewed more than three million times and has been translated into thirty-two languages. Geena is the founder of Gender Proud, an award-winning media production company that tells stories to elevate justice and equality for the transgender community.

Geena Rocero

BEAUTY PAGEANTS MIGHT AS well be the national sport of the Philippines. The way Americans watch football or basketball is how Filipinos watch pageants. They take place in mountain villages, provincial coliseums, and concrete stages next to rice fields. They are so embedded in mainstream culture that you can catch one almost any month of the year. Because they are a part of Fiesta celebrations where we honor Christian saints and patrons—and because nearly 95 percent of the population is Catholic—Fiesta pageants are just another wholesome activity that nearly everyone enjoys.

I still remember the feeling of neighborhood Fiesta celebrations as a kid in Manila where I grew up. It was a fun and exciting time, with people on the streets drinking, going from one house to another without formal invitations—and somehow you were always just welcomed into the homes of random people. Kids, grandmas, aunties, friends, and entire families sitting outside, eating and applauding, all eyes on the stage. Fiesta included singing contests, dancing contests, and transgender beauty pageants. The irony of transgender beauty pageants being a popular shared custom in one the most conservative religious celebrations is not lost on me. Even though there was no word for *transgender*—and certainly no acceptance of being transgender in the church—these pageants were hugely popular. No one called them transgender beauty pageants, but that's what they were. There was no shared vocabulary or context for explaining to your parents that you knew you were not the gender you were assigned at birth. So I wore T-shirts on my head to pretend like I had long flowing locks and walked down our hallway like it was my runway. And when Fiesta came around I was sitting in the front row at every single pageant.

I remember seeing my first one around seven years of age. The contestants—mostly teenagers—all lined up in their costumes, striding out with such poise and glamour. I was transfixed—especially by one contestant who was a Phoebe Cates impersonator. I had no idea who Phoebe Cates was at the time, but I was fascinated. She and all the others were compelling, and I couldn't take my eyes off them. Immediately I felt a connection. *Maybe I am like them. Maybe I can be them.*

I never shared this dream with my mother, but I made it very clear that I was pageant material. I used to steal the lipstick from her purse before she'd leave for work. I chose to play with little girls and dress up Barbies for fun. She was an elementary school teacher, always surrounded by young children, so she must have noticed what was different about me, but she never made me feel shame. I told her I was really a girl, and she just said, "Okay, if that's who you are . . . whatever makes you happy."

When I turned eleven she left for America, something we always knew was coming. Members of the older generation in my family had fought for the United States in World War II and were granted opportunities to come to the United States and bring family members over to become citizens. Going to America meant that my mother could be with her mother and some of her eight siblings who had already been there for several years. It meant more opportunities for her children. It meant she could work and send money home until she could petition to get us there. This had always been our family's destiny, so it did not come as a surprise, but it still sent shock waves through my whole existence.

After my mother left for San Francisco, my sister and I stayed with our dad in a small province outside Manila and attended school. I wore a boy's uniform every day. Most of the subjects were taught in the formal version of English that I have spoken from a very young age, but at home we spoke Tagalog—and cried for our mother, who we missed every day.

And then I met Tigerlily, my trans mother figure for two of the most important years of my life. I was fifteen years old—still a die-hard fan of pageants—and had just gotten a taste of participating in my first one when a friend of mine asked me to be a backup dancer for the opening number of one in our province. A few days later, my friend Reynald invited me over to her house because a pageant troupe from Manila was going to be getting ready for that night's pageant at her place. Reynald knew how exciting it would be for me to see these queens in person, who I normally only saw onstage or on TV. When I arrived, Tigerlily, the manager, and all her girls were there, doing hair and makeup, sewing costumes, and blowing my mind. When Tigerlily saw me, she told me I was tall, fresh, and beautiful. She asked if I was interested in being in pageants, and within a few minutes I put on another girl's swimsuit and showed her my walk. She offered me a spot in that night's pageant. It was like a fairy-tale moment for me, where the small-town girl gets discovered by her fairy godmother.

That night was unforgettable and surreal. Tigerlily quickly threw together a set of garments for me to wear, and I lined up with all the other girls for this most exciting rite of passage. My swimsuit was a two-piece bright orange number that looked great with my dark skin, and my gown was borrowed from another girl on Tigerlily's squad. For my casual wear, I dressed like a young ballerina in fuchsia pink and super-high heels. I looked like a living Barbie doll. It was thrilling. I impersonated Assunta de Rossi, a beautiful actress who's very popular in the Philippines. When I walked on the stage, I felt a sense of validation I had never felt. To hear a crowd cheer for you at your best, brightest, and most beautiful—it was the most exhilarating thing possible. I made it all the way to the semifinals. Out of forty-five candidates, I was in the top twelve.

And that is how I became a fifteen-year-old beauty queen literally overnight. The rest was history, and I was hooked.

Tigerlily was like a coach and a manager and a mother all rolled into one, helping our group of young trans girls define and perfect our performances. We not only needed guidance on our clothing, talent, and poise—we needed help with our makeup, preparing for the interviews, finding resources for travel, and developing our impersonations. Every village or town had a pageant mom who ran the pageant scene in her territory. Although we all competed against one another at pageants, we were each other's best support system too. Tigerlily's girls were my new family. I still technically lived in my house with my father and sister, but my new home was with my pageant sisters, where I completely immersed myself in a community that provided validation and fun for a young trans girl. We traveled all the time, and when I would come back home to my father and sister, I loved sharing my winnings, taking my sister out shopping or to the movies. She could see how happy I was that I'd found this group of friends.

It changed everything for me. I remember a few pageants in, thinking, *This is me now. I am going to go full-time as myself! No more boy's uniforms at school!* I started wearing female clothes all the time—not just onstage—and used my pageant winnings to buy hormones—something many trans girls were beginning to do. It was dangerous because it was unsupervised by medical professionals, but it was also crucial in our journey to become more authentically ourselves. It was survival for us.

The pageant community was my survival too. Tigerlily not only helped us manage our careers, but she also served as a mentor and emotional supporter in a very tumultuous teenage time. I found a sisterhood of best friends who accepted me and understood me in a way I only dreamed of when I was a kid. Pageants are considered sexist to many people all around the world. I am a feminist, but where I grew up pageants were the only place where I could express myself and earn money for my performance. Through pageants, I learned how to command a stage, speak without fear, and love who I am— not to mention I found a community of women who had my back no matter what. The skills I learned being a beauty queen are the same skills I used several years later in my activist work.

We were competing in so many pageants—sometimes two or three per week—that I was able to make hundreds of dollars and it became my full-time job when I finished high school. By then I had done nationally televised pageants and become one of the most prominent queens, winning most of the big titles. I was more happy and secure than I'd ever felt in my life.

And then at the age of seventeen, everything changed. My papers had come through for me to immigrate to San Francisco to be with my mom. It should have been good news—and it was. But it was complicated. I had missed my mother so much, but leaving Tigerlily and my pageant girls was devastating. We didn't have Facebook or texting then. I remember landing in San Francisco and writing Tigerlily a letter because even a phone call was very expensive. I felt so cut off from the family who had been my only home for the last two years. They were my safety net and my mirror, showing me it was okay to *be me* for the first time in my life. It felt like cutting myself in half to leave all that behind.

It did not help that San Francisco felt so foreign to me. Even though I spoke English, my version of the language was formal and polite—and slang or everyday idioms were completely lost on me. Even the fresh, balmy air was strange to me—it was wonderful of course—but I was used to the gritty, dirty smell of the city. Where I grew up houses were literally stacked up next to each other, separated only by thin plywood walls. This new white-picket life was very alienating to me. San Francisco felt isolated compared to Manila, where kids played out in the streets at all times. And even though a lot of people were Catholic in San Francisco, they didn't celebrate Fiesta. I missed the rowdy outdoor parties and wandering from house to house to talk to neighbors.

And no Fiesta celebrations meant no trans beauty pageants. I was heartbroken and homesick.

"This is America; it's not the same as the Philippines," my mother would say.

She fully accepted me as I was, and allowed me to be me—but she had to get real with me about the fact that I wasn't going to make money from pageants in the United States. And I had to find work because I needed to earn money. It was so hard to let go of "trans beauty queen" as my job title. My mother knew the feeling—she went from being a teacher in the Philippines to being a factory worker in America. She kept suggesting that I apply at a grocery store or maybe try for some sort of customer representative job. But I was hardheaded and seventeen and had just left the most affirming, exciting career I could have ever hoped for. It was more than a career—it was a lifestyle—and a glamorous one, which is not something most seventeen-year-olds get to enjoy. So I was having trouble signing up to work in a food court at a mall. I felt so disconnected and needed to find my people.

And I wasn't just a beauty queen without a pageant. I was an immigrant now, trying to find a home in a completely new country. Something told me that the secret to my survival was to find other immigrants from Manila. I started asking my pageant friends back home to see if anyone had a friend in San Francisco. A friend of a friend in Manila told me about Lucy. She'd been living in San Francisco for a few years and invited me to visit her apartment and meet other Filipinos.

That night was the beginning of my new life in America. Lucy introduced me to a great group of girls. We went to a late-night Thai restaurant and danced until the wee hours of the morning. The next day, we had Filipino brunch in Daly City—otherwise known as Little Manila. What a welcoming place for any Filipina immigrant! After our brunch, one of the girls mentioned that there might be a job opening at the cosmetics counter where a bunch of the girls worked in a big department store. Even though my only experience with makeup was when it was being applied to my face by someone else, I insisted I would be good for the job. She laughed at my resolve and set up an interview for me.

I went to that job interview like a true beauty queen, ready to conquer the world. I looked like my best self. I got my hair done, in a nice, understated way. Not a pageant style, but a nice blowout with layered waves that didn't move no matter how hard the wind blew on my way there. Somehow I got the job. The first day at work made me feel at home. It may not have been a pageant, but I was surrounded by makeup and lovely women and a lot of the girls I'd gone dancing with a few weeks before. In no time at all, this group of girls had become my new family. Instead of sharing a love for pageants, we had our love of cosmetics, dancing, and garlic fried rice.

The Asia and Pacific Islander Wellness Center became a regular hangout for me and the girls, every Wednesday. It was a place that served the immigrant and LGBTQ communities, and Wednesday was trans-girls' night. We would meet up to share our stories, have a potluck, connect, and learn about ways to improve our health and our relationships with ourselves. API Wellness became my refuge, where I could get critical information about things like taking hormones and finding doctors who would provide compassionate care. This new source of information and community-building gave me a better sense of my own worth and belonging in America. As I developed deeper friendships, I was able to share more about my passions and dreams until I finally felt determined to find a trans pageant in San Francisco.

If you're lucky there's maybe one per year there, but a girl at API Wellness had mentioned she'd heard about one coming up. Lucy helped me sign up for the pageant and helped me find the supplies I needed. I got right back into my old rhythm, putting together a look and costumes. If it couldn't be my career anymore, I was still going to work this pageant like it was my job. I couldn't wait.

The pageant was at the Palace of Fine Arts, a beautiful old building in the Marina District. It had a huge stage. I had borrowed a red halter gown from Lucy and was most nervous about the interview portion, since my English was still a little too formal and I had trouble communicating my real personality. But as soon as I arrived and began getting ready in the dressing room, I felt so inspired. Unlike the Philippines, where most of the girls are Filipina, here there were contestants from so many cultures and nations. Samoan, Taiwanese, Polynesian, Thai, Latina, and a lot of Filipinas too, of course. As I looked around at all these American faces, I loved seeing all the many ways there are to be trans. There's not just one way. And beauty is more diverse than we imagine too. I thought of Tigerlily and all my Filipina girls back home. In the Philippines, trans people were highly visible—even celebrated in pageants—but they weren't politically recognized. In America, it seemed just the opposite—at least at the time. Trans people were more politically recognized in America, but not nearly as visible and celebrated. *How lucky I am,* I thought, *to experience both of these cultures.*

I couldn't wait to sashay out on that stage and give it everything I had. If I was only going to get to do this once a year as a hobby, I was going to make it count. As I predicted, I struggled a little in the interview portion with my English. I didn't say anything grammatically incorrect, I just had trouble conveying my intelligence and personality. I wanted them to see who I really was. One of the judges asked if I was enjoying my new home in the United States. I smiled and nervously replied, "Yes, I love being here with my family."

As I uttered these words, I looked out across the audience to see dozens of Filipinos smiling and rooting for me. They had come out in droves to enjoy their favorite pastime—just like at Fiesta.

I ended up winning second runner-up. Not bad for my first American pageant, but mostly I was just happy to be home.

PHOTO BY MARY WALN

Frank Waln is an award-winning Lakota hip-hop artist, producer, and audio engineer from the Rosebud Rez in South Dakota. A winner of three Native American Music Awards and recipient of the Native Arts and Cultures Foundation 2018 National Artist Fellowship for Artistic Innovation, Frank Waln travels the world sharing his story through music and presentations focusing on finding our truth and reconnecting to our roots.

Frank Waln

MY GRANDMOTHER IS AN alchemist trapped in a death camp. Mother of eleven, grandmother of too many to count, and relative to many, my grandmother's spirit forged gold out of scraps in spaces and places that were built to kill and destroy her people. Foreign invaders took everything she would have used through countless acts of physical, spiritual, and emotional violence. Still she found a way to turn everything she made into gold, including me.

I, like my grandmother, was born and raised on the Rosebud Indian Reservation in south central South Dakota. What I didn't know until I was in my midtwenties was that our reservation was historically a concentration camp where the US government marched my people to die. I later learned this happened to more than 560 different nations of people in a historic and ongoing effort to systematically eliminate indigenous people. Why would the government want to do this? Why would they want to destroy the people with whom they signed hundreds of treaties? Because they broke the treaties and built their country on stolen land. To erase us is to erase the evidence of their violence. Once Native Americans cease to exist, the United States can rewrite the history of this illegal settler colony.

I learned that the US government not only trapped my great-great-grandparents on concentration camps called reservations, they also limited and regulated our travel, food, education, housing, health care, and day-to-day lives within those concentration camps. We had to get permission from white settler men called "Indian agents" if we wanted to get food, fix our own houses, or travel between communities on our reservation to see relatives. If we didn't get permission from the Indian agent overseeing our district, we were violating US law and would be arrested. This was also a time when it was illegal under US law for us to practice our cultures, ceremonies, or ways of life. We weren't free to even practice our religions until the American Indian Religious Freedom Act of 1978. Growing up, I didn't realize each and every person on our reservation descended from those who survived genocide. We carried the strength and trauma of the Indians they couldn't kill. We became alchemists out of acts of survival. We were left in death camps with nothing but scraps. My grandmother became an alchemist like the ones before her. She taught me to be an alchemist like the ones before me.

My grandmother spent many years as the head cook at the elementary school in my home community of He Dog. This is a small community of about thirty to forty families. She tells me one year, long before I was born, the state sent pears to the schools on our reservation to serve at school meals. It was the first time many of the children on our rez had ever even seen a pear. Many of the students wouldn't even try the new foreign food being served at lunch. They didn't know what to think of it. Fruit doesn't grow in death camps.

When my grandmother realized many of the children at the school she cooked for weren't eating the pears because they didn't know what they were, she asked the principal if she could go into the classrooms to teach the kids about pears and then let them try the new fruit. The principal gave her the green light and her idea became a successful food education campaign.

My grandmother would also bake fresh bread every day for the whole school because, according to her, "They deserved fresh bread every day too." My grandmother's bread is famous on our rez and I almost find it hard to believe that a whole school got my grandmother's fresh baked bread every day, because now she only makes it on special occasions. Soon the state came in to investigate, and in a surprising turn of events, mandated that every school in the district bake fresh bread for their students every day. My grandmother was magic like that. She took the scraps they gave us and transformed them into gold. She impacted lives in real ways that still resonate back home when folks older than my mother come up to my grandmother and tell her she's their favorite cook of all time. The food she made was medicine that healed the spirit wounds of children who weren't even granted the privilege of knowing they were undergoing food violence.

Enduring food violence has become a necessary survival skill for Lakotas. Lakota people's main source of food, tools, hide, and life was the buffalo. We followed their migration, and they provided us with all sources of life. We lived in balance with the buffalo nation until colonizers decimated the buffalo population on this continent in a coordinated, systemic effort to annihilate our main source of food, tools, and clothing. This is why buffalo are an endangered species today. When foreign invaders took all our food and left us with nothing but processed, unhealthy, death-camp rations to eat, people like my grandmother found ways to turn those rations into meals filled with love and stories of survival.

I was twenty years old when I realized for the first time that I too was an alchemist. My mom's brother had just died tragically in a ranch accident, leaving behind a gaping wound in my family that nothing could fill. Like most rez families, my family is no stranger to trauma and tragedy, but when relatives die unexpectedly, there's always this sort of numbness that pervades within everyone. Being an artist and an empath, this meant for me taking on the burden of feeling everyone's pain and sadness—in addition to my own—and it seemed almost too much to carry. I did the only thing I knew how to do—I started making a beat and writing a song. Along with my cousin-in-law from Virginia, I wrote a song called "Heavy" about my uncle's death. I broke into tears while recording my verse of the song, but I held it together enough to get one of the most emotional vocal takes I've ever done. Before I took the song to the local radio station on our rez, I gathered my family to let them hear it first. It had been hard for my family to talk about my uncle's death, because sometimes surviving means not talking about the pain. But by the end of the song, everyone was silently in tears. My grandma asked to hear the song again and we played it over and over until we all felt a little less heavy. I realized I can take the pain, frustration, and loss I feel and transform it into a song that can help others process and heal. I realized I'm an alchemist like my grandmother before me.

Being Lakota and being from a reservation gives me a unique perspective as an artist. Even though I am an American citizen and was born and raised in America, I don't consider myself American. I am Sicangu Lakota. I don't recognize the colonial borders that were forced onto our stolen lands. I do not believe settlers in an illegal settler colony have the political or ethical right to label other colonized people "illegal" or "alien." Everything illegal and alien on Turtle Island* was brought here by settlers.

My grandmother never had the privilege to think about things like this.

---

* North America

She was too busy raising eleven kids with my grandfather on one of the poorest Indian reservations in the United States. I feel like it's my duty to carry these stories and truths with me and sing them around the world. I always tell people I come from a family of artists who don't realize they're artists. My grandma taught us all to be survivors in our own way. We're all alchemists. It's in our blood. My music is my gold.

My grandmother is an educator, an artist, and a change maker. My grandmother is many things to many people. However, all those labels and Western terms still can't fully capture the beauty and depth of her spirit. My grandmother is an alchemist trapped in a death camp, or you can just say my grandmother is Lakota.

PHOTO BY PUANANI CRAVALHO

Auli'i Cravalho is a singer and actress. She is of proud Hawaiian, Puerto Rican, Portuguese, Chinese, and Irish heritage.

Auli'i Cravalho

THIS IS WHAT I remember from my childhood.

I always woke with the sun in my eyes. The warmth and light seeping through the panels. I grew up in my mama and papa's plantation home in Hawai'i where its single-wall construction will do that: allow you to wake with the sun. I grew up in the same house my father did; Mama and Papa were my paternal grandparents. I slept on top of my mama's quilts, in my papa's worn shirts, and left the windows with their ripped screens wide-open. The tangerine trees outside were warm, bright orange and robust, fruit I held with two hands pinching the skin, tasting it through my nose like my papa taught me. Running across the lanai, across the front yard, across the driveway. Past the hibiscus hedge, through the macadamia nut grove, down, down, knowing every dip in the concrete, jumping over, skirting around the memories of skinned knees in the past. Barefoot and sweaty. Face flushed with warmth, cheeks in a constant blush. I ran hot those days. Hot with curiosity and love and adventure. I begged for stories of the past and barreled over the worry of rudeness or sensitivity to get them. I read until my head was full of adventure, and listened to my papa tell me stories about Puerto Rico and the humid tropical nights until my heart ached for its waters. The floor of the living room was my stage, and I spent hours reenacting fact and fiction; kissing mirrors and dancing to seventies radio. I knew exactly who I was. *Exactly who I was*, at that early age of five.

By the time I hit double digits, I felt as though I knew everything about everything. And thirteen-year-old me? Forget about it. I've come to learn that "*who I am*" is not exact at all. That each piece of my character was spontaneously created years ago, and nurtured since. Culture, held together with glitter glue and adorned with googly eyes. Genealogy, forever branching with love from each and every family member. "Growing up" taught me that my dreams were supposed to fit in standard-size envelopes. But Five-Year-Old Me covers the page with Dora stickers and hand-delivers it instead. Sixteen-Year-Old Me types my aspirations in Times New Roman and writes in MLA format but allows Seven-Year-Old Me to go in with a pen to add hearts over the *i*'s in my name. And yes, my college essay is going to be totally dope and possibly covered in stickers. But it will only be so because I keep looking back to that bright-eyed kid and asking her, "Does this feel right?" And in the future, when I look back—even just five years from now—will I be able to see my own growth?

Take sixth grade. Ten-Year-Old Me had a show-and-tell, and I was so proud to talk about my family. I shared stories that had been told by my paternal grandparents. How my mama was full Portuguese, and my papa was all Puerto Rican. How just before Mama passed, my father told me she never wanted to stop holding me, even though her Parkinson's disease was so bad she could hardly walk. I told them how I used to dance and constantly step on my papa's tired feet because all I wanted to do was twirl whenever I heard a mariachi band play on the old cassette tapes. I shared everything I remembered about them with the class: their food, their cultures, their love. I shared about my maternal grandparents too, how my mother was the seventh child of seven children, how family get-togethers meant three-day-long parties and sleepovers filled with music and an endless supply of food. I learned how to weave flowers into *hakus* (flower crowns) and how to fish like the best of them (the best I could anyway).

Each of my grandparents had passed by the time I was able to share their stories with my class. In an unselfishly selfish way I talked about them because I wanted my show-and-tell to be radically different from the rest of the class. I didn't have a hamster or a goldfish. I didn't want to share my favorite book or a favorite fictional superhero. I wanted to talk about the heroes of my life. I talked and talked, and probably took up more than my allotted time of five minutes, but no one could stop me. I had pride coursing through my veins. And I remember how I glowed with it when I sat down at my table, until my classmate said, "You're too white."

Now let me clarify—this classmate wasn't being rude. Sure it was unfiltered, but she was merely stating a fact. I was fairer than most of my classmates, though all of us were of mixed descent. Let me also clarify that I am only able to say these thoughts as Seventeen-Year-Old Me. But Sixth-Grade Me turned to this chick. Paused. And said: "What?"

My mind connecting my heart's emotion to this week's vocabulary word: *confused*. "You're too white to be Mexican," she continued. As if my ethnicity was just beyond my understanding.

"I'm not Mexican," I started. "I'm Puerto—"

"Yeah that," she interrupted. "You're definitely not that."

I paused again. "Okay . . ." I smiled tightly, trying to laugh it off.

"I'm just saying," she continued. "If you're going to say you're Port-o-Whatever you should at least look it."

She proceeded to barrel into a more in-depth explanation before I rushed to explain "I'm Puerto Rican, Portuguese, Hawaiian, Chinese, and Irish." And suddenly her eyes lit up. *Finally*, I thought, *she gets it.*

"Oh! Well, then you just look, like, 'super Irish.'" Shrugging her shoulders, with her two fingers dancing into an air quote. Yet another awkward pause.

"What the heck does 'super Irish' look like?" I asked, my eyes narrowed into slits as I aggressively quoted her and her air quotes.

"Well . . . Um. You. I guess." She had finally stopped herself, looking around, realizing the surrounding tables were now her audience. When my stare was her only response, she made her final remark. "You just . . . don't look like anything you said you are."

I didn't say anything after that. I turned away from the tables of searching eyes and hid my flaming cheeks with my hair, my lips pressed tightly together to keep my eyes from revealing my hurt. My mind spinning a hundred miles an hour trying to think up a retort, something, anything, that would make her eat her words. Something about how I grew up in a Puerto Rican–Portuguese-Hawaiian household, and that I knew how to say "you're stupid" in all three languages (*I didn't* really). How I could stick it to her by knowing dozens of stories of Puerto Rico and that I could eat a whole bowl of poi if it was left in front of me (*Well . . . not the* whole *bowl*). And if she wanted to keep arguing with me, I would argue that she was mixed too! She was Hawaiian like me, Portuguese like me, simply darker-skinned in all her glory. But if all she saw was my "whiteness"? If all else failed? We could take it out at recess! And then she'd *really* see my Latin temper!! (*Now* that *I could do.*)

Instead, I stayed silent. My pride ripped from me. Wishing my culture would show itself. Wishing my mama and papa looked a little more like me. Or me a little more like them. My easily tanned skin, not quite as light as my mama's, but too light when compared to my Hawaiian mother's side of the family. Soft curly hair that matched my papa's, but with baby hairs that refuse to grow, so unlike the long flowing locks of my Hawaiian cousins. It took a long time of defending myself to realize I didn't have to. Not to anybody. I am who I am. I am what I am. I grew up as a loving Hawaiian Portuguese, running around barefoot and climbing trees, eating fried plantains until I fell asleep still chewing. I grew up in the land of my Pacific ancestors and could recite their folklore before I could even think of writing it down. I celebrate Chinese New Year eating noodles for a long life, and Saint Patrick's Day cooking corned beef and cabbage, leaving our household smelling it for days. I'm mixed. And you can bet damn well I'm proud of it.

And if I could go back (because you know I would if I could) . . . If I could sit where I sat, argue the entire sixth-grade conversation again, I would finally have the perfect retort that would make my family proud, and Me-of-All-Ages proud too. She'd say, "You just . . . don't look like anything you said you are." I'd notice she was as embarrassed as I was. I'd take in her own mixed features, so different from mine, and everyone else's. I'd take a breath, look her right in the eye, smile, and say, "Well, then, I guess I just look like me." And I'd sit again in pride.

A Palo Alto native, **Jeremy Lin** is a guard for the Brooklyn Nets and is the NBA's first American-born player of Chinese or Taiwanese descent. He became an overnight sensation in 2012 for his performance with the Knicks, commonly known as "Linsanity." Lin has played with the Warriors, Knicks, Rockets, Lakers, and Hornets, and most recently signed with the Nets as a free agent in 2016.

Jeremy Lin

WHERE I GREW UP, in the main part of Palo Alto, California, the population was predominantly white. So before Steven showed up, our basketball team had been a bunch of white kids and me. Thanks to Steven, I was no longer alone.

East Palo Alto didn't have a YMCA, so Steven always came to our Y to play basketball. When he walked into the gym on that first day, I was in awe of his height. I was nowhere near as tall as he was—and still am not to this day. I spent my entire childhood trying to get taller. I was a little intimidated by Steven, but together, we killed it on that court. It was unfair to all the other third graders in the Palo Alto Y rec league that Steven and I were on the same team. We destroyed everyone else.

Steven was the first black kid I ever played basketball with, which was weird to me since I saw so few white NBA players on TV. In my house, we only paid for cable TV during the few weeks of the NBA playoffs to watch Michael Jordan and the Chicago Bulls. My parents are immigrants from Taiwan. Both of them worked as engineers to make a comfortable life for me and my two brothers, but we didn't have a lot of extra money for cable after they paid for our basketball gear, all the food I ate trying to get taller, and piano lessons (yeah, you read that right).

Even though my parents made me do things like practice piano and put school before athletics, they always supported my passion for basketball. Not every Asian parent will do this. My mom had high standards for us, but she always encouraged us to do what we loved. She would even sometimes watch NBA games with all her boys. I used to turn on the TV in my living room and watch the games through the window outside while trying to copy Jordan's moves.

Before I met Steven, most of my friends were white or Asian. Steven and I weren't exactly friends at first. We were solid teammates for sure, but we went to different schools and lived on different sides of town. Yet the more we played ball together, the tighter we became. And by high school, when we finally attended the same school, we were bros and took our team all the way to the state championship. We became the only two players from our team to go on to play in college.

It took me a long time to get there. I had a chip on my shoulder from day one. And day one was when I was six years old, frozen in the middle of the court during games, standing still and sucking my thumb. I was terrified. Every night before games, I tried to will myself to do better. I would wake my mom up and tell her I was really going to play the next day. Then, come game time, little man froze up again. You can see why my mom thought piano might be my calling.

When I finally did come out of my shell and played ball, I was in it for life. But when people look at an Asian kid, they don't see "basketball player." At public pickup games, I always struggled to gain respect from other players, or even get a spot on the floor to play. Coaches assumed I would be a second-string benchwarmer. I would watch guys on opposing teams argue over who got to guard me, because they thought I'd be the easy one.

This killed my game for the longest time. I would get hung up on proving myself. It's not exactly good for your game to be stuck in your head.

A few years in, as coaches started to see that I could play, they pushed me to build my confidence. By fifth and sixth grade, I was going all out, playing on multiple teams, trying to get as much time on the court as I could. I had gotten pretty comfortable playing on my Palo Alto teams. I was still the only Asian kid, and sometimes Steven was on the team too, but all my friends and coaches saw what I brought and let me do my thing. I worried less about what everyone thought and really started to have fun. It's amazing how much better you play when you're not thinking about everyone else.

In sixth grade, I was on two teams in the Amateur Athletic Union, or AAU, the nation's best youth basketball league. The two teams were different, but they had one thing in common: they both had just one Asian kid. Metro Mirage was mostly white kids and me. Bomb Squad was all black kids and me.

Something amazing happened when I played for both of these teams at the same time. I saw how expectations influence my success. With Metro Mirage, I walked in just knowing I was the guy. I grew up playing with all these kids, so I didn't question myself. I was relaxed and confident—and became the best player on the team. But on Bomb Squad, I was so nervous all the time. No one on this team knew me, and everyone else on that team seemed to fit the mold of looking like all the good basketball players I looked up to on TV. I put a lot of pressure on myself and started thinking that I would never be as good as the Bomb Squad guys. I was convinced I couldn't hang with them, and they were probably just laughing at this small Asian guy.

Of course, I was wrong. They were great players and great kids who never made me feel like I didn't belong on the team. But that didn't matter. What mattered was the way I sabotaged myself. I convinced myself I didn't fit in, and it showed.

One weekend, there was a tournament where Metro Mirage and Bomb Squad had games that just so happened to be back-to-back in the same gym. The first game was with Metro Mirage where I played starting shooting guard. I had an amazing game where I ended with twenty points and sunk a buzzer-beater to win the game. I was amped and running around celebrating, feeling great. Meanwhile Bomb Squad was all there watching on the sidelines, warming up for the next game. They had never seen me look so happy— much less play so well. When I changed jerseys and headed over to join them for our next game, they were yelling at me, "Man, why can't you play like that when you're with us?!"

It was a good question, and it planted the seed for me. I had to change my way of thinking. I couldn't let perceptions hold me back anymore.

As high school approached, I got a lot of digs from other teams. People still saw this short Asian kid and expected I wouldn't give them any competition. I got yelled at by people in the crowd or other kids on the sidelines who would tell me I was an import from China. Even though I had only ever known a life in the United States, these comments reemphasized to me that I was different from everyone else and made me feel like I didn't belong. It wasn't until much later in college with the wise advice of my assistant coach Kenny Blakeney that I finally found a way to tune out the racism. I'm not going to lie, it still makes me mad when people make fun of my ethnicity. But I decided I wasn't going to let it drag down my game. And I wasn't going to accept the underdog status anymore. I got better and better at tuning out their perceptions and negativity, and just focused on my own goals to shut out the haters.

Just before high school I started focusing on my other major objective. Get taller. I made this a goal—as if it were actually within my control. I knew the odds were stacked against me, but I was determined. I had to play high school ball, and it wasn't going to happen if I remained this short. So I prayed, and I ate, and then I ate some more. I used to drink more milk than you want to know about, because I thought it would make me taller. I already ate more than anyone else in my family. My mom says when I was really young and we used to eat lunch at church, I would finish eating my food first and then stare at other people's plates until they felt bad and offered me more. Luckily people were nice to me, but my mom was mortified.

I would always complain to my parents, "Why couldn't you be taller?" In reality, they are both five foot six, which isn't short for the average Asian person. You could even say my mom is pretty tall compared to other Asian women. But I was still way shorter than my parents, and I knew I would have to surpass them by several inches. I did all kinds of crazy stuff to achieve this impossible dream. I would hang off the monkey bars at school and stretch my body over the side of the bed to try to lengthen it. Every morning I would wake up and measure myself to see if I'd grown while I was sleeping. I was obsessed. I just had to make it to six feet. Freshman year, I was the smallest guy on the team at five foot three. But somehow, my efforts paid off. By junior year I was six feet tall. By the end of my senior year, I was six foot two. I guess sometimes you really can exceed your highest expectations. But I still don't recommend anyone drink that much milk.

As I grew both physically and mentally, I started setting my sights on college basketball. At the time I was in high school, only one out of every two hundred Division I college basketball players came from Asian-American households. And no American player of Chinese or Taiwanese descent had ever made it to the NBA. There were only a few Asians to play in the entire history of the league.

No one expected me to get very far, but my parents got behind me because they saw how passionate I was. My dad would get me and my brothers nosebleed seats when the Houston Rockets were in town to play the Golden State Warriors so we could see Yao Ming play in person. Our seats cost, like, $10 and we could barely see the court, but I had to be there to see him in person. Seeing a Chinese athlete play so dominantly in the NBA meant so much to me.

By this time I was doing whatever it took to show my parents I was serious. I kept my grades up and my mom, Shirley, became one of the most involved basketball parents anyone had ever seen. She traveled with my team to all our tournaments and kept an eye on all my teammates. All the guys on my team shared the kind of bond that you share with teammates, but our lives off the court were very different. The white kids mostly lived in insanely huge houses. Meanwhile, most of my black teammates lived in East Palo Alto, which at the time had the highest crime rate per capita in the entire country. When the team was together, we were all pretty tight. But when we weren't hanging out before or after games and practices, all the white guys hung out with their white friends. All the black guys hung out with their black friends. And I hung out with my Asian friends.

It made for some interesting road trips when we had out-of-town tournaments. Traveling together allowed us to spend a lot of time with each other's families, chill together, and break bread together. A few of them were so wealthy that they would pay for private jets to fly our team to out-of-state games. One of the dads who paid for the team to take a jet would sometimes take us all out to eat at big restaurants. This was always my favorite because it meant I could order a drink. My parents would never pay for a beverage in a restaurant. I was only allowed to order water. So getting a soda with my meal was a real luxury for me. One time, this dad told us he was taking us to the Old Spaghetti Factory. I was bummed because I don't really like spaghetti. My teammates teased me: "No, stupid, they have other things on the menu!" But I don't even remember what I ended up ordering for my entrée because I was so excited to get a strawberry lemonade. I spotted in the fine print that refills were free and drank two glasses before the waitress had even gotten our food orders. She brought me three or four more, and my teammates started to laugh at me. I didn't care. It seemed too good to be true. I ended up finishing eight glasses.

My mom wasn't impressed, but I was still glad she got to witness her son enjoying a nonwater beverage at a restaurant. It meant the world to me that she was always there. She was there when I had a great game, and there when I got called names on the court for being Asian. She was there when I acted stupid or lost my temper on the court. And she always believed in me. I know a mother's confidence in you is not the same as a coach's confidence, especially when you are a teenage boy. Back then, I probably discounted how much it meant to me. *Mom, it doesn't matter that* you *think I'm great. You* have *to say that.* But looking back, I really appreciate how present she was. My dad was too. They were always right there believing in me. Not every kid is so lucky.

And when you're young, you believe what people tell you about yourself. Everyone's expectations become your reality. When people didn't expect me to be a good player, I froze up on the court. But when people like my parents expected such great things of me, I gained the self-confidence I needed to be strong. When people bless you with high expectations, you rise up to meet them. There's something pretty powerful about just being told you're good enough and you belong.

Now, so many years later, I still think about expectations a lot. Even through my college basketball career, no one expected me to become the NBA player that I am. The first time I got to play in Madison Square Garden with the Knicks, the security guards asked me for ID—they thought I was one of the trainers. Now I just laugh it off because I know who I am. Sometimes when I go talk with kids at basketball camps, I tell them what I learned growing up and spending so much time being one of the only Asian kids on the court: *It doesn't matter if no one else looks like you. You still belong as long as you believe you do. You can't let anyone else's expectations hold you back.* When I first showed up to play with the Golden State Warriors, I rolled up in my old Toyota Camry and parked it next to all the other players' Mercedes and Porsches. My ride really surprised everyone that day. It's not the only thing about me that has defied expectations, and I'm pretty cool with that.

America Ferrera

I'M STANDING ON MY father's grave. It's twenty years since the last time I saw him. I'm here on accident, or by chance; maybe it's a coincidence, or perhaps it's fate. I can't decide because my body is numb, and my head is blurry, and my hearing is growing duller by the moment. I'm trying to grasp on to one single thought, but my focus is split between the tombstone with my estranged father's name on it and the dozens of tombstones that surround his, which also bear the last name Ferrera. I vaguely recognize the name of my father's father on the gravesite next to his. The rest of the names are brand-new to me. The birth and death dates reaching further back in time, but the name Ferrera stubbornly sticking to all the headstones that seem to be surrounded by the same rectangular mound of dirt. "There used to be an iron gate around your family, but in this country everyone steals everything for money," the old woman says to me. This country she speaks of is Honduras. This country is where I am from, and also where I have never been, until now.

I did not come here to find my father's grave nestled between generations of his family. I did not come looking for this small mountain village called La

Esperanza, the village in which he was raised and where he died. I did not come in search of a connection to my Honduran identity. I am in Honduras with an organization that funds US programs to empower women and their children. It is a trip like many others I have taken through Africa, India, Australia, and the United States to educate myself on the struggles, solutions, and deep resilience that reside in women living under disempowering and oppressive systems. I am living out my childhood dream to know more about the world and to understand my role in making it better. Except this time, I'm doing it in my parents' homeland. I spend the day with some incredible women in the stunningly gorgeous and lush green mountains of La Esperanza, marveling at the physical beauty of this country. Even though I did not come looking for my father, or his childhood, or his history, I do wonder to myself whether he ever walked these same paths in these gorgeous mountains. So when the head of our Honduran security team pulls me aside to tell me that he grew up with my father in this village, and that he's contacted the woman who cared for him while he was dying, and that she wants to take me to his gravesite, I say, "Okay."

We only have forty-five minutes to visit the cemetery and meet back up with our crew. We have to start driving back to the capital city of Tegucigalpa before the sun goes down and the cartels get on the roads. First we stop to pick up the woman who nursed my father while he was dying. She is about eighty years old. Not what I expect. She is holding fresh flowers and immediately hands me a program from my father's funeral and says, "I always bring him flowers on the anniversary." I look down at the funeral program and realize that today is the exact two-year anniversary of his burial. It is also the two-year anniversary of when I stopped looking for him.

I was eight years old when he left the United States to return to Honduras. My mother told my five siblings and me that he was gone and that he wasn't coming back and that we were better off without him. We didn't ask questions or speak much about him after he left. I can't say it was a surprise that he left. I was well aware of the tensions in my parents' marriage. My mother worked multiple jobs, while my father had trouble holding down a single one. He was home a lot and spent a lot of time closed up in his bedroom. He was a slow, gentle, overweight man, while my mother was an energetic and tireless fighter. The six of us kids were never shielded from the frustrations that would sometimes erupt in argument and at times trigger long periods of silence between them. There's nowhere to hide from your parents' unhappy marriage when you're a family of eight in a two-bedroom apartment.

While the divorce wasn't so much a surprise, I had a very hard time understanding why my dad would go back to Honduras. I had heard my whole life just how lucky I was to be American-born. How my parents had left everything they'd known in Honduras to come to the United States and give me and my siblings opportunity, a good education, and the chance to live out our dreams. Occasionally, I would overhear my mother reminiscing and laughing with my aunt and grandmother about the life, friends, and family they had left behind, but that was mostly when they thought none of the kids were listening. Conversations about Honduras usually centered on how hard life was there, how corrupt and dangerous it was becoming, and how little opportunity there was for anyone there to live a good life. My mother would often remind me of this reality when I'd complain about things like how boring the long summer days were and how unfair it was that my friends were all off at camp or traveling to adventurous places with their families. "In Honduras you'd be working to help support the family, so be grateful for boring," she'd say. I would often wonder about the life I narrowly escaped living in

Honduras—no college, no acting, no Saturday-morning cartoons. I'd thank whatever universal force made sure that I was born an American, and I would stop complaining about my long, boring, camp-less, travel-less summer days.

Honduras was my phantom limb. I always felt its presence, but I couldn't see it, or touch it, or wave it in the air to prove "this right here is a part of me!" I could barely picture it for that matter. Whenever I tried to imagine Honduras as a child, my mind would flash to an improbable collage of images I snatched up from the adults' conversations or made up altogether. The Honduras in my mind had Catholic schools and school uniforms. It was green and lush and hot with pink and green and yellow buildings that were faded, not from neglect, just from time. In my imagination, Honduras was an old place with important buildings that soldiers stood outside of with big guns to protect the powerful men inside. Girls and boys would arrive to school in straight lines and quietly wait to be dismissed at the end of the day before they skipped home down sidewalks lined with fruit trees. My mom and dad were always children in my picture of Honduras. To me, it was a country that existed in the past. It remained elusive, unknowable, and frankly, a bit terrifying, since I had come to think of Honduras as the fate I had been spared from. When my father went back, he too became like a phantom. He now belonged to Honduras, and therefore to the version of my life I would never live. I never thought to mourn that life. I was taught only to celebrate the one I had in the United States; the one in which I had freedom, school, abundance, wild dreams, and opportunity. When my father chose Honduras over the United States, over his family, over me, I came to believe my mother's words: he left me, he's not coming back, and I'm better off without him.

For a very long time I believed that I had no curiosity about my father. I even came to believe that being abandoned by my father had absolutely zero impact on my life; that who I was had absolutely nothing to do with who my father had been, or not been, to me. Sure, some surges of emotion would overcome me now and then, like during the father-daughter dance at the thirty bat mitzvahs I attended in my thirteenth year of life. But I chalked that up to the dim lighting and corny lyrics about butterfly kisses that made it all seem much more magical than it probably really was. Whenever I needed to cry in a scene for drama class, thinking about my father would often get the job done, and I thought that was a useful trick to have up my sleeve as an actor, but I definitely didn't think it was a sign of deeper, unexplored feelings about my dad abandoning me.

When I was twenty years old and filming the first *Sisterhood of the Traveling Pants* movie, I had to do a scene where my character, Carmen, calls her dad to confront him about feeling abandoned by him. For twelve takes I tried to act my way through the scene, to do my best impersonation of a child who was angry and confused and deeply hurt, but my director wasn't buying it. Take after take I would pray that I had acted well enough so we could move on to another, less uncomfortable scene, but take after take my director would gently ask me to stop holding back the emotion he could tell I was not letting through. On lucky take number thirteen, the dam broke. I felt the truth of my character's pain hit me in the gut. "Just tell me, Dad, what did I do wrong? Why did you leave? Why did you have to go?" I said the words as Carmen for the thirteenth time, but it was the first time that I had ever spoken those words out loud for myself. Whenever I watch that scene I see the waves of pain crashing over me and taking me completely by surprise, but other people just see acting, and that was why I felt safe and free performing. In everyday life, my big emotions made me a "drama queen" at home. I was told all the time to "save it for the stage." I was a small kid with very big feelings that were often dismissed or ridiculed whenever I did things like sob through my sister's class performance of "We Are the World" when I was five years old, or declare in the first grade that I was going to grow up to be an actress *and* a civil rights lawyer. Onstage, my tears and passion were applauded and rewarded. And the best part was that the emotions were accepted as make-believe, so I didn't really have to own them as my own or deal with them. It was an arrangement that for quite a long time allowed me to believe I didn't want or need to think about my dad's role in my life.

Then suddenly one night, when I was twenty-six years old, a switch flipped in my head. I had spent my whole childhood avoiding thoughts about my dad, and then like a flash, the thought entered my mind: *I don't have forever to get to know my dad. I should start now.* It surprised and scared me. I didn't know where this sudden urge had come from, but I decided I would follow it. I spent time talking to my close friends and therapist to figure out why I wanted to contact my father and what I expected to get out of it. I wanted to understand my feelings before taking the plunge, or maybe I was just terrified and stalling. It's not like I knew how to start looking for my long-lost father who lived in a country I had never been to.

I had never spoken to my siblings about my father, and I wasn't going to start now, so instead I reached out to an aunt who I thought might be in touch with him. She sent me his direct phone number, and I almost had a heart attack. "No, no, no, I don't actually want to call him! I just want to know if you know how he's doing." I was absolutely not ready to make contact.

And it turns out I wasn't quite prepared to find out how he was doing either. My aunt answered my question in a long email I received on my way to meet friends for dinner. The news that he was not doing very well was more than I could digest in the back seat of a New York City taxicab. He was obese and sick with complications from diabetes. He was living alone in a room he rented in his friend's house. He couldn't work and was struggling financially.

The heaving sobs that were emanating from my body as I read this email were as surprising to me as they were to the cabdriver. I didn't know where this grief was coming from. It felt like a hole had opened up beneath me and these emotions were flooding in from some underground storage unit I had lost the key to a long time ago.

This involuntary wave of emotion terrified me. I was obviously opening up way more than I was prepared to deal with. So instead of reaching out to him, I spent more time thinking and talking about these newfound feelings I never realized I had toward my father.

Weeks passed, but no matter how much I talked it out, I couldn't imagine what I would actually say to him if I had him on the phone, so I decided to do a little exercise and write him a letter. It amazed me how easily the words came. After three months of processing my feelings and preparing myself, I actually knew what I wanted to say and why I wanted to say it. I decided that as soon as I was back home from my work travels I would pick up the phone and call my father.

Two days later, I was boarding my flight home when my phone rang. It was the same aunt who I'd reached out to for info on my dad. She was calling to tell me my father passed away that morning. Thirty-six hours after I had resolved myself to making contact, he was uncontactable—for good this time.

It did not escape me that during the final hours of his life, I had been writing my father a letter of all the things I wanted to say to him, all the things I wanted him to know. I wanted to believe that somehow he had received my letter, that some part of him was communicating with some part of me, that without knowing it, we had spent the last three months preparing for the end, saying goodbye. At times I believed that this whole journey had been some sort of divine soul communication, and then other times I was convinced it was nothing more than an unnecessarily cruel coincidence.

But the hardest times were when I felt nothing, believed in nothing, did absolutely nothing. The numbing depression I fell into was more unexpected and surprising than anything else I'd experienced on this journey. I had barely thought of my father before the light switch moment three months before. How could it be that I was now in a full-on debilitated state from his death? Hadn't I lost him when I was eight? Hadn't he been gone essentially my whole life? Nothing on this journey had made any sense to me. But one thing I could know for sure was that he was dead now. Gone. And any hope I had of knowing him, or knowing more about myself through him, was gone too.

———

And yet, here I am, standing on his grave in La Esperanza, Honduras, two years to the day he was buried, by complete coincidence. I read his name over and over: GREGORIO FERRERA, 13 JUN. 1948–22 AUG. 2010. I am also standing on what appears to be many graves belonging to generations of his family. The Carlos Ferrera who died in 1978 must have been my grandfather. The old woman points to another stone that also reads GREGORIO FERRERA and declares "That's the general," which jogs some faint memory of my parents' talking about a military man somewhere in my father's lineage. There is no denying I am standing on the right family plot, communing with more Honduran relatives, and more of my own history, than I ever imagined possible.

There are no tears, no sweaty palms, no racing-heart palpitations, at least not that I can feel, because my senses seem to be shutting down. My limbs are numb, my ears are plugging up, and I can't hear what the old lady is saying to me. I am dizzy. I sit down for a moment to breathe. And then I remember my forty-five minutes are running out. I have to get back to my crew and on the road. We drop my cemetery companion off at her house, and she insists that I come in for some tea and a quick chat. She wants to show me some pictures. I don't want to be rude, so I go in but tell her that I only have a few minutes.

She pours me some tea and produces a picture of two young boys riding horses. One is my father and one is her son Rumi. "They were always inseparable. Brothers," she says.

"How long did you know my father?" I ask.

"Oh, since I started breastfeeding him. Your grandparents lived next door and your grandmother couldn't make milk. I had just had my daughter, so I breastfed both her and Goyito." Goyito is short for Gregorio, and it's what we used to call my brother as children. I try to picture my father as a Goyito. "Your father was like a son to me. When his mother left him, he was always at our house." This is the first time I'm hearing that my father was abandoned by his mother. I am all of a sudden holding my breath. "His father would go in to the city to work for months at a time, and he would live here with us. When he came back to Honduras from the States he came back here. He spent his birthdays and all the holidays with us. All my grandchildren adored him." I picture my father spending Christmas with kids who are not me and my siblings and feel a sting of pain. "Did he ever talk about us?" I ask. "Oh yes. He had a box filled with pictures and videotapes of you kids growing up. Occasionally he would sit down with that box and cry."

This is a lot to be learning in the final rushed minutes of our time together. My group is waiting, and I really have to go now. The old woman, whose name I've learned is Doña Maura, walks me to the car. I thank this woman who breastfed my father as an infant, who cared for him as a child, who nursed him while he was dying, who buried him in his grave. I give her a hug, this woman who mothered my father, and I try to imagine what she sees when she looks at me. Does she see him? There is no time to ask. I get back in the car. I didn't come looking for my father. I didn't think it was possible to find him. But as I drive away from Doña Maura, past the building that used to be his childhood home, past the cemetery where he rests next to his father, and grandfather, I know there is more to discover. I know I will be back.

———————————

Two years later, I went back to Honduras with the explicit purpose of learning more about my father's history. I was given the most amazing opportunity to be the subject of a TV show called *Who Do You Think You Are?* A show that takes people back through generations of their family history, a journey that would have been way too daunting and scary for me before my dad's death.

They took me back to La Esperanza. This time I got to spend more time with Doña Maura, and Rumi, who was my father's lifelong best friend. It was wonderful to be back with people who knew and loved him. They shared more pictures and memories. But it wasn't long before I realized that they couldn't give me the answers I was really looking for: Why did he leave? Why didn't he come back? Did he miss me? Had he loved me? It was dawning on me that only he could answer the questions I'd been holding my whole life, the questions I would probably be holding for the rest of my life. But there were other answers to be uncovered on the journey. Answers to questions I had never even thought to ask. Questions that would lead to unexpected and life-changing discoveries. Questions like, who exactly was that enigmatic military man my parents spoke about in my fuzzy childhood memories? A question that the producers of the show set out to ask and answer for me.

General Gregorio Ferrera was my father's grandfather, my great-grandfather. He was the son of humble farmers Sebastián and Gregoria Ferrera. Gregorio spent his life as a revolutionary general, calling the people of Honduras to rise up multiple times against dictatorial regimes and to take up arms for free and fair elections. He was a passionate man who died at the age of fifty fighting on the battlefield for the rights of his fellow citizens.

My great-grandfather, the man my father was named after, was an activist. Like me. I sat there on camera, reading a letter General Ferrera had written to his countrymen and -women, calling them to take up arms to defend their right to democracy. My limbs began to tingle, my hearing dulled, and my vision blurred. For the first time in my life I was recognizing a huge part of myself in my family history.

I recognized the five-year-old me who wanted to be both an actress and a civil rights lawyer; and the fifteen-year-old me who rushed from after-school play rehearsals to late-night political science classes at the community college; and the eighteen-year-old me who doggedly completed her International Relations course work while traveling between film sets. I recognized the ambitious young woman who struggled to juggle her passion for acting with her passion for engaging with the wider world; the forever curious student who continued to educate herself on the issues that mattered to her, like access to education, immigrants' rights, voting rights, and the empowerment of girls and women around the world; the lover of democracy who traveled the United States campaigning for candidates and registering people to vote.

Even though I fought to follow my passions, I had spent my whole life questioning the legitimacy of my activism. I battled a critical voice within that said I was just an actress pretending to be an activist; an egomaniac with a God complex. The voice was constantly asking, *What gives you the right to try to change the world?*

But as I read my great-grandfather's letter to the people of Honduras, calling them to "rise to the defense of liberty, justice, and the law," I all of a sudden knew what Harry Potter felt when Hagrid found him in the lighthouse and declared, "You're a wizard, Harry!" So much became clear to me in a matter of seconds. I wasn't a hack, or an imposter, or an egomaniac! I was a wiz-ard! Okay, maybe not a wizard, but I was the great-granddaughter of a general! A revolutionary! A man who went to battle for the betterment of his country and for the rights of his fellow citizens! My urge to fight for what is right, which I had felt deep down in my bones since I was a child, was not made up or phony, it was in fact rooted deep down in my bones; in the blood that coursed through my veins. This part of my identity, which I had doubted and struggled with for decades, was not only my right; it was my inheritance.

It was always hard for me to imagine what I had inherited from my father beyond the almond-shaped eyes and the sharp peaking brows. I never got to fully know him, and what I did know about him seemed so distant from my own nature. I assumed there was very little of my identity defined by his side of my gene pool. I could have never imagined that he would be the link to an ancestor I so deeply identified with, an ancestor who reflected back to me such a vital and unexplained aspect of myself.

As I walked through the village of San Jeronimo where my great-grandfather was born, past the tiny church where he was baptized and married, past the land that used to be his father's farm, past the local community center named after him, I was struck by a brand-new and complicated feeling. I had only ever been taught to think of my family's immigration to the United States as a great gift; to give thanks for my life in the United States and to appreciate what I'd gained. It had never crossed my mind to mourn what I'd lost: hun-dreds of years of history, of connection, of identity, of family, of knowing the people and the land that I come from, of knowing myself.

I stood in the mountains of Honduras wondering what else there was to discover about the blood I carry, wondering who I might have been if my par-ents hadn't left, imagining the life they could've lived if Honduras was a coun-try that held promise and opportunity for them and their children. For the first time I caught a glimpse of the unlived version of my life, and it wasn't as simple as I wanted it to be.

Of course I am grateful for the life and rights I have as an American. The harsh reality is that it is very unlikely that a young, working-class girl like me would find the opportunity to express her talents and fulfill her wildest dreams in Honduras. Honduras is a country where women who speak up for social justice, women like the fierce environmental activist Berta Cáceres, who was assassinated in the very town of La Esperanza, are targeted and systematically silenced. My parents knew that, and they knew that the United States held a brighter future for me, but they probably also knew that Honduras would always be the only place that held the richness of my past and the links to my historical identity. I stood on the land that generations of my family stood on before me and let myself feel the full depth and complexity of the role immigration played in my life. The opportunities and the gifts and the dreams it afforded, and for the first time understanding what it truly cost.

PHOTO BY RAVI V. PATEL

Ravi V. Patel is an actor, director, writer, and entrepreneur. He codirected the Emmy-nominated documentary *Meet the Patels*. Ravi has also appeared on numerous popular shows over the course of his career, including but not limited to *Master of None*, *It's Always Sunny in Philadelphia*, *Scrubs*, *Hawaii Five-0*, and *Grey's Anatomy*. He is also the cofounder of the snack company This Bar Saves Lives, which has recently expanded to over 8,500 Starbucks worldwide.

Ravi V. Patel

DAD WANTED TO "TREAT" us. That was the premise of this family vacation. And when Dad's "treating," that means only one thing: *savings will be had*. It was Labor Day weekend (actually, it was the three-day weekend *before* Labor Day weekend, because *Patel*), and Dad had booked an all-inclusive Carnival cruise for the entire family. We were to board this giant vessel of economies of scale at a port in Long Beach, and on the drive down there—we were late, because *Patel*—my wife, Mahaley, asked me if I had brought our passports. "Why do we need passports for a cruise?" "What do you mean it goes to Mexico?"

Cut to my wife, Mahaley, and I sitting in the Carnival cruise lines holding area, a sad place for sad people who just found out the vacation they spent all year saving up for may not happen; it was like the opposite of a carnival. My wife was understandably mad at me—I guess she had told me to grab the passports when I was doing that thing where I don't hear her talking. Probably worth mentioning about the last twelve months: we got married, bought and renovated a new home, got pregnant (during which time Mahaley vomited almost every day for nine months) just after I had visited three Zika-infested countries. Since we had our daughter, Amelie, I worked an average of twelve hours a day every day including weekends. We were out of the country most of that time because of acting work, meaning sleep training was not going well, meaning my wife was essentially a single mother to a constantly cranky baby without any of her close friends nearby. I guess you could say our marriage was under a lot of stress. I had gained twenty pounds. All in all, this just didn't seem like the right time to share close quarters with a crying baby, overwhelmingly happy grandparents, and unlimited amounts of ice cream.

We had called our neighbors at home, telling them that if they could locate our birth certificates and email copies, that we could get on this boat. We had zero confidence that we even possessed these documents at home. I was secretly hoping we didn't.

Dad must have called me twenty times to reiterate the urgency of getting on this cruise (as if somehow that was helping): this was the first family trip with Geeta's new boyfriend and our new baby daughter, but more important, the tickets were nonrefundable; *savings were at risk*. Cheap travel was a great joy to him. Along with the giant Patel nose I inherited from him, it was a part of his legacy.

Fifty years ago, he had come to America for the first time.

He came here so he could "make it" for his family. He is a Patel, and that means something. With Indians, last names aren't just familial, they are tribal. You can meet an Indian, ask their last name, and identify what part of India they are from, what language they speak, their religion, and (if you were born in India) a bunch of inappropriate stereotypes like:

1) Patels are cheap and loud.

2) Patels are adventurous and entrepreneurial.

3) Patels stick together.

Patel is one of the most common last names in India, and because of said stereotypes, one of the most successful communities worldwide. Patel is a Gujarati last name, meaning we descend from the state of Gujarat, and we speak the language of Gujarati (yes, it's different from Hindi). To be a Patel is to be part of the biggest family in the world.

In 1945, my dad was born in Utraj, a small farming village in the state of Gujarat—the kind of village you see in *National Geographic*: no electricity, no shoes, small bungalows with patios made from dried cow dung. Water was retrieved daily from the village well, which was then boiled for consumption and bathing.

One of five brothers, he stood out academically right away. And the better he did, the farther he had to travel to attend a better school. By the sixth grade, he claims to have walked many, many miles each day along a dirt path, "often shoeless." He loves talking about the time he got bit by a scorpion yet still went to school. What a student. What a Patel. High school sent him to the prestigious Vidyanagar School, which required a move to the dorms in the big city of Vadodara, a couple hours outside of his village (though today the roads are paved, and the drive takes less than half an hour). In that day and age, staying in school meant not making money for the family, so you only continued schooling if you did well. Two of Dad's brothers had dropped out to work on the farm, and the other brothers worked toward professional jobs in the city after graduation. So the real pressure to ascend was laid entirely on Dad, and his father never ceased to let him know. If Dad could make it to the top high school in the state, and become one of the top students in that school, then maybe he could get accepted to a college in America, which meant eventually making more money in a week than the family made in an entire year.

When Dad got into an American college, he became famous, a local celebrity. Everyone wanted to shake his hand. They even threw a celebration for him, which included a giant feast, schoolchildren performing choreographed dances, and a puja to give him good fortune in America. The day he left, the entire village followed him in a procession led by a band. The village wept as their favorite son walked with his small suitcase down the lone dirt path leading to the village entrance, where a rickshaw awaited him. Usually, this would have been a bus ride, but today was special.

Dad's dad had borrowed money from the entire village just to pay for his plane ticket and tuition. Make no mistake about it, this was *a lot of money* to the village, but they jumped at the chance to loan their life savings to him; this was an investment. His mission was clear: *get to America, and you will change the lives of everyone around here.* The minute he made enough money in America, he would send every extra penny back to repay the village. And then he would start bringing the village to America.

In the winter of 1967, a four-foot-eleven somewhat-chubby Dad landed at O'Hare International Airport in Chicago. He claims that he and his friends—six other nerds who placed in the top 1 percent in the state—threw their bags into their small studio apartment* and immediately walked down Lakeshore Drive looking for work. They worked three jobs while also attending college full-time. The math doesn't really work out there, but these immigrant stories cannot be questioned.

Dad became a civil engineer (or is it civic?), eventually working for a

---

*I recently filmed a piece for Sarah Silverman's show *I Love You, America,* during which time we retraced Dad's arrival to America fifty years later. We visited that apartment. Turns out it was huge (you can google the clip).

company called Honeywell. In 1975, my sister, Geeta, was born, also a nerd. And in 1978, I was born in Freeport, Illinois, a couple hours outside of Chicago, not a nerd, but blessed with the ability to communicate with nerds. I was also blessed with Mom's allergies and Dad's nose (big, yet ironically bad sense of smell). At this point, Dad had built a house and married Mom, who had a similar story to his—in terms of being "the savior of a village." However, she later told me that she used to sneak out of the house every night as a teenager and that she didn't want to get married or fly to America to live with this "short and chubby guy" she had met only once during their (arranged) wedding ceremony. But the instructions Mom was given were very clear: *get to America, and you will change the lives of everyone around here.*

Another Patel truth: Patels do not like working for other people. So Mom and Dad somehow decided that buying a résumé and career-consulting business would be a good idea for people with accents. Of course, their business did well. And while they were doing that together, they started importing the rest of the Patels in the world. Growing up, my house was like a Patel immigration halfway house. It was not uncommon for me to wake up and hear that we had to go pick up another family from the airport. Another family who spoke little to no English who would be taking over my bedroom, my home. Another set of kids I would have to show a good time, despite having nothing in common with them. It was the same drill every time: Mom and Dad would not only loan them money to get their lives started, but they would also assist with their immigration paperwork, job interviews, driving lessons, and learning English. This was a full-service program. And I had to go along with it.

Actually, all the Patels in the world had to go along with it too. See, this was part of a larger business plan Patels had for world domination. Every other Patel who came to this country with my parents ran the same halfway house, and the relatives and villagers they brought over would eventually do the same. Here's the tricky part: my parents' generation was the cream of the crop, but the next generation they brought over was not necessarily the same. Many of them were not as educated or skilled in English. So how would they keep this Patel Ponzi scheme going?

The motel.

Dad's generation said, "Look, we have the capital. We will loan you money to buy a run-down motel, your whole family will live in the first three units, and the whole family will work there as well. We will train you to run the business, and we will help you find ways to run the business even better. All you have to do is work hard and drive a Toyota Camry and you will be rich." When Patels like something, they all do it, and the motel business became *our thing*. It became our front for Patel-laundering for the next thirty years. Guess what? Today, all these motel Patels are millionaires. . . . I sometimes regret that I did not go this route instead of trying to be an actor, especially all the times I wish I had more money, which is all the time.

In childhood, I visited extended family members at their motels, often staying weeks at a time in a Super 8 motel room owned by a family member. I was always put to work for people I'd often never even met and would never see again. When I got my driver's license, I became much more valuable to the village. A typical (and actual) request from my mom I recall is being asked to pick up some guru from the airport and drop him off at some random auntie's house. On the way home, I was to stop at a different auntie's house to pick up some snacks for a dinner party our family friend was having. Mind you, Indian aunties don't let you leave their house without eating a full meal and then some, so what I'm telling you is: that guru and I had two lunches together. Never saw him again. *OMG, I just figured out why I was chubby.*

Food is a big deal in my culture. The Indian dinner parties were part of the cheap, loud, stick-together adventure that was Patel life in America. Every weekend, some innocent Caucasian neighbors would be walking their dogs and come upon a scene of two dozen cars and five dozen Indians dressed up, carrying trays of strong-smelling food that wafted up the street, mingling with all the loud Indian kids playing outside. This happened every weekend, all weekend long.

In 1990, we moved to Charlotte, North Carolina, for warmer weather, where Mom and Dad would start what would eventually become Charlotte's largest résumé and career-consulting company. By the time high school rolled around, I was a typical Southerner with a Southern accent. I played a ton of sports, loved drinking and stealing the car at night to go toilet-paper a friend's house. I smoked weed and pursued my favorite hobby, which was finding new ways to break old rules—my friends described me as an Indian Ferris Bueller (why not just say Ferris Bueller? I'll tell you why, because back then, white people couldn't stop noticing that I was Indian). I also cheated on literally every test, and I was class president every year (except for my senior year, because of said cheating addiction). When I would spend time at my non-Indian friends' houses, it was always shocking how much privacy and space those kids had from their own immediate families. Another thing I found weird about my American friends was when they would say things like "I don't care, it's my parents' money, not mine." I wondered what it would be like to have that kind of freedom and sense of individuality, and to spend your parents' cash as if it were Monopoly money. Especially as a teenager or a struggling young adult, there are times when you just want to be left alone. There are times when you do not want the input or audience of your parents, or your aunties, or your parents' friends, or your distant cousins. But Patels don't ever leave you alone. This is why I didn't want to get on that cruise.

College was more of the same. Despite being a terrible Patel (I was not into school at all), I was an incredible Patel in the sense that I could take any test and do well without ever having attended class. That's how I double-majored in economics and international studies. That's also how I got a job in investment banking after college (though I may have also faked my transcripts a bit).

I was a *horrible* investment banker. I was always late, couldn't focus. Hated the work. And they hated me. A few months into the gig, my boss Mike called me into a conference room to show me something. The TV was on—the Twin Towers had been hit. A couple of months after that, I got the call that our firm had been bought and I was being laid off. They were giving me something called a severance, and it was more money than I had ever seen. What they didn't know was that I was already planning on quitting: I had decided I needed to be doing something on my own. Around the same time, Geeta had quit her finance job in NYC—she was also a terrible employee—because she decided she wanted to become a screenwriter. So in the same twelve-month span that all brown people became the antagonist to terrorist-fearing conservatives, my parents discovered that they had raised two unmarriageable kids. And it was because in part we were more Patel than your average Patel: my family does not like bosses!

Within a couple of years, I had joined Geeta in Los Angeles. She was assisting a screenwriter, and I had begun my career as an entrepreneur, starting a poker magazine called *All In Magazine*. Soon thereafter, Geeta's friend asked me to come audition for something, and a few months after that, I was a full-time actor and Geeta and I became roomies. A couple of loser Patels who had thrown their parents' hard work away to become struggling artists. Of course, Mom was begging Geeta and me to just let her buy a motel for us in Los Angeles, not only because of the financial stability, but also because she felt being able to say "Ravi owns a motel" was way more marriageable than "Ravi was the other guy in the McRib commercial."

Fast-forward to 2008. Geeta and I are now in our thirties, still poorish, still unmarried, and our parents were in *Code Red*: you-guys-need-to-get-married-now mode. After a family trip to India where relatives badgered us relentlessly to find spouses, I had an idea. What if Geeta and I made a documentary together featuring us and our parents about this crazy pressure in our family to get married the way our parents did? Geeta had zero interest. Documentaries take too long to make and nobody watches them. And also they make no money. But in the end, she said yes. Why? Because Patel. She cared more about me than herself.

For the next six years (yes, *six years*) that we were grinding away at making *Meet the Patels*, I regretted this decision. Geeta and I had entirely different sensibilities, and we were *horrible* at working together. What we were trying to do was fairly ambitious for people who didn't have much experience—we wanted to make a *romantic-comedy documentary*, because it sounded like something sexy that people had never heard of, because we made it up. We would regularly spend many hours debating small ideas, and the debates would consistently devolve into passive-aggressive conversations or full-on shouting matches. Like many siblings, we had a lifetime of baggage. But like Mom and Dad's arranged marriage, divorce was not an option. We couldn't fire each other from our lives, and we had put too much into this film to let it crumble. We had no choice but to find a way to love each other, to find what was *there* instead of what was missing. It didn't happen overnight, but by the time we finally finished the movie—six years later—Geeta and I were best friends.

We thought the movie was *great*. Nobody else did.

After being rejected by every major festival, *Meet the Patels* was finally premiering at a documentary festival called Hot Docs. Even though this meant that the film we just spent six years making was surely going to never be seen by anyone, and would bring zero return on our investment, Dad insisted on making a big deal about the premiere. He wanted to "treat" everyone.

The night before the premiere, there I lay in this motel room that I was sharing with Geeta. Dad had gotten a Patel discount on a gross spot in downtown Toronto. I was lying on top of the sheets because I wasn't emotionally prepared to see the sheets. Geeta lay next to me in her bed two feet to my right—it was *kind of* a separate bed, and it kind of wasn't. I was trying to sleep, but I had anxiety. Maybe it was that I was worried about my career. My life. Geeta had fallen asleep and started snoring. Mom and Dad had their own room across the hall but came over to do their usual party: Indian snacks, chai, and opinions. Mom was busy with what can only be described as an Indian-snack assembly line. At the end of this assembly line was Dad, who loves *eating* snacks (he loves saying that's why he and Mom go well together, because she likes making food and he likes eating it). He was sipping on tea, sitting on my bed announcing all his Facebook notifications. He had decided to send messages to every Patel he could find in Toronto—this is literally tens of thousands of Patels—inviting them to our movie's premiere the next day. I may have rolled my eyes or cringed, so he changed the subject.

"Ravi, guess how much I got this room for? You won't believe it," my dad said.

"I'll believe it."

"Thirty dollars! Downtown Toronto. Thirty dollars!"

"I believe it."

But I didn't believe what happened next.

On the ride over to the theater the next day, Dad told us about a few local Patels who had responded to his Facebook requests and planned on showing up to the movie; he had promised free tickets to some of them, because Patels will even do things they have no interest in if they get a good deal on it. His excitement was contagious, and I found myself feeling moved that he tried so hard to invite people to show up. I realized I wanted to say something and made a little speech in the car.

"Guys, how many families get to have an experience like this? Look how much closer it's brought us. We got to make a movie—this was film school to me. I feel like I found my voice, and I'm actually excited to be an artist now, because I now know how art can impact my personal journey. This experience has made me a better person. A better brother and son. It's been the most introspective journey of my life. Let's be grateful. Whatever happens tonight doesn't matter."

It was the kind of speech a coach gives a team that's about to lose.

As we approached the venue for the film festival, we saw what appeared to be one of the more successful movie screenings in the festival. There was a crowd of people lined up along the entire side of the building. We turned left after the building and the line continued around the block.

The car stopped next to this long line, and we got out.

"Hey, do you know where *Meet the Patels* is showing?"

"Right in here. I think the back of this line is on the other side of this building."

That night, a packed theater of something like four hundred people gave us a five-minute standing ovation. People were going nuts. Mom was crying. We ended up winning the Audience Award at the festival. And then after winning more festival awards, the movie was released in real theaters, prompting Dad to Facebook the entire country. He basically set up a call center in his house to get the word out. He even made *Meet the Patels* yard signs that thousands of people displayed around the country to market our little movie. It ended up being one of the highest grossing documentaries and one of the most-watched films on

Netflix that year. It was a true grassroots movement. It took a village, and fortunately for us, Mom and Dad know *everyone* in the village.

Making that film was one of the best experiences of my life. What nearly destroyed my relationship with my sister resulted in a movie that affirms our friendship and our love of family. We heard from people all around the country telling us it made them feel better about their own family relationships. And my family is still having fun because of it. People approach my parents constantly, and it's always such a scene because they are as wonderful in person as they are in the film. They are kind of famous now because of *Meet the Patels* and they also kind of love it. They have both retired and gotten acting agents. They started a "club" with their retired Indian friends called the Life Is Great Club, which involves going on field trips around the world, playing a lot of golf and bridge, and consuming a lot of snacks and wine. After running their own business together for more than twenty years, they focus even more of their efforts into volunteer and charity work here in the United States and in India. Dad now talks about *Meet the Patels* as if he made it himself. His current obsession is funding a movie for us to make together. It's so cool that this is even a thought in any of our minds.

———————

Fast-forward to the Carnival cruise sad place. My phone rings: our friends found the passports. We had to go on this cruise. My first thought is that I had let my daughter down on the occasion of her first vacation. I remember thinking, *I have to aim higher for my kids, to break this cycle of poverty-themed vacations.*

As we walked onto the boat, the smells started almost immediately. It was as gross as expected. Maybe it was the Trump times I was living in, but watching people gorge themselves on buffets, alcohol, and hot tubs really bummed me out. Mahaley and I were both sleep-deprived, and the stress of almost not getting on the cruise (coupled with the stress of unfortunately getting on the cruise) had given her a terrible headache. When we arrived to our room, Mom and Dad came out of their room, adjacent to ours on the left, and then Geeta and her boyfriend popped out of their room, adjacent to ours on the right. They were all excited and ready to party. I had to deliver the bad news: I think the three of us need to relax for a few hours, but maybe we can just catch you guys for dinner. Dad said, "Tonight is the big opening-night gala! Seven p.m. Dress up!"

Great, a cruise gala, I'm sure it's gonna be a hot event.

Dad continued, "It's going to be a hot event!"

Cut to Mahaley and me, eyes barely open, seated at a large empty table. Just us and the baby monitor, which was transmitting the sounds of my daughter's white noise machine from the bathroom of our cabin where she was sleeping. Geeta and her boyfriend showed up first. "Sorry we are late; we were partying in the hot tub." Then Mom and Dad showed up. "Sorry we are late; people keep recognizing us from *Meet the Patels*. What can you do?"

It was a six-course meal of lackluster cruise food, and my dad loved every last bland filet of fish, every last soupy casserole, every soggy vegetable, every watery cocktail, every overly sweetened dessert. My mom on the other hand did that thing where she complains about how she could have cooked every single dish better. Mahaley loved laughing at Mom, and I loved seeing both of them laugh together. I couldn't believe I had found Mahaley, this incredible woman who loves me back and was willing to enjoy the world's least luxurious vacation with me. I watched her nervously eyeing the baby monitor, pushing away more plates than she ate, sweetly enduring this floating-Patel-motel experience. People love telling me that she's way out of my league, which is totally true and offensive. Sure, this first year of our marriage and a new baby had not been easy.

But it was getting better. It was clear to me how much I love being her husband. And how much I love being my daughter's father. Geeta was drinking more wine than I'd ever witnessed her drinking, which was a good thing. She was completely relaxed, at peace, in love—I hadn't ever seen her this happy. Next to her was her boyfriend, Sean, who would propose to her a couple of months after that. I remember everyone in tears laughing at so many points. I remember my mother toasting to the fact that none of us had had a boss in several years. We were all living life, making our own work, healthy, happy, and building things together. It was a very Patel ending to my hectic year.

By the time dessert showed up, Dad was on his second glass of merlot and seemed to be making a toast every five minutes. It seemed the older Dad got, the more sentimental he'd become, and the more he felt the need to constantly point out how lucky we all are to have one another. I had gotten used to it—we all found it adorable—but this time felt different. The only reason I can give you is that becoming a father had done all the things they say it does to a person. My perspective had changed in life, my priorities. I realized I don't want to work so much anymore. I don't even care as much about achievement and adventure. I still want to do cool things, but only if they give me a lifestyle that brings me closer to my wife, daughter, parents, and sister. A few months after that cruise would mark fifty years since Dad stepped foot in this country with the weight of an entire village on his shoulders. And now here he was with our new village. For the first time, I felt his pride—his achievement as a father. I thought to myself: *I want my daughter to spend more time with her grandparents. I want her to have what I have. One day, I want her to want off this Carnival cruise as bad as I do.*

Toward the end of dinner, a dance party started in the middle of the dining room—a lame cruise-ship kind of dance party. Everyone at the table got up to dance. My plan was to stay back—I was embarrassed. Then Dad came and grabbed me—he's strong when he's drunk. As we walked toward the dance floor, he put his arm around me and whispered in my ear—as if it were a secret—"You know, I've been waiting for this night my entire life."

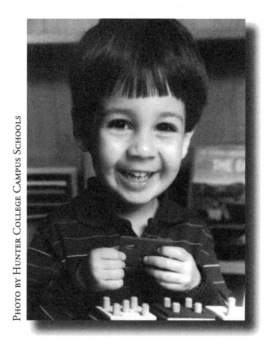

Lin-Manuel Miranda is a composer, lyricist, and performer. He is the proud son of a Puerto Rican dad and a Puerto Rican/Mexican mom.

Lin-Manuel Miranda

"WHAT'D YOU GET?"

"What'd *you* get?"

It is January 5, 1988, school is back in session, and we, the second graders of Hunter College Elementary School, are comparing our holiday haul in the mini gym. The Hanukkah/Christmas split within our grade is pretty close to sixty/forty—whether we got small gifts for eight days or a lot of gifts on the twenty-fifth, the requests are the same. He-Man/She-Ra action figures. Voltron. ThunderCats. Transformers. Raphie Posner got the G.I. Joe aircraft carrier, which is almost eight feet long, so several of us make a mental note to book a playdate with Raphie ASAP. We speak in hushed, excited whispers, envious sighs, a postconsumerist reverie.

I look across the mini gym and catch eyes with Jillian, with Pacho, with Jason, and with Jiman.

We share a smile. The holidays may be done for all the other kids but not for us.

For the five Latino kids in the second grade at Hunter College Elementary School, the holiday haul is not over. For Jillian, Pacho, Jason, Jiman, and I will gather hay for the camels that are on their way to our respective houses and apartments that night. There is no hay in Manhattan, so we will likely dig under piles of snow in Central or Riverside or Inwood Hill Parks for just enough dead grass to fill a shoebox. We will set these humble offerings, our shoeboxes full of dead New York grass and dirt, by our beds, too excited to sleep. We will meditate on the Three Kings, those same ones who came to Baby Jesús, pronounced with the accent, and we will hope that those same Three Kings will bring us anything that Santa may have forgotten the week before.

January 6. Three Kings' Day. A school day.

We wake up and are dazzled by presents, right at the foot of our bed. There is no waiting for parents to wake up on Three Kings' Day, no homilies about the giving being the best part—Kings are only interested in gifting children, and we are here for it. There, at the foot of our beds, that missing He-Man doll, that rare Pound Puppy, that fancy lunch box—that hard-to-find toy that is perhaps more affordable in whatever postholiday sales the Three Kings frequent.

Then we look around the house and our minds are blown.

The grass, for the camels—it's *everywhere*. These camels are sloppy eaters, and for a moment our minds blaze with the mental image of *real* camels, climbing our stairs, somehow clopping in from our fire escapes, navigating Washington Heights apartments, leaving behind toys and a mess of dead, half-devoured grass. We look around and wonder, did we hear them in the night? Do we remember hearing a bump or a snort? Could it be?

We barely have time to play with our new toys. We scarf down Cheerios and *café*, heavy on the milk, and race to school, where Pacho, Jason, Jillian, Jiman, and I, for one day a year, are the chosen ones, our new toys in hand.

We are the only Latino kids in our grade, and on most days we are friendly but not close, each in our respective corners, unsure of how to share a world and a culture we ordinarily keep at home. But on January 6, we are basically on par with Jesús, because the Three Kings picked the five of us, and all the other Latino kids in the world, and bestowed us with gifts, just like him.

"What'd you get?"

"What'd *you* get?"

Tanaya Winder is a poet, vocalist, writer, educator, and motivational speaker from the Southern Ute, Duckwater Shoshone, and Pyramid Lake Paiute Nations. She is the founder of Dream Warriors, an indigenous artists management company and collective.

Tanaya Winder

WHEN I WAS A little girl, Granny sang to me about leaves in the fall, colors changing from yellow to orange or red; the beautiful process of letting go embodied in each leaf slowly turning away from green. I can't recall all the details exactly, but I remember the wind. Every time Granny sang I pictured leaves dancing in concert as the wind twirled one after the other, carrying them from one destination to the next. Granny said something about silver, so maybe the song was really about the winter; I think I'd prefer it that way because I was born in December, and I came out screaming like most babies do as they take their first breath of air. In that way, I like to think I've been singing since birth, a life song our people have held in their hearts and spirits for generations, songs to always help us find our way back home.

Granny was my maternal great-grandmother. She was Pyramid Lake Paiute, and she lived on that reservation in northern Nevada. The Pyramid Lake Paiute reservation is also where my mother grew up. Each winter, Granny would come visit my mother, older sister, and me on the Southern Ute reservation in southwestern Colorado, my father's reservation and home where I would grow up and spend my school years. Each summer, my sister and I would go visit Granny and my maternal grandparents in Nevada. This time of year was always my favorite, because it meant we got to swim in Pyramid Lake.

We grew up hearing different stories of how the lake was created by the Stone Mother. Long ago, there was a mother who had four daughters: North, East, South, and West. The mother raised them alone, their entire lives spent in the desert and the extremes of its environment. In each grain of sand, the daughters felt a rooted connection to the land, but still, each wanted to travel in her own direction—inevitably, leaving her mother behind. When they finally grew up, their curiosity about the world beyond the desert, along with all the wonders this other realm held, took hold and they ventured out on separate paths. The mother, both saddened by their loss and willingness to leave her and their home, cried so intensely the skies envied her ability to create such moisture. She carried on this way for days, which turned to months and years. Finally, her tears gathered in salty pools so strong they gravitated toward one another's weight. The mother created a lake out of tears, but the bitterness she would not let go of turned her into stone. She is called the Stone Mother, and to this day, she sits watching over the lake—waiting. I imagine her singing through the lake in waves: *Come back to me, my children. Come back to me.*

As a child, I feared different things, but I was never afraid of drowning. Floating on my back, I trusted the water to carry me. I could be vulnerable with the lake. I could let go. I loved nothing more than swimming with my family, reenacting favorite scenes from musicals like *Funny Girl*, singing "Don't Rain on My Parade" at the top of my lungs. The water was my stage, and the sandy beach was my make-believe audience. My entire life I've always felt different, like a Fanny Brice outcast because I didn't exactly fit the mold of beauty standards in American culture; I was never the best at sports in my high school or anything like that, but I was smart. I got good grades and could lose myself for hours in a good book. Sometimes I even felt like an outsider with my friends, and occasionally with my family, but the lake always made me feel at home and like I belonged. To this day, I've never known freedom like swimming in a lake, treading water, diving, and imagining everything I could be. Swimming in the same lake my ancestors swam in made it all the more magic.

Grandma, my mom's mother, is another person who always made me feel like I belonged. In her own way, she was water too—adapting to any situation and circumstance she found herself in. Grandma always found a way; she too was magic. Each summer, when we weren't swimming or watching musicals or movies, Grandma would have us help in the garden, or she'd teach us how to bake and knit and embroider. With Grandma, I learned how to put things back together. From her laugh to her hugs and the food she made, Grandma was and is all the best things about love.

When I was a little girl, Grandma would sing, " 'Ain't got no home, no place to roam,' ooo-OOO-ooo," to make me laugh. She did the twist-and-shout move, swinging her arms back and forth, spinning me during all the *ooo-OOO-ooo*'s. She made it so silly I thought she made up the song. It wouldn't be until I was in my early thirties that I'd hear that song on the fifties XM radio station and I'd realize Grandma wasn't lying; it was a real song. By then, the song would hold such a different meaning because I knew more about the world; I could never look at anything the same.

As a young girl, I didn't understand how complicated living in America was and is as an indigenous person. The idea of citizenship and belonging to a sovereign nation while also being a US citizen didn't really cross my mind. I knew we lived on my father's reservation during the school year and visited my mother's reservation during the summers. I knew I was enrolled in a different tribe, Duckwater Shoshone, my maternal grandma's tribe. But, I had no idea there were 562 federally recognized tribes at the time. In the history books my school used, Native Americans were erased, relegated to the past, and portrayed as uncivilized savages. I remember having to memorize the beginning of the Declaration of Independence, but they didn't let us get to (or left out) the part where the text called us "merciless Indian savages." Imagine growing up in a country whose founding documents don't recognize you or your people as human. There was so much truth I did not know. But I did know who I was, where I came from, and where I belonged.

I was raised to honor all parts of me. As a little girl, my family encouraged me to honor my voice through singing. My mother has been taking us to ceremonies since I was a baby, and as soon as I was able to, I contributed by singing along with everyone else. One of our neighbors even started a drum group for the kids in our neighborhood; the boys would drum, and we as girls would stand behind them, singing the tales of each song. I still carry those songs with me, and I thank my mother for that; she always made sure we were grounded in our culture, traditions, and ceremony. Today, my mom cruises while listening to ceremony songs so loudly in her car every time she picks me up from the airport I can hear the drum beats before I even open the door. It's a sound that reminds me I am home. Most days, my mom will slip into a song, humming different melodies or songs from ceremony, pausing to say, "Sing songs until they become a part of you"—because of her, I know they are. Those songs let me know that I am never alone; my ancestors are always with me. Just being around my mom gives me that feeling of safety and protection—all the things that should come with what "home" means. It is hard to imagine what growing up without that looks like.

My grandma is a survivor of industrial schools, also known as boarding schools. These "schools" were created by the US government with the intent and purpose of assimilating and "civilizing" indigenous people under the praxis "Kill the Indian, save the man." I didn't learn about boarding schools until I became an adult. I did not learn this history in my US education. I did not know that Native children were forcibly taken from their homes, land, and families. In some industrial schools they cut off children's long hair, beat them for speaking their Native language or singing their medicine songs. Some children had to shine shoes or had needles stabbed through their tongues or soap put in their mouths just for speaking and singing the only language they'd ever known. The government wanted us to feel cultural shame, forcibly training Native people to be ashamed of being Native because it wasn't safe for us to be who we always were, who we have always been.

My grandma did not experience this in her boarding school; at least she doesn't talk about those things. Once, I asked my grandma, "Why didn't you run away? Why didn't you go home . . . ?" She told me, "I didn't have a home to go home to." She talks about boarding school as having food and a warm place to sleep. The memory she likes to tell from her boarding school experience is about her winning the talent show by singing "Blue Moon." When she shares this story she sings: " 'Blue moon, now I'm no longer alone, without a dream in my heart, without a love of my own . . .' " and I can tell she's happy each time she tells this story to me because Grandma did find love with my grandpa and the family she made with him. For me, the best part is: my grandma never stopped singing. She stills sings to us to this day in her Native language.

It is a miracle that my grandma survived and is still here. It is a miracle that any of us indigenous people are still here; to me, this speaks to our strength as a people. My mom reminds me of this each and every day as she tells me to pray and give thanks for everything I've been blessed with. I include all my family in my daily prayers; I am especially thankful for my granny, my grandma, my mom, and my sister—without them, I wouldn't be here today. They survived in a world that tried to kill our people. They and our people continued singing our songs even when it was still illegal to do so up until the American Indian Religious Freedom Act was passed in 1978, just seven years before I was born. I will always be grateful that I was born in a time where I am able to sing ceremony songs, belt out ballads, write and perform poetry using the breath and air I am thankful to hold in my lungs, and none of it is illegal. I am grateful that I get to sing, and it is all because my grandma and all my ancestors never abandoned who they were. I can sing Clarence "Frogman" Henry's song that I'll always consider my grandma's "Ain't Got No Home" song, but I can give the words "I've got a voice. I love to sing . . ." new meaning. I get to sing and not have to be ashamed of who I am or the cultures I come from.

There's another version of the Stone Mother story. One of our elders tells it like this: She is our mother of all mothers. She had children who all got along when they were little, but as the kids got older, they misbehaved, argued, and fought. So the mother had to separate them. She sent a boy and a girl to the south and a boy and a girl to the north. She told them to build a fire each night so she'd know they were okay. She saw the fire from the kids she sent to the south, but she never saw a fire from the kids who went to the north. So she cried and cried; her tears formed the lake. Her heart turned so cold she turned into stone.

In this version of the story, the Stone Mother teaches us the importance of lighting one's fire. We need to show each other and our ancestors that we are okay; we do this by lighting our fire—sharing our gifts, living our purpose, and not being afraid. The Stone Mother gives us the greatest gift a mother could give. She gives us a way to heal. We can swim in a lake created out of tears, which means we can learn how to navigate any hurt or trauma that comes our way, we can fight and swim and tread water and learn how to balance.

I think stories and songs come to us at different points in our lives. I believe they are told and sung in different ways to reflect the mirror we need to look into. I carry many stories and songs. Some have been passed down for generations through tradition or ceremony—as blood memory. And some have yet to be written. But I am always one song away from my next destination. I light my fire to show respect for the journey. I am an indigenous woman who heals not just my heart but also all those whose blood I carry inside me. Each time I write and sing I am lighting my fire; I am honoring my ancestors, because singing makes me feel alive and my ancestors live through me.

Wilmer Valderrama is an actor, producer, and activist raised in Venezuela. He, along with America Ferrera and Ryan Piers William, founded Harness, a group dedicated to connecting communities through conversation to inspire action and power change.

Wilmer Valderrama

I HAVE BEEN ACTING and performing for as long as I can remember. But the first acting job that put me on TV regularly was playing the role of Fez on *That '70s Show*. Fez was short for *foreign exchange student*, and the running joke on the show was that no one knew what country Fez was really from. No one knew his native language or what his real story was. They just knew he was this funny, overly confident, and kind of crazy dude with a mysterious accent. So my job was to create a made-up nondescript accent for Fez.

Little did people know that, as I was creating that unique accent for Fez, I was working through my own very thick accent. In fact, the first year playing Fez is how I finally truly became fluent in English. I was seventeen years old, spending every day learning my lines, reading scripts, and performing with a group of other mostly native English speakers. It was the best language training I could have hoped for.

If you would have told me when I was a little boy in Venezuela that I would learn English on the set of an American TV show, I wouldn't have believed you. Even though I was born in America, my parents moved the family back to Venezuela when I was still a toddler. I grew up there in a small town—Acarigua in the state of Portuguesa—where there was only one movie theater. It showed *RoboCop* all year round. Are you feeling bad for little Wilmer right now? Well don't, because I freaking loved *RoboCop*. I must have watched that movie a million times. I was obsessed with the bad guy, Clarence Boddicker—who is one of the greatest villains in cinematic history. I knew that movie backward and forward, and my favorite scene was when Clarence and his gang are standing in the back of a moving delivery van with the rear doors flapping open, exchanging gunfire with the police who are chasing them. One of Clarence's minions, Bobby, has made a critical mistake in the robbery they just tried to pull off, so Clarence viciously ejects him from the moving vehicle, saying: "Can you fly, Bobby?" This line rang through my head all the time as a kid. I thought it was hilarious, and I ran around trying to act like Clarence as a little boy.

But besides "Can you fly, Bobby?" I didn't know much English. Technically I was supposed to be learning it in school. I was pretty much always enrolled in a language class, but it was not at the top of my list of favorite subjects. I hate to admit it, but I barely paid attention in English class. I was way more interested in singing, dancing, and acting. Realistically, there was no future in the performing arts for little boys in Acarigua. In case the *RoboCop* year-round feature didn't tip you off already, they didn't make a lot of TV or movies in Venezuela. But doing plays was one of the main forms of recreation for a lot of kids. The whole community pitched in to write the plays, make our costumes, build the sets, and do our hair and makeup for our shows. For a place with so few resources, we were surprisingly well equipped for the performing arts.

So I had my thing. And it was not learning English. It was performing. I was a pretty happy kid with great parents and a great hobby. But one day when I was thirteen years old, my dad came to me and said: "*Mijo*, the good news is, we're moving back to the United States. The bad news is, you're about to be really sorry you never paid attention in English class."

My dad's prediction was dead-on. I was excited to go to the United States, but was incredibly stressed that I didn't know English. My parents were risking everything to give me and my sister a better life and provide us with opportunities they never had. They worked very, very hard, but where we lived, working hard couldn't save you. During that time in Venezuela, you could turn on the news and pretty much every single day see stories about decapitations, school buses getting sprayed by AKs, drug-cartel violence, bombings, senators getting murdered, police corruption, rioting, and more. The problems there affected the rich just as much as the poor. And you couldn't just move out of your neighborhood or get a better job in order to escape the violence and corruption. It was everywhere. I know America has its own problems—every country does—but compared to where I was, America seemed like Disneyland.

Even so, leaving Venezuela was a huge risk for my parents, but they were fearless. They had to be. From my experience, many immigrants are fearless. They leave so much behind to brave something so new and challenging. My mother was a native Colombian and my father a native Venezuelan, but they knew America was the best place to bring their kids. They didn't speak a word of English, but that wasn't stopping them. And the least I could do was learn English and help them learn it too. I wanted to be as fearless as my dad. So I took my job seriously, thinking, *I'm going to be unstoppable in America! All I have to do is learn English!*

You know. No big deal. Just learn an entirely new language at the age of thirteen and then go ahead and conquer the world. Never mind that I couldn't even count to three in English, didn't even know the word for *hello*. I was petrified.

When we landed in Miami, we began the long drive across the country to settle in Los Angeles, where some of my dad's relatives lived and could help him find work. I remember spending several days in the car, traveling from coast to coast. This is such a massive country, and there was a lot to take in, a lot to think about. In every town, city, or rest stop I would spot the American flags. They seemed to be everywhere. I would look at the flag and think about this wonderful place I was so lucky to get to live in. My dad talked to us during the drive to make it very clear that "we came here to start again. We came here to work. We didn't come here to go to Universal Studios and Disneyland!" My job was to keep that candle burning. I knew I had to roll up my sleeves and get an education. Take advantage of the opportunities of this amazing place where I had been lucky enough to have been born.

But then shit got *real*.

There I was—suddenly a seventh grader in Los Angeles at a regular public school. Sure I was coming back to the place where I should *feel* like I belonged—it was technically my home country. But I didn't speak a lick of English. I was held back a year, since I couldn't speak the language, so I was now in the same grade as my twelve-year-old sister. They put us in all the same classes so we could help each other out. We were always together and became so close that people thought we were dating. But we tried not to care what people thought. We didn't have time for teen angst—we were serious and determined to become successful. Neither one of us had friends at first, so we just hung out with each other. Then when we finally made our own friends, I hung with the Mexican and El Salvadorian soccer players and she took up with a lot of white girls. So naturally, she lost her accent a lot faster than I did.

Having a thick accent and a sparse vocabulary didn't make school easy—socially or academically. Math class was especially hard. Can you imagine learning pre-algebra in a language you don't speak? Neither can I. So I didn't. I started missing home in Venezuela, where all the kids would hang out doing plays or musicals. I wanted to feel that connection again and that amazing feeling of getting onstage. I started taking drama class and realized my drive to act again was much stronger than my embarrassment about my English. I was determined to get onstage.

The drama department was putting on a production of *Beauty and the Beast*, and I decided to audition. I loved the story—like so many kids, Disney movies were the backdrop of my childhood and provided me much of what I knew about morality and fantasy. My English was still very, very limited, and my accent just as thick. But I thought to myself, *You can't let these things be barriers. Throw yourself to the wolves and fight! Be fearless!* I went right up to the drama teacher, who could already detect my extreme devotion to acting, and I said, "I'll do anything. Just give me a chance. How about the beast? Let me play the beast. He doesn't speak English, right? He's not even human!"

"Wilmer, the beast does have some lines. And of course he speaks English."

This did not deter me.

"I can do it! I know I can do it!"

She could see how bad I wanted it and couldn't say no to me. Plus, no one else wanted to wear that terrible costume, which was a giant mascot-type head. I was willing, and she was probably the most generous casting director in the history of time. She offered to let me play the beast if I would allow her to be the voice. Meaning, I wore the beast's giant costume head and did all the dancing and movements onstage, but she would yell all my lines from the side of the stage. That's right. I was lip-synching the role of the beast, who was actually voiced by a very kind woman. But I didn't care at all. I was just happy to get some stage time. You might expect there was some sort of calamity around this—her voice not synching with my movements, the head falling off to reveal the truth. But it went off without a hitch. I delivered the role perfectly, if I do say so myself. I didn't even care that they had to sub in a white kid for me at the very end of the show when the beast turns into a prince. When the costume head came off, I went off-stage too. I literally had to step aside to let this other actor deliver the lines and pretend like it had been him inside the beast costume the whole time. It was the opposite of having a body double. I had a voice double. But I wasn't bothered. I made my exit with absolutely no shame. No one in the audience was even aware of the swap-out. And I didn't need the glory, I just wanted to be a part of the show. Looking back, it's pretty amazing to me that I didn't have an ego about this. I knew I was just as good as that white kid who played the prince. All that mattered is that I was up there with all the other kids, doing my best.

Maybe I was fearless, or maybe I was just young enough to be able to disregard the kind of negative perceptions and assumptions people start having once they get a little more experienced in life. I didn't care how people perceived my accent or my skin color. I had big shoes to fill—my parents deserved to see their kids do their best in everything. So from that point on, my intensity only grew. I took every theater and performance class I could and tried out for every play. Just like in Venezuela, I had a bad habit of paying less attention to the classes I disliked (math) so I could focus more on the ones I loved. Not only would I ditch geometry class to go sit in on drama classes I wasn't even enrolled in, I would also ditch school altogether to attend special workshops or drama classes outside of school. That's right. I ditched school for school. What a rebel!

I also spent time studying American TV to find people who looked like me and sounded like me. Watching old reruns of *I Love Lucy*, I remember seeing Desi Arnaz with his handsome good looks and his real Cuban accent. *I got this*, I thought. *I can do it too*. And I learned a lot of English by watching that show. There were other Latino men on TV who inspired me—like Antonio Banderas, Jimmy Smits, Edward James Olmos, and Anthony Quinn. It's true that up until pretty recently, Hollywood featured exactly one Latino male star per decade, but I wasn't deterred. I just looked for the inspiration I needed until I found it.

Pretty soon, my English was getting much better—at least passable enough that the theater directors would let me say my own lines onstage. No more lip-dubbing for me. The beast was coming out of the shadows! There was a great group of drama kids, and we put on some funny plays that were really well attended at school. Suddenly people were starting to notice me. I remember getting lots of laughs onstage and feeling so proud, only to find out that the audience was only laughing at the way I had mispronounced a word. When I delivered a line about eggs being "hatched" everyone thought I said the eggs were "hash," and I guess this was pretty funny to them. Sometimes after a show, kids would come backstage to meet the actors. They'd tell me how funny I was in the play, and when I would respond to tell them thanks for coming, they'd say, "Oh, wow! That's your real accent! I thought you were just doing it to be funny for the show!" I didn't know whether to take this as the best compliment or the worst diss.

Either way, I decided not to get too discouraged or embarrassed. I couldn't be too bothered by it because I was getting parts and making people laugh. I even got to have my first kiss with a girl, onstage of course, because it was part of the script. But I was proud I was good enough to play the love interest. And when my high school did *A Midsummer Night's Dream* I actually came out sounding better than all the native English speakers. When you're trying to speak in Shakespearean iambic pentameter—which might as well be a foreign language—it doesn't hurt to have a nice rhythmic Latin accent to make it sound better.

Sometimes my parents' other immigrant friends would make comments to them suggesting that immigrant kids should work harder in academics if they wanted to get anywhere. More than once my parents were made to feel like I might be going down the wrong path by doing theater. It's not like I was joining a gang. I was playing Peter Quince in one of the world's greatest Renaissance plays. Pretty sure my parents didn't understand a word of that show, by the way. Even the white kids' parents didn't understand what was going on, the way we butchered that flowery incomprehensible Elizabethan English. But anyway, no matter what kind of criticism my parents received or how unlikely it may have seemed that I would become a working actor one day, they always held their heads high and supported my dreams. And while I was dancing around in tights onstage, they were working very hard, and struggling to pay the bills.

One night when I was about sixteen years old, I woke up in the middle of the night, hearing a commotion in the living room. I could hear my parents talking. My mother was crying and my dad was trying to comfort her. I figured out by what my mother was saying that someone had stolen our car. In Los Angeles, you need a car to do everything, especially if you are in the working class, doing several jobs every day like my parents did. We only had one car and we barely made ends meet. We would never be able to afford getting a new vehicle. My dad would be lucky to keep his job if he could figure out how to get to work every day. My mother was fretting over specific details like the fact that my sister and I were now going to have to walk to school, and she was going to have to walk to get groceries, and my father would miss out on work or would have to find something that was within walking distance.

When I asked what was going on, my father did what he always does and put on a happy face. He is strong and fearless and always finds the humor in everything.

"Well, *mijo*, the bad news is someone stole the car. The good news is, we're all going to get new shoes."

We all laughed in the moment, realizing that we could get through whatever hurdle or disaster came our way. My dad taught me in moments like these that life is only as complicated as you want it to be. And it can also be as beautiful and simple as you want it to be.

It was a big moment for me, seeing my parents struggling and my dad handling it so well. I wanted to be like him in that way. And I wanted to help out the family and be the best actor I could be. So after that night, I went for it as hard as I could. I studied harder in my academic classes, I worked on improving my accent, I exercised more, I ate healthier and stayed focused on my goal to become a real actor. I performed my heart out onstage. My teachers noticed how driven I was, and pretty soon one of my acting teachers told me that I should really consider trying to make acting a real career for myself. I took more acting classes outside of school and had an acting coach who took me on for free and got me auditions for small parts in commercials and TV shows. My parents were cool with it as long as I kept my grades up.

So I kept my grades up and kept auditioning for professional paying roles. I got a lot of good feedback and a few small roles in commercials. My first commercial was an all-Spanish commercial for Pacific Bell Smart Yellow Pages. Ironically my only line was the one English phrase in the whole thing. I said "Pacific Bell Smart Yellow Pages." But it worked out because I made just enough money to become a Screen Actors Guild member so I could audition for the good roles. But the money just wasn't rolling in at this point. Usually I was told by the casting directors that they loved my "ethnic" look but not my "ethnic" accent. I would walk in a room and see that all the other actors auditioning were white guys. It started to become a thing: "If we don't go white, we'll go Wilmer," they would say. But they pretty much always went white. And I'm pretty far from white, in case you haven't noticed. Nonetheless, I saw it as a great compliment that I was even in the running. At some point, they were gonna "go Wilmer," and I just had to be ready for it.

One day around this time, my mother and I were walking home from the supermarket and I looked down at her hands. They were so red from gripping the bags of groceries that my parents could barely afford. I knew we were having a hard time even paying for things, and we were several months late on rent. My mom stopped and put the grocery bags down to take a break. I could see how down she was, and I started telling her about another audition I had coming up as a way to try to cheer her up. It was for a pilot TV show and I was going to get to read for a pretty good part. I was seventeen years old and was constantly being told my accent was "too ethnic." I still struggled with speaking English the way you'd expect an American actor to speak it, but somewhere I had it in me to tell my mother anyway: "Don't worry, Mom. I'm going to get this part, and I'm going to make enough money to take care of everything."

A week later, I was sitting in the audition room for the pilot TV show with my dad. We both knew that if I got this part, I would make $15,000 just to film the pilot. And if the show got picked up, I would make a real salary that was more than my dad had ever made. We both knew we could really use the money. But my dad never wanted me to feel pressure to support the family. "Remember, *mijo*, if you get this part, great. If you don't get the part, that's great too. You'll still learn something, and we will be okay." With that advice, I walked into the room completely stress-free and fearless. I was doing this for *me*, for my love of acting. This wasn't about winning the part. It was about going in there and doing my best.

With all his hard work and bravery, my dad showed me what fearlessness really looked like. So I walked into that room with my "ethnic accent," and nailed the part of a guy who was supposed to have an entirely different "ethnic accent." And that's how I became Fez on *That '70s Show*.

And maybe the craziest part of all? I came face-to-face with my favorite childhood villain. That's right. Clarence Boddicker himself! Well, actually it was Kurtwood Smith, the actor who had been cast to play Red Forman on *That '70s Show*. How crazy is life? Just five years earlier, I was in a dark movie theater watching him throw Bobby from a moving vehicle, and now he was walking up to shake my hand. I pretty much flipped out. I told him all about the movie theater in Acarigua and was obnoxious about constantly quoting my favorite line to him: "Can you fly, Bobby?" It was a dream come true: he had been a part of my childhood imagination in Venezuela. And now he was my real-life *coworker* in America.

The pilot got picked up and stayed on the air for eight years and two hundred episodes. My life completely changed. It was my confirmation that I was living in a land of opportunity where hard work really does pay off. I helped my parents get their own house so they'd never have to worry about rent again, and thanks to the fun I had with Fez's accent, people were finally laughing at me for all the right reasons. I've been working and doing what I love ever since. Not only did I get to help support my family, I also got to bring more Latin characters—like Handy Manny—to life on the screen so kids like me watching might feel a little more visible. And beyond playing these parts, I also get to *create* them. I just finished producing and starring in an animated movie about Prince Charming, who will be the first Latino fairy-tale prince. And unlike that first role in *Beauty and the Beast*, this time I get to be the *voice* of the prince too.

Anna Akana is an actress, producer, director, and comedian. She is the proud daughter of Japanese and Filipino immigrants.

Anna Akana

THOUGH MY MOTHER IS Filipino, she refused to raise my siblings and me with any semblance of her heritage. She thought that her own culture was too crass and low-class, opting instead to enforce my father's Japanese values: shoes off in the house, rice cooker always full, bowing to elders, and a deep respect for the collective group's well-being. Though my father encouraged her to teach us Tagalog so we could grow up bilingual, she refused. "Tagalog is a poor man's language," she said. So the only words we ever learned of her native tongue were by accident. We picked up that *ainakoyabatantouya* was a sign of exasperation and that *kikilinakikai* was a stern warning when we were in trouble. If we heard my mother start to mutter that under her breath, we ran. We knew the slipper was soon to follow on our heads if we didn't.

We knew nothing of customs of the Philippines, but we did realize the extent of its poverty by how our mother could consume an entire fish (eyes and brain and all, down to the bones) and how quickly she could patch up a hole in our jackets. She was an excellent thrifter, always somehow managing to find the best brand-name pieces on any given rack. She haggled with people at flea markets with reckless abandon and ruthlessness, drilling into us that you should *always* be willing to walk away, because that's when you'll seal the deal at the price you want.

I used to be embarrassed by my mother's shamelessness. Her poor upbringing made her rambunctious and loud. When she walked into a room, you knew she was there. She was the life of parties, the loudest laugh in the room, and the drunkest karaoke singer. She would drop us off at school and scream *yahoo!* out the window as she drove off. She'd tell our friends embarrassing stories of our childhood and show them pictures of us as naked babies. She knew how to crack a dirty joke, and she did it often, loving the adolescent shocked faces that she could evoke.

My father, despite a similarly poor upbringing, was a stark contrast to Mom. Being the eldest of six and raised by a single mother, he valued hard work, responsibility, and rigid routine. He was pulled out of poverty and into the middle class through the military, so he tried to instill a similar work ethic in us. Whenever mom would visit the Pacific Islands, we would cry and beg her to take us with her. Being left alone with Dad meant 5:00 a.m. wake-up calls, an extensive chores list, required reading, and physical training. The few weeks where we'd be under his care felt like being in the Japanese militia: expected uniformity, respect, and a complete lack of individuality.

Despite his regimented way of raising us, Dad was also unbelievably generous. Growing up in poverty had the opposite effect on him. Where Mom was frugal and wanted us to learn the best way to save a buck, Dad wanted us to have everything (as long as we were willing to work for it). He'd take us on spontaneous trips to Disneyland, sightseeing at Yellowstone National Park, and enrolled us in local schools when we were overseas so we could be fully entrenched in various cultures.

Growing up with a wild animal of a mother and a robot of a father was entertaining, to say the least. Where Mom would often gross us out with the creatures she was willing to eat (frogs, dog, insects), Dad would try to train us to become prodigies. There were no limits to the skills he tried to make me excel in: golf (the only reason he stopped is because I crashed the cart into a ditch), tennis (I had no knack for it), and math (I will never understand math).

Mom, however, would push us into artistic talents. She tried teaching us crochet, cross-stitching, and painting. She would shove clay into our hands and pens and paper under our noses. They put their dreams upon us. We were a clean slate, a fresh start, in the land of freedom and opportunity. *If only their kids knew how good they had it! The somebodies we could become with this middle-class income and security!* Though both had exact opposite ideas of what being well-rounded meant, my parents agreed on one thing: success was defined by accomplishments. Whether academic, artistic, or physical, they wanted their kids to be the best at whatever they did.

Growing up, we were required at all times to be on a sports team and learning an instrument. We were allowed to quit and hop to another if we wanted (diversity was highly encouraged, because you never know what your kid will be a genius at), but we had to always be learning something.

They knew how to motivate us as well: *money.* We got a penny per page of books we read, ten dollars for every A grade earned, and a weekly allowance so long as we completed our chores. Any extracurriculars were always verbally encouraged. My parents would compare our accomplishments to each other to breed "healthy" competition. An emphasis on our college educations and the need to prepare for that was relayed as early as elementary school. My parents believed that we could be anything we wanted to be. As long as it was a respectable, successful occupation, of course.

Being the child of poverty-stricken immigrants has given me a work ethic, ambition, and many causes for eye rolls over the years. I have heard every tale there is: that the people back in the Pacific Islands are starving, that I am lucky to have unrestricted internet access unlike communists, that I am in a land of privilege and should be proud. And all of this is true, but only because I have my parents' upbringing to highlight it for me. I am able to appreciate being an American from a middle-class family because the stories from their childhoods demonstrate it. My mother had to watch cartoons through a neighbor's screen door. My father was never quite sure if he was going to eat each evening. They were both children in families of seven or more, often had holes in their hand-me-down clothing, and dreamed of days when they didn't have to worry about money.

Because of my mother, I am artistic, vulnerable, honest, and always up for exploration. I owe my *need* to express myself artistically completely to her. She taught me that when something hurts, I can make something beautiful. And my entire career has been built on expressing my pain: the loss of my sister, the disappointments of love and friendship, the struggles of being an Asian woman in the entertainment industry. It was she who taught me to not only find my voice but to also use it freely.

Because of my father, I am organized, disciplined, and an entrepreneur. He instilled the values of hard work, integrity, and accountability into my life. He gave me the structure that I needed to be a prolific artist. He encouraged me to never stop learning, whether that be knowledge I can use to fuel my art or make my business more efficient.

Between my two parents, I feel like the perfect balance of artist and businesswoman. They gave me the best of their worlds, which happened to be exactly what I needed in my life's passions and pursuits. And because of these skills drilled into me, I am able to have a thriving career, a deep appreciation for art, and an eye for business.

It is because of my immigrant parents that I have a fulfilling life. It is because of their lessons that I have a career, the willingness to work hard, and the gratitude for what I sometimes take for granted. So thank you, Mom and Dad, for giving me the life that you consciously wanted me to have. For instilling the skills in me to maintain it. And for all the wonderful qualities that make me both Asian and American.

Laurie Hernandez is an American-born, second-generation Puerto Rican gymnast, an Olympic gold medalist, and the youngest-ever champion on *Dancing with the Stars*. At the 2016 Olympic Games in Rio de Janiero, Laurie won silver in the individual balance beam competition and gold in the team final.

Laurie Hernandez

IT WAS ONE OF the greatest moments of my life. I was sixteen years old and I'd just heard my name called. My lifelong dream had just come true. I was going to the Olympics! This was something I had wanted since I was five years old.

I will never forget the feeling of finding out I'd made the cut. This was before gymnastics fans and journalists started calling me the "Human Emoji," but I am pretty sure I was making alllll the emoji faces that day. Especially the ones involving laughing and crying at the same time. 😄

But another very memorable thing happened that day. Right after they called my name, the journalists were lined up, asking me questions. And one of them said with a huge excited smile:

"Laurie, how does it feel to be the first US-born Latina gymnast to make the US Olympic team in more than thirty years?"

This caught me off guard. My whole life I didn't plan to be "the First Latina Gymnast to Make the Olympic Team." I never really thought about it in those terms. So when this highly specific question was asked, I might have been making that emoji face where the yellow bald guy is showing all his teeth, and it looks like he's cringing and sort of fake smiling at the same time. You know the one who looks like something really awkward just happened? 👉 😬 Or maybe I made the surprise emoji face. The one where the mouth and eyes look like perfect little o's. 😮

I wasn't *upset* about what the reporter said. It was pretty cool to hear. But the truth is, I didn't even *know* I was the first Latina to do this in thirty years. The even deeper truth is that I'd never even put much thought into the idea that I was a "Latina gymnast" in the first place. I was just Laurie, the girl who loved to work really, really hard at gymnastics. 👧 🤸 The girl who clowned around a lot but was also super focused on being the best she could be and making her family proud.

Of course I *knew* I was Latina. But I never thought about the idea that I might be *representing all* Latinas. 🤔

My grandparents came to New York from Puerto Rico and had my parents in New York. My mom and dad grew up living around lots of other Puerto Ricans in New York. But by the time I came along, in 2000, my parents had moved to a quiet middle-class town called Old Bridge Township, New Jersey. They thought it would be a good place to raise me and my older brother and sister. They wanted us to be able to pursue our dreams—to be able to go to good schools, take gymnastics, and have a comfortable house with enough space for my grandma to live with us. And plenty of room for family dance parties, of course.

I remember coming downstairs as a kid and seeing my parents salsa dancing in the family room. They would be blasting the music—my dad loved Marc Anthony, Sergio Mendes, Ricky Martin, and Toco. I just referred to it as "Spanish music." You know. Music where they sing in Spanish. 👧 Maybe it was Puerto Rican, or Mexican, or Cuban, or American. I'm not really sure. Either way it was a lot of fun. I'd reach the bottom of the stairs, and my dad would extend a hand and pull me onto the "dance floor." My grandma would always be there too.

"When I was a young girl in Puerto Rico, *this* is how we danced," Grandma would say, while she demonstrated a very funny version of a merengue, moving her body as confidently as she would have if she were forty years younger.

"Okay, Grandma, but when *I* was a young girl in New Jersey, *this* is how *I* danced," I would say, being super sassy and doing my best whip and nae nae.

Grandma would just laugh and shrug her shoulders watching me demonstrate my moves. We all had fun no matter what style of dance we were doing, and we all had good rhythm. I didn't even realize how good my sense of rhythm was until I was working on floor routines at gymnastics practice. The dance part of it always came so easily to me. Meanwhile, some of the other girls would have trouble finding the beat. But me and my Puerto Rican grandma could always find it just fine. 🐵 💜 🎵

When we told my grandma I had made it onto the Olympic team, she just calmly nodded her head and said without any emotion, "Great. Good job, honey." My mom and I exchanged a look. We knew what was going on. Grandma hadn't really understood what we told her and was just doing her smile-and-nod thing. Even though her English was pretty good, she would sometimes tire of translating everything in her head and just kind of tune us out. She missed some major news that time. But she made up for it two weeks later when she came running and screaming from her bedroom. She had been watching her favorite telenovelas on Univision and had seen a commercial come on about me and my teammates going to the Olympics.

"*Mamita! Mamita!*" (She always called me this.) "You're going to the Olympics! I'm so proud, *mamita!*"

And then a stern but smiling glance: "Lauren, why didn't you tell meeeeeee?!"

She didn't get to attend the Olympic games in Rio de Janeiro when I competed. Her health wasn't good enough to handle the traveling. But it didn't matter, because she had been there every step of the way—my whole life, helping me become who I am.

My parents worked a lot, and my brother and sister are several years older than I am. So when I was a kid, I spent a whole lot of one-on-one time with Grandma. Since she lived with us, she was always there for me. She used to help me get ready for school in the mornings. I had wild curly hair—I still do—and my grandma used to try to keep it out of my face. She was a practical and tough woman who would not allow herself to lose a battle with a pigtail. 👊 My mom was a lot gentler and didn't always win the war, but when Grandma set her mind to it, she made perfect pigtails. She would pull my hair so tight that she'd end up ripping hairs out of my head trying to get my kinky hair to behave. Then she'd drop me off at school on her way to the senior center every morning. My hair always looked amazing, and hers did too. 👩🏿👩🏿 If it was raining, she'd tie a plastic bag over her head to protect her do. Maybe most kids would have been embarrassed by their grandma walking around with a bag on her head. But I wasn't. I just couldn't be. Because that's just who Grandma was, and I didn't care who saw it.

One of my friends at school was a girl named Jessica Hernandez. It was a crazy coincidence that she had the same last name as me—especially because she was Chinese. 😂 We were some of the few kids in our school who weren't white. But we never really thought about it. The other kids in the class used to ask us if we were related. We would just giggle and shrug our shoulders. We couldn't have looked more different, but we both loved playing hopscotch and running relay races. And that was really all that mattered.

When I would come home from school or gymnastics practice, Grandma would be there cooking in the kitchen. She made a lot of her favorite foods from growing up on the island—things like rice, beans, chicken, or pork. To this day, her beans are the only beans I have ever liked. I know, I know. I'm supposed to love beans—I'm Puerto Rican. But I never really liked beans too much. Except for when my grandma made them.

If I didn't eat all the food she served me, she'd get mad and ask me in Spanish when I was going to finish my plate. Then she'd get annoyed because she'd have to switch to English to ask me again—because I didn't understand Spanish very well. It was so funny to me as a little girl to see someone so fired up about a clean plate. Some people might assume she was annoyed I liked American food more than Puerto Rican food. But it wasn't that. She was just so practical that she didn't like to see food go to waste. Especially not food *she* had cooked.

She would always make me laugh with her persistence. She never, ever gave up when she wanted something. If she felt someone else was in the wrong, she would not rest until the other person agreed that *she was right* and *they were wrong*. In the kindest way possible, she cared about justice and righteousness. She was very persistent, aggressive, and strong. My dad and I have inherited some of her traits. 😉 💪

My parents never talked much about her life. I knew that Brunilda Esther Hernandez had left Puerto Rico when she was a young woman. My dad used to say that she moved to New York for a better life. I knew her early years had been hard somehow, that she'd lost her husband before I was born and that she still had a lot of family back in Puerto Rico. But to me, Puerto Rico was a beautiful, magical vacation place I went to a few times, where I danced to the sound of the coqui and ate *quenepas* by the branchful like any other wide-eyed, salivating tourist. 😎 ☀️ I might as well have been *Jessica* Hernandez on Luquillo Beach, digging for sand dollars and drinking Maltas. This was the place where Grandma was born, yes, but she never showed any sadness about being disconnected from it, and she never tried to make me feel guilty for not knowing enough about it. She just let me be *me* and enjoy my life in New Jersey. She let me see her as someone who was right at home wherever she was. She was a happy, funny, intense lady I loved so dearly, who made me *horchata* pops and tolerated my constant dancing and clowning around.

She was always laughing with me. But when something would upset her she would curse in English—and *only* in English. Don't get me wrong. She didn't curse very often. She was a devout Catholic and hung crosses all over the house. But when she did feel upset enough to curse, it was going to be in English. Even if she was alone in her bedroom where no one else could hear, she'd switch to English to utter the bad word. The hilarious thing is that I didn't really understand much Spanish, but I sure understood the English curse words my grandma was slinging around.

If I could change anything about my truly wonderful, fortunate life, it would be to go back and speak Spanish with my grandma. I would love to learn to speak it better and would be so proud to be able to share that with her. I'm learning it right now even though I will never get to talk to her again. She passed away in 2016.

The last time I saw her, I was standing next to her while she delivered a special message to me (in English) for the viewers of *Dancing with the Stars*. I was competing on the show, and as I made it further and further along in the competition, they wanted to show more about my family and give my grandma a chance to wish me luck. My family might have been more excited about seeing me on *Dancing with the Stars* than they were about seeing me on the Olympics. 🖼 When you see footage of my mom and dad in the stands at the Olympics, they look pale, nervous, scared, and almost sick. It's such a hard thing for a parent to watch their kid in that level of intense, global competition. Nobody can relax in that environment. But *Dancing with the Stars* was a whole lot easier to take in. I was *dancing* after all. And that was the Hernandez family's thing! And Grandma couldn't have been happier to see me on TV shaking what she (and God) gave me. 💃

When the camera crews first arrived to film her, she pretended like she didn't want to be on TV. But as soon as they fixed her hair and made it look really amazing, she was immediately ready for her close-up. I'll never forget what she said when the cameras were rolling:

"Hi, Lauren, this is Grandma. I'm very, very proud of you, *mamita*. Continue doing the way you want it: fantastic. Okay, mama?"

Continue doing the way you want it: fantastic.

She said it so clearly in her less-than-perfect English. *Be whoever you want to be. Do it your way. You are fantastic.* 🏴 Puerto Rican, 🇺🇸 American, 🥇 Olympian, 🤸 gymnast, 👩🏽 Latina, 💃 dancer, 😄 goofball, 😂 Human Emoji, 💜 granddaughter, ✊🏽 Lauren. She accepted me no matter what. And she brought our family to this country where we were allowed to follow our dreams, where we had room to dance!

She died a few weeks after she filmed that interview for *Dancing with the Stars*. She didn't even live long enough to see me win the mirrorball, but I think of her every time someone comes up to me and thanks me for being an inspiration to the Latino community. Or every time a group of excited Puerto Ricans crosses the street in a hilarious, loud frenzy to come tell me (while practically dancing on air): "HEY, LAURIE! WE'RE PUERTO RICAN!!! YOU'RE PUERTO RICAN TOO! WE'RE SO PROUD OF YOU!!" It's like

I have a big extended family everywhere I go, and I couldn't be more honored. ⊖ ⇥

In the year after the Olympics I got more and more questions from journalists and gymnastics fans about how it felt to be representing Latinas. I have thought about the significance of it more and more. I am pretty grateful that it has never been hard to just be *me*—regardless of my heritage or my dreams of being an Olympic gymnast. Sometimes finances were pretty tight for my family, but we always had one another and it was never hard to be strong when you could lean on family. We were just a regular, tight-knit Puerto Rican family who loved dancing, eating pork and *arroz con gandules*, and who treasured family and faith.

And I feel so lucky that I never even had to second-guess any of this. We live in such a diverse country. A little girl in America with the last name Hernandez can be Puerto Rican or Chinese. And gymnastics has been a mostly white sport in the past, but my Olympic team in 2016 was one of the most diverse in history. We had a Latina (me!), a Jewish gymnast, and two African-American gymnasts. Some kids have had to struggle to figure out how they fit in, who they are, or what their heritage means to them. But I've been so lucky to have the permission to be exactly who I am. To *continue doing it the way I want.* Nothing less or nothing more.

The other day, a mom and her daughter came up to me in the airport and started talking to me about my hair.

"Hi, Laurie . . . ? Excuse me . . . I know this might sound strange, but I just wanted to tell you thank you so much for never straightening your curly hair." The mother smiled nervously.

I immediately thought of my grandmother's hands in my hair, pulling my insane curls through her fingers until she had created two perfectly placed poufballs on either side of my head.

"My daughter has really curly hair like you," she continued. "And I'm so glad she can see that a curly-haired Latina is out there in the world making history!"

"Thank you," I said. And I felt so proud. Then I paused and sent a big juicy emoji-face wink straight up to my grandma. 😉

Kal Penn is an actor, producer, and former Obama White House aide. He has appeared in a number of productions, including the Harold and Kumar franchise, *The Namesake*, *How I Met Your Mother*, and *Designated Survivor*. His first book is being released in 2019. Follow him @kalpenn for updates.

Kal Penn

THE FIRST TIME I rode on Air Force One, as we cleared the runway and climbed into the sky, I thought to myself, *Well, this was all supposed to have been impossible.* Then, I picked up the white unsecured phone next to my seat and called my parents. My folks are amazing. They had always borne the burden of my comical and ridiculous life choices. "We didn't move to America for you to become an actor"—I remember them telling me in eighth grade, when I first expressed an interest in the arts as a potential profession—"but it's a very nice hobby." Impossible life choices had been a common thread all along.

In middle school I was a huge nerd who got bullied (before there was a name for this). By high school, I was petitioning the board of education to let me take multiple honors programs. We had a fantastic public high school district where I grew up in New Jersey, with both an international studies *and* a performing arts honors program; I applied and got *accepted* to both, so why shouldn't I be allowed to *attend* both?! It certainly wasn't *my* fault if the other kids didn't want to apply themselves. My parents pay taxes too! The school board rejected my proposal on the grounds that it offered me an unfair advantage on my GPA (cry me a friggin' river). They made me pick one.

I picked performing arts. Not taking no entirely for an answer, I convinced the school board to let me wake up every day at 6:00 a.m. to go take AP history at another high school in a different town so that I could spend the middle of the day in my actual high school auditing a global history class that the cool, supportive young teacher Mr. Krais was in charge of. Then I'd go do the rest of my academic classes, including the honors performing arts ones. In high school, I was *that* kid. Insufferable at times but ignoring laughter from the bullies and rejecting the irritating answer adults best liked to use: "No, you can't do that. That's impossible."

By the time I got to college, I had heard *impossible* a lot more from adults. When I graduated and began many years as a struggling, aspiring actor, I heard it more than I thought possible. "This is impossible. You'll never get cast. You'll never get a job. There are no roles for Indian-American actors. Impossible!"

This was very similar to what I was being told within the Indian-American community: "Don't go into a career in the arts. You should have majored in something stable. Why are you doing this?" Why couldn't I just be a doctor or engineer like Sadena Auntie's kids?!*

Self-doubt finally gave way to confidence and opportunity. Some of which I had to create myself, and some which I was fortunate enough to have the chance to earn through more traditional venues (internships, climbing the ladder of jobs, and so on). Finally, after years of struggle, I had a few movies under my belt and a regular, steady acting job on the TV show *House*.

---

*"Why you can't be doctor or engineer like my kids?" —Sadena Auntie, circa 1997.

In the middle of 2007, I decided to sign up to make a trip to Iowa to help then senator Barack Obama out with his presidential campaign. At the time, Obama was trailing in the polls and was fairly unpopular within his own political party, which was very busy telling him that what he was doing was quite impossible. This was something I could relate to. He was also honest and shared many of my core values.

By my second day in Des Moines I had met most of the Obama campaign team (who were also idealistic and in their twenties). Seeing their hard work, dedication, and refusal to say no to conventional thinking (which said that a black guy from Hawaii shouldn't run for president among other "impossible" things) was enough to make me join them full-time by moving to Iowa until the caucuses took place.* In these new campaign friends I found my people. More than ten years later, I regularly find myself thinking, *Man, the goal may have been to get Barack Obama elected, but if you had told me that these people with whom I was having late work nights (and sleeping on floors and couches of campaign offices) would become some of my best friends, I would have looked at you like you were crazy.* Not because I thought we couldn't do it, but because I didn't realize what would come next.

After Barack Obama became president of the United States, I left my lucrative TV job on *House*, took a sabbatical from my acting career, and joined those amazing campaign friends at the White House. We had the honor of serving in the halls of the highest office in the greatest democracy on Earth; we had the chance to work on some small part of the history-making progress, and again had late work nights (and were sleeping on floors and couches, this time at the White House, across the government, and around the world).

I think the reason we were able to overcome the impossible in this realm

---

*Iowa is the first state in the country to weigh in on the presidential primary process. It's totally nuts.

is in part because we were doing things for the right reasons. We never set out for the coveted West Wing job, or the ride on Air Force One. We volunteered for Barack Obama because we had friends overseas in Iraq, and buddies who couldn't afford tuition. We are all normal people. What business did we have changing the world? It still brings a smile to my face.

My story of going from Hollywood into public service is not unique. My story really is the same as thousands of other young Americans who volunteered for then Senator Obama's campaign, took a leave of absence from school or a private-sector job, and served for a few years in the federal government as a presidential appointee. The only reason that my appointment garnered more press attention than some of the others is because I am an actor, something else I'm deeply proud of. Something else that was supposed to have been impossible.

It's hard to explain what it feels like when former Obama White House aides see each other now. Our hearts instantly feel ten times bigger and our faceholes involuntarily smile when we bump into each other on the street, or at an airport, or on the subway. We knew that things were not mutually exclusive in our America. We didn't take "No, you can't do that" for an answer. We don't believe in impossible.

Which brings us back to Air Force One. The unspoken rite of passage says that when you first fly on Air Force One, you're allowed a personal phone call or two. This is really more selfish and emotional than anything else; you pick up the phone at your seat, and the operator says, "Good afternoon, Mr. Modi,* how can I help you?" You tell the operator that you want to make a phone call, give her the number to dial, and wait for her to call you back as

---

*Kal Penn is just a stage/screen name, sort of like Whoopi Goldberg (at least I assume that's not her birth name, but I could be wrong). At the White House, you go by your legal name for security clearances, IDs, et cetera. I went by Kalpen Modi, which is my legal name.

soon as a connection is made. The whole thing is pretty patriotic and extremely badass, because when the person at the other end picks up, the operator says to them, "Hello, so-and-so, you have a call from Mr. Kalpen Modi aboard Air Force One, please hold." The phone at your seat then rings, and you say hello to whichever stunned human you've decided to call. So, as I said, for my first call, I knew I was going to phone my parents.

Thirty-four years before, my dad had left *his* parents, who had marched with Gandhi, behind in India. Like many other beautiful immigrant clichés, he moved to America with $12 in his pocket and the dream of a better life for his kids, and here I was flying aboard Air Force One as an aide to the first black president of the United States. What the heck were the chances that *any* of this could happen? America is the kind of place where the impossible becomes possible. We can take our deepest insecurities, our communities' worst fears, our neighbors' greatest hesitations, and with a lot of work, a lot of hardship, a lot of turmoil, turn them into something incredible for each other. Let's support each other. Let's keep doing those beautiful, impossible things.

Anjelah Johnson-Reyes is a comedian, actress, and music artist most well known for her character Bon Qui Qui from MADtv and her joke "Nail Salon," which has more than eighty million views on YouTube. She has four comedy specials under her belt and continues to tour the country to sold-out crowds. She hails from San Jose, California, and lives with her husband in Los Angeles, where they sit on the board of the anti–human trafficking organization Unlikely Heroes.

Anjelah Johnson-Reyes

GROWING UP, I WANTED to be more Latino than I felt I actually was. My name is Anjelah Nicole Johnson. Legally it's spelled *Angela*, which isn't exactly the spicy Latina name I wished I had. You know, like Jazmine Sanchez, Yvette Gonzalez, or really anything that ends in *ez*.

Johnson is a white last name (or black, depending on how you say it), I don't speak Spanish, and I didn't grow up in a super Mexican area. But like many Mexican-Americans, I have a huge family who takes pride in honoring Latino traditions. But we'd always throw in the good ol' American ones as well. For example, we eat tamales with rice and beans for Christmas, but we have ham and mashed potatoes on the side. We have a family reunion every two years with more than five hundred people in attendance. Only a Mexican family can pull that off. However, at this reunion we take part in some good ol' American traditional things like bingo, potato-sack races, bobbing for apples, barbecue, and a game of horseshoes.

I grew up in a neighborhood in San Jose, California, that was home to many different ethnicities. We had Latinos, Asians, Portuguese, white people, approximately three Indians, and one black guy. We lived down the street from big technology companies right in the heart of the Silicon Valley—Cisco Systems, 3Com, Sun Microsystems, and IBM, just to name a few. My neighbors were some of the smartest people in the Bay Area, but I didn't aspire to be smart and work for a tech company.

My dream was to be a chola.

Around the age of twelve, I had made up my mind. I wanted to wear the dark lip liner, the bandanna, the feathered hair. I wanted the Nike Cortez with creased-up Dickies pants held up with an oversize belt buckle that was engraved with my initials. Or better yet the initials of a guy I could be dating who had tattoos all over his neck and looked like Benjamin Bratt in the movie *Blood In Blood Out*. So dreamy. I wanted to listen to oldies and go cruising downtown in a lowrider. A '64 Impala with hydraulics to be specific.

Unfortunately for me, cholas didn't exist in my neighborhood—they lived in downtown San Jose or on the east side. And even more unfortunate for me, I was just your run-of-the-mill prepubescent brown girl. My typical afternoon activities included doing Pop Warner cheerleading and playing with my friends outside. When I was first allowed to wear makeup my mom wanted me to start off light. So she got me just one lip liner and a ChapStick. Little did she know she had handed me the chola starter kit I had always dreamed of. Now all I needed was some eye liner and a can of Aqua Net hair spray and I'd be on my way.

There was just something so appealing about being a tough chick. They didn't care what other people thought of them. They didn't wish to be more Latino than they felt they actually were—the way I did. Plus, I think my parents' divorce may have had a bigger effect on me than I let on, making me want to avoid ever feeling vulnerable. I became driven in my early teens to protect myself from ever getting hurt. And what better way than to surround myself with a gang—or at least people who looked like they were in a gang? My mind was set on it—except I couldn't really handle being in a gang, because that would mean I would have to get "jumped in." And I have a very low tolerance for pain. I can hardly handle emotional pain, much less physical. I can't even watch sad movies because I think about them as if they were my own life and my body doesn't know the difference. After a movie I walk around depressed—visibly so. People are like, "What happened?" And I'm like, "She had room for Jack on that piece of wood! He didn't have to die!"

Maybe this is also why I wanted to look tougher. I wanted that life where I could just call my homegirls if I ever needed backup in a fight (even though I would try to avoid fights at all costs). I got myself a voice mail pager to feel more like I had a huge crew at all times. For those of you young kids who have no idea how things used to work, the pager was a device I would wear on my belt or sticking out of my pants pocket that would beep at me whenever someone called a number to leave me a voice message. I could then find a landline or pay phone and call the number to check my voice messages. It was a three-step process. Very gangsta. Or they could just page me their call-back number and it would appear on my pager screen. Everyone had their own pager code. Mine was the #7. So I could page a guy I liked my phone number with code #7 and he would know that it was me paging. Kind of like texting through a landline phone. You could also send coded messages. For instance, if you wanted to say "I miss you" to someone, you would page "1 177155 400"—because that is supposed to look like the words "I miss you." Some popular shortcut codes were 143 for *I love you*, 823 for *I'm thinking of you*, and, on a different note, 187, which meant *death* or *I will kill you*.

My homegirl Monica and I would change the voice mail greeting every week to tell people to leave a message but also to either give a shout-out to a boy we liked or to call out some girls who were trying to fight us. It would sound something like, "Yeah, what's up what's up, you know who you got a hold of. Go ahead and drop that message after the beep and we'll get back to you. I just wanna say, What up to Hector, a.k.a Little Smiley. And if this is that one chick who keeps paging us 187, why don't you just go ahead and leave a time and a place and we can meet up and you can tell us that to our face. Yeah, that's what I thought. You ain't down. Aight then. Late, peace, outtie, I'm gone. *Al rato vato.*"

I also started romanticizing what it was like living on the east side. They had taquerias and panaderias on every corner. Meanwhile, in my neighborhood we had one Chinese restaurant, a liquor store, and a bunch of airport hotels because I lived five minutes away from San Jose International Airport. In my part of town we didn't have easy access to tacos and pan dulces. The best we could do is walk over to the liquor store and stock up on chile picante Corn Nuts and a Charleston Chew.

The only time my sister and I ventured to the east side was to pick up our friends or go cruising on the weekends. Cruising was our favorite thing to do as teenagers. We would get all dressed up in our "going-out pants," which were basically black leggings and whatever cute top we bought at Contempo Casuals, 5-7-9, Judy's, or the brand-new Forever 21. We would pile on makeup, use foundation and powder that were too pale for our faces, dark lip liner with ChapStick, and we'd have some freshly plucked eyebrows. We would jump in the car and drive down Santa Clara Street all the way to Story and King Roads. Then we would just turn around and drive all the way back. It was obviously a complete waste of gas, but when you're not old enough to get in the club, or can't afford the cover charge—or didn't get on the guest list by calling in the radio station—then you settle for pitching in for gas money and cruising.

Cruising music depended on the mood or the car we were in. If we were in a lowrider car like an Impala, Cutlass, or any classic car we would listen to oldies. If we were in my sister's Honda or my friend Ana's Jeep we probably listened to freestyle/high-energy music. Windows would be rolled all the way down. If it was a packed night and cars were bumper to bumper, we would sit on the windowsill and talk to all the guys who were either driving next to us or pulled over on the side of the street. Motorcycle clubs would all park at the 7-Eleven or our favorite taqueria. Those guys would always have extra helmets in case any of us girls wanted to go for a ride. Sometimes we did, but don't tell my mom.

After we went cruising, we would get dropped off back at home in our safe neighborhood on the other side of town. No drive-bys, no drug deals— just families, senior citizens, and working streetlights. And I resented it. I wanted to be tough and cool. I wanted to change the first three numbers of my phone number from 452 to 279 like all my chola friends' phone numbers. Because if your phone number started with 279, then you were legit from the barrio.

I wanted to accept a collect call from prison like all my chola friends who knew somebody who was locked up. They were always visiting prisons, but I didn't even know where the prison was located. I would ask my mom if we had any family members behind bars, and she would just laugh. My mom was doing her best to raise four kids on her own and keep us out of trouble, and all I wanted to do was pretend to be in trouble.

In the early days of my stand-up career, I was no longer pretending to be a chola, but I was sometimes trying to be who I thought people wanted me to be. I didn't yet have a grasp of my own point of view, and the feelings of being embarrassed for not speaking Spanish as a kid were still too fresh for me. The only shows I performed in at first were the Latino shows like Refried Fridays. Most of the comics would use some Spanish in their sets or speak with an accent. I thought to myself, *Oh. I can do that accent.* So I would tell stories about my parents, doing voices for them where they spoke in broken English.

But the truth is, they were born in California, just like me. They didn't speak Spanish either. The only time I ever heard Spanish in my home was when my grandma was watching her "stories" on Telemundo or when she was on the phone with her sisters. Her calls would always end with *ande pues*, which means "alright then." I only know that because I just googled it.

Just so you know, I downloaded Rosetta Stone in 2006, but I'm still on level one. Much like my chola aspirations, I never really made it too far. But I am so grateful that my mom never fully let me walk down the road to Cholaville. It's not an easy road. Most, if not all, of my childhood chola friends had kids in high school. Some went to prison. Some got heavy into drugs, alcohol, and partying. I tried my best. I got about halfway down the road and heard my mom's voice telling me dinner was ready and also don't make terrible decisions. Or maybe it was God's voice, or maybe it was God speaking through my mom. Either way, I made a swift U-turn and came home.

But when I look back on my entry-level chola days, I understand part of where I was coming from. Aside from just wanting to feel tough and protected, I wanted to be proud of my culture and my heritage. And cholas have that down. Cholas are strong, proud women who know who they are and aren't afraid to show you. Or tell you. To your face. To be a chola you have to have a badass quality about you. You can't just dress the part of a chola. You have to *be* the part. I admire this kind of loud strength and have carried it with me ever since my chola days. Today, I am confident in who I am. I say what I mean, and I mean what I say. And I hope you don't like it! Sorry, that's my inner chola talking.

As an actress and a comedian, I want to unapologetically tell all types of stories, including Latino stories, because they're important. (Not to be confused with my grandma's "stories." The kind I want to tell will have less slapping and dramatic music and more laughing and heartfelt tears.) Back in the eighties and nineties when I was a kid, there weren't many proud, educated, normal, hardworking Latino families on TV or in the movies to help point me in the right direction. There were no Latino Huxtables. No Huxtables-ez. So now, I want to tell chola stories, family stories, relationship stories, English stories, and Spanglish stories. I want to show the world that being Latino and American doesn't just look like one thing.

I don't want other kids to feel the way I did—to want so badly to be more Latino than I felt I actually was. Even in the early days of my career, I thought I was supposed to prove myself. But how can you be more of something that you just inherently are? You can't. And you shouldn't. Instead, you just *do you* and *do you well*. Regardless of what that looks like. I've learned you can be unapologetically proud of your culture, your heritage, and your heart, and you can celebrate everything about yourself without justification.

I try my hardest not to compare myself or my journey to anyone else's. I trust that my path is specific for me and I live fully in that. It's okay that I've ditched my brown lips for a soft pink. Today I'm surrounded by amazing family and friends who love me just as I am. I even connect with some of my old chola friends every now and then. We support each other, pray for each other (cholas go to church too, that's a whole other story!), and sometimes we just share old pictures and reminisce. When I go home to San Jose to do stand-up shows I make sure to have my chola friends I grew up with come and experience the show VIP style. I want them to know that they are a part of who I am and how I got to where I am today.

And I'm still going to learn Spanish. But my motivation is no longer to prove myself. I just want to enjoy the gift of being able to connect to my culture and people on a deeper level.

And also so I can confidently say in Spanish, "*Sí, sé que el guac es extra.*"

Martin Sensmeier is an American actor of Tlingit, Koyukon-Athabascan, and Irish descent. He has appeared in several film and television projects, including *Westworld* and *The Magnificent Seven*. He will star in *Bright Path: The Jim Thorpe Story*, a biopic on legendary Native American athlete Jim Thorpe. He is also an ambassador for the Native Wellness Institute and the Boys & Girls Clubs of America.

Martin Sensmeier

WHEN I WAS A kid I had four T-shirts I loved, and every other article of clothing I owned didn't matter. There was the shirt with a cartoony Maine crab on it, the shirt with Figment the Disney dragon on it, the shirt with the Teenage Mutant Ninja Turtles on it, and the top pick in my small rotation: my La Bamba shirt. Under the gold print words was a winged guitar hovering over a musical staff with music notes. The shirt was white at one point but turned yellow—because I wore it so much—and it hangs on the wall in my parents' house to this day. Around the ages of eight, nine, and ten, I would wear it several days in a row until my mother would pull me aside and say, "Son, it's time to wash La Bamba."

These shirts were important to me because I was obsessed with the fictional characters I saw on TV or in books. I wanted to be a part of their stories and would tell anyone who would listen about my favorite plots or characters. I come from a long line of storytellers and have inherited a deep love for stories. I still consider storytelling my greatest strength, and as a kid, that took the form of wildly imagining I lived within the world of all my movie heroes—even thinking cartoon characters actually existed. In my mind, they were just in some alternate reality somewhere that I could probably find if I just looked hard enough. When I was six years old I was found kneeling down in the street in front of city hall, trying to pry off the manhole cover to the sewer. I was looking for the Teenage Mutant Ninja Turtles. Luckily, I lived in a very small town where everyone knew everyone, so the city hall employee just called my mom to let her know they had found me.

I grew up in southeastern Alaska in a little fishing village called Yakutat. There are about six hundred people who live there, many of whom are from the Tlingit tribe like me. It's a beautiful place, surrounded by the Saint Elias mountain range. There are no roads going in and out of Yakutat, but you can hop on a forty-five-minute flight to Juneau any day of the week—or take an unbearably long ferry ride. But I didn't really leave very often, because we couldn't afford it.

My dad worked as a fisherman—like so many in our village—and my mom worked as a physician's assistant, but with six kids, they had a lot of mouths to feed. We were never hungry or deprived of anything, but we were poor no matter how hard my parents worked. When they couldn't pay the electric bill, we'd go days without power in our double-wide trailer. I remember those times as especially fun. Instead of wiggling the TV antennas to find something fuzzy to watch, my mom would bring out candles and oil lamps and we'd play board games or listen to my dad reading books to us. The propane stove still worked, so my mom would cook a great dinner. Other times, when we ran out of oil and went without hot water or heat, I'd simply shower in the school locker room, and in the evenings, we'd huddle around the stove for warmth. I never thought of these as "hard times" or even sad. It's just how it was.

Our village was small and peaceful. We were completely satisfied running around outside all day for fun. An example of an especially exciting day is when we'd find a particularly large snow drift to jump into from a rooftop. But mostly we played basketball. I played on competitive teams all the way up through high school. *Everyone* plays basketball in Yakutat, the boys, the girls, the parents, the grandparents, the doctors, the teachers, the carpenters— the janitor at my grade school named Betty played too. Basketball wasn't just for entertainment—it was one of the many ways we stayed strong and healthy, which was a priority in my family. We either spent long spans of time inside a gym or full days playing outside. My dad was an athlete and a soldier in his younger years, not to mention a great hunter and fisherman. Discipline was a part of our everyday life. We never ate candy or junk food. We had a traditional Tlingit diet of wild game—venison, or moose if we were lucky— or fish every night for dinner, and we would work our way through a monthly $10 bag of rice.

I did grow tired of eating the same meat and rice dinner every night. I re-member one day watching the 2000 Olympics on TV and eating another plate of smoked salmon—a wild fish caught by my father and smoked by my mother, something I now consider the most amazing food on earth—that at the time seemed like no more than repetitive sustenance. While eating, I re-member seeing a commercial for Burger King come on TV, seeing the burger slapped down on the bread, the juicy crisp lettuce, pickle, and tomato all fall-ing into place in slo-mo. I thought it looked so delicious, and I couldn't wait to one day eat food like that. All the while, I was mindlessly consuming what I now save in my freezer for special occasions, because my mother's smoked salmon gets shipped to me in California, and I have to savor whatever amount of home I can.

But every now and then as a kid, we'd get a treat of chicken nuggets and french fries. Or pizza, the food that I and my cool friends, the Teenage

Mutant Ninja Turtles, all loved best. Sometimes my dad would take me to the local tavern in the middle of the day, before adults were drinking there, so we could order from the bar menu—always a pizza—for lunch. I'd drink a Roy Rogers and play music on the jukebox. My dad patiently allowed me to spend all his quarters to play the same song over and over again.

Para bailar La Bamba!
Para bailar La Bamba se necesita un poco de gracia!

My dad would humor me, and get up and dance with me in the middle of the bar. He let me relive my favorite movie, perform the song in my favorite shirt. I barely noticed how annoyed all the other adults in the bar were to hear the same song start up again and again. I mouthed the words and spun around with my air guitar, just like Lou Diamond Phillips.

That movie was a light turning on for me—a kick-ass story about a guy just like me, who came from a poor family just like me, and dreamed really big just like me. Ritchie Valens was a Chicano character who looked like me—and he wasn't even wearing beads and feathers. He was just a real person who I could identify with. In one scene, Ritchie's mom angrily yells, "They don't know who the hell they're dealing with. My granddaddy was full-blooded Yaqui Indian." And that was more than enough for me, because up to that point, the only Natives I'd seen on TV were Indians in John Wayne westerns, which I was also obsessed with watching. But John Wayne's Indians were usually played by Italian actors, and they weren't recognizable to me in any way. They made crazy yodeling sounds and behaved like animals. Even as a kid, I understood them to be made-up movie Indians, not real people we were supposed to care about.

To me, Native people weren't the Indians you saw in westerns. They were regular people who made up half the population of my town. They were the folks you'd see every day, the mechanics, welders, teachers, doctors, and wait-ers. Except for in old pictures, or at very special ceremonies, I never saw any-one wearing regalia. Everyone in my town dressed more like John Wayne than the Indians, and no one spoke the old language of my Tlingit tribe. But our kind of Native was never shown in any movies I saw. TV Indians were depicted as bad guys, hooligans, or wild, strange villains. So we always rooted for the good guys—the cowboys. My best friend across the street was a white kid, and when we played cowboys and Indians, I was always the cowboy and he was always the Indian. I had more in common with a Teenage Mutant Ninja Turtle than I did with a John Wayne Indian.

But *La Bamba* changed everything because it showed me a face and a story I could relate to. I used to drag my well-worn VHS copy of *La Bamba* to my friends' houses and beg them to watch it again with me. They would cringe when I'd bring it up. It's not exactly a movie intended to appeal to pre-teen boys, but I was finally old enough to know that mutant turtles weren't actually living in the sewers. And the struggles Ritchie and his family experi-enced felt like my real life. I daydreamed all the time about growing up to be-come an actor like Lou Diamond Phillips, but it was maybe the most unlikely profession for a Tlingit kid—or any kid really—from Yakutat. At the time I would have settled for being a basketball player too. Even though I was a little bit chubby, I was a good ball player, as long as you could look past the Sharpied-on goatee I drew on my face for game day so I could look like Seattle Sonics power forward Shawn Kemp, my other idol. I was committed.

I was teased for my chubbiness, and who knows what else. My head was in the clouds, and I didn't care that I wasn't a popular kid. Nobody was rich in our town, or if they were, it just meant they had slightly better TVs and trucks. Mostly I wasn't very jealous or too harmed by their bullying, but I admit that popularity was an advantage I wished for when the school plays came around. There wasn't a big performing arts emphasis at my grade school, and the teachers assigned roles solely through preference and favoritism. In other words, the popular kids got all the leads, and I didn't even get the chance to audition for them. When we did *Huck Finn*, I was given the role of the runaway slave, Jim. And when we did *Robin Hood*, I played the sheriff of Nottingham—because nobody else wanted to play the villain. But joke was on them, because I had the most lines.

I remember standing backstage before the first show, after rehearsing for four months, looking out into the audience, sweating with excitement through my costume and knowing this must be the life I was supposed to live. I was bitten by the acting bug, but unfortunately, these two plays were the extent of my theatrical career for my entire childhood. I would have jumped at the chance to do more acting, but I guess our school was just too small to put on any more plays.

Fortunately, movies and school plays were not my only outlet for storytelling. The elders in my community had exposed me to tales of Tlingit people for as long as I could remember. Even though we never learned about our past from school textbooks, the elders made sure we knew our history—sharing stories passed down to them through the oral tradition. From memory, they would name your father, your grandfather, your great-grandfather, and carefully lay out your story that began hundreds of years ago. We would sit for hours, keeping their stories alive by listening. It was during my time sitting at the feet of elders that I learned my people had been here in Southeast Alaska for thousands of years, before the gold rush, before the fur trades, before manifest destiny or the United States of anything. But I had already seen this with my own eyes, and felt it with my own body and spirit—that this place had been our home for a long time. This tiny town without a movie theater was where my friend Anthony and

I found a seven-hundred-year-old Tlingit bow out in the forest, which now sits on display in a Juneau museum.

Even though I loved Yakutat, anytime we had a chance to visit Seattle or any other part of the Lower 48 I was all over it. Somehow I rarely thought about the world outside Yakutat as a child—it barely even existed in my mind because it was outside the bounds of my town with no roads out. But suddenly in my teen years, the world beyond Southeast Alaska became a place of opportunity and excitement. When I got to visit other cities, I'd head straight for a movie theater. Once, during a high school field trip to Seattle, with my older brother as a chaperone, we got to see the movie *Training Day* on the big screen, with Denzel Washington and Ethan Hawke. It was a very memorable day for me. Denzel was my *guy*. And there was something so compelling to me about the two of them riding around LA in their car, with the palm trees in the background. I was mesmerized by those trees and wanted to go there. That was where people went to bring stories to the big screen. I never forgot.

But acting was still a figment of my imagination. Like a town with no roads in, there was no charting a course to that destination. I had become a great basketball player, and going out for a college team was a real option for me, but it wasn't a dream I thought worth chasing. I had never seen a Native player in the NBA. I also couldn't picture myself becoming a fisherman, because the fishermen never leave Yakutat, and I'd internalized the universal advice that *in order to be successful, you have to leave home.* So I settled for college in Anchorage, where I could learn welding and make a good salary.

Attending the University of Alaska Anchorage was not easy. I was just a village boy who grew up in the country, and now I was living in a big city of three hundred thousand people. I missed the community and the pace of Yakutat, and I was scared. I comforted myself by finding a gym where I could play basketball and make some friends. I settled in, and eventually loved the electives more than the welding classes. I took courses on Native American studies, philosophy, and psychology. For the first time I learned the confusing and devastating history of genocide, and all about the people who are fighting for my human rights still to this day. I started considering the effects of history on my life and began to recognize the power and mandate in me to tell stories—my story, or any stories that would inspire others.

I longed for home, but at the same time the palm trees were calling me. I wanted to take my desire to tell stories to the big screen and become an actor, but I couldn't afford the pursuit in any way, shape, or form. It seemed crazy to choose an acting career when I could make $75K per year in an entry-level position with an oil drilling company—something a lot of my friends were doing. So I took a job on Alaska's North Slope that paid me more money than I knew what to do with and gave me two weeks off every single month.

For a young man who has never had any money, this was thrilling. The combination of having a lot of money and a lot of free time was a win-win. With my first big paycheck I flew to California to see a Lakers game. And it wasn't too long before I spent all my time off the rig in Los Angeles. Two weeks at work, and two weeks in LA. I would go months without flying home to Yakutat, and every time I visited, it was like a punch in the gut to see my parents getting older, my nieces and nephews getting bigger, and the town ever the same—beautiful and peaceful. It was painful to stay in Yakutat for just a few days and turn around and leave again. But acting classes compelled me to return to Los Angeles any time I could. Maybe just maybe, I could be like the poor-boy Ritchie Valens who finally made it big because he never gave up on his dream. When I finally took the plunge and moved to California full-time, I wasn't getting acting parts, and I slowly spent all my oil money until I found myself delivering pizzas to get by. Cowabunga, dude, it was not the future of palm trees and artistic expression that I had dreamed of.

Then one day in California, I got a phone call from my parents that an elder in our village had passed away. It was not the first funeral or important occasion I had missed, being away from home so often, but it was especially difficult news as this elder had been very close to me and my family, and I had been called to serve as a gravedigger. In our tribe, when there is a death, we band closely together as a community to care for one another and ensure a safe passage to heaven for the dead. We do not send the deceased to a morgue, funeral home, or cemetery all alone. Their spirit is still with us until they are in the ground, so someone is always by their side, accompanying them on their journey. We do not fear the dead or believe in the kind of ghosts invented by Hollywood. We celebrate the dead and connect with them in their presence until the burial is complete. To be asked to dig this elder's grave was a deep honor and an important spiritual responsibility, but I didn't have enough pizza money to buy myself a plane ticket home. I was gutted.

I beat myself up pretty badly over this. It was a huge sacrifice to both me and my family to live so far away from home, and I started to wonder if it was really worth the cost. I had grown up daydreaming about being the next Lou Diamond Phillips and tried to justify leaving Yakutat as the only way I could ever become an actor who could bring important stories to the screen. I wanted to change kids' lives the way mine had been changed by *La Bamba*. But I also began to feel very suspicious about that idea I had been sold for so long that *you can't be successful unless you leave home*. I would often hear famous actors, athletes, or musicians give speeches or interviews and say if they'd never left home, they would still be stuck in whatever horrible small town, inner-city hood, or suburban nightmare they grew up in. But I wasn't buying this idea anymore. I didn't have to leave Yakutat to become a story-teller. Yakutat *made me* the storyteller I *already was*. The elders, the people, the landscape, and the rhythm of the whole place made me who I was. And yet, it also shaped the very dreams and goals that compelled me to leave it. This was a very confusing position to be in.

I imagined myself going home and forgetting California altogether. It was—and still is—easy to picture myself being very happy going back to Yakutat to stay forever. There are people there revitalizing the Tlingit language, running day cares, coaching basketball, preserving our history, sharing our ancient stories, hunting for game to feed our elders who would otherwise eat off government assistance. When a child is sick, the village pitches in to care for him or her. When my brother-in-law has a day off, he goes around fixing everyone's boilers for free so they have hot water again. My nephew watches movies on DVD over and over again, just like his uncle did, and children all over town run around in the sunshine and snow, under the shadow of the mountains, with the water sparkling light and life into their everyday. It is a beautiful place—not one you need to escape. And even if you *wanted* to escape from Yakutat, it is not a place you can ever truly leave.

This struggle—and the grief of mourning for the elder I would not be home to bury—led me to an epiphany. I realized I could use my little home village as a positive motivation rather than a negative one. Yakutat was not the *opposite* of my success. It was the *source* of my success. And if I was going to be so far away from it, I needed to work harder than ever to make my acting dreams come true.

Fast-forward to today, and I've been lucky to work with some of the same actors and directors I idolized when I was younger. If you would have told me in high school that I would one day be in a movie with the same Denzel Washington and Ethan Hawke from *Training Day*—and that I would get to help create a Native character to portray in that movie (*The Magnificent Seven*), I never would have believed you. But storytelling has always been my calling. I've been given a gift from the Creator, and it is a great honor to tell stories of ordinary people whose journeys and struggles should be shared with the world, because they matter. I have been even more lucky to have a platform through the Native Wellness Institute and the Boys & Girls Clubs of America to speak to kids who grew up like I did. I tell them to follow their dreams and that if they stay in their small towns, they still matter. They can still do good work wherever they are. And every Native kid I've ever met tells me I'm their favorite character in *The Magnificent Seven* (except my nephew, who ranks me third, behind Denzel Washington's and Chris Pratt's characters). But he sent me a photo of himself dressed as Red Harvest for Halloween, and it meant the world to me.

Now when I visit home, I make sure to stay for weeks at a time. I play basketball with my old friends, eat the moose from my mother's freezer that was hunted by my eight-year-old nephew. I go camping, fishing, or just drive the back roads by myself. It is quiet, peaceful, and a part of me forever. When I walk the streets with my dog, people always smile at me and say, "Welcome home!"

Carmen Carrera

Carmen Carrera is a mother, an actor, a model, an advocate, and one of the world's highest-profile transgender women. As an actor, she has appeared in HBO's *Outpost*, *Jane the Virgin*, *The Bold and the Beautiful*, and *Ricki and the Flash*. Carmen is a dedicated international human rights and HIV prevention advocate. She has lectured around the world and works with organizations like SUEÑOS LGBT to fight discrimination against young transgender women.

———————— *A Letter to My Ten-Year-Old Self* ————————

Dear Chris,

You are ten years old, and I thought I would write you a letter because there are some things I want you to know. First, you are beautiful. Right now, exactly the way you are. In the future you are beautiful too. In fact, you will grow up to become a strong, proud, beautiful Latinx woman. A model and an activist. Yes, you!

Right now I'm guessing you are finding this hard to believe. You want to feel comfortable in your skin, but you are surrounded by beautiful women who see you as their little boy. You hide your femininity even though femininity is everywhere—within you and constantly surrounding you. Literally radiating from these four beautiful Peruvian angels: your great-grandmother (La Mama), grandmother (Grandma Chela), mother (Mommie), and sister (Arissa). It is only a matter of time before they fully see inside your heart and soul.

You are just like them. Strong. They came to this country with just their religious beliefs and the strength to carry God and responsibility on their shoulders at all times. In your grandmother's culture, being a strong woman means being a good mom and a good wife. This seems complicated to you—to become a woman who fits that mold. But that's okay. Because, trust me, you will make your own mold. And you will do it without discarding the traditions that made you who you are.

You will never lose your love of your Peruvian culture, the

food, and the stories. You will always taste the richness of *papa a la huancaína*, smell the bright spices, see the bold yellow shades of turmeric in the sauce. You will reach for the same *alfajores* cookies when you are grown up and savor them your whole life. They remind you of family and love. You will always remember the Sundays at La Tia Delia, the Peruvian restaurant where your community would gather after church. You will never discard this part of yourself. In fact, you will reconnect with it and find some of the most important parts of yourself within it. You will always savor the stories your grandmother told you about the strong Inca warriors, the architects, the farmers, the spiritual builders of magical places you will visit one day in Peru. *You will build something one day too*, your grandmother told you.

And you will.

But in the meantime, I want you to look at your mother. She has broken the mold, and she is building something too. Right now. Take a look at what she is doing. Raising you and your sister without the help of a man. Working several jobs to make ends meet. Doing the best she can to give you your middle-class life in New Jersey. Did you know she was only a child herself when she came to America? Maybe she was trying to be the woman her religion wanted her to be when she married so young and had your sister, enduring hardship and abuse along the way. But then she divorced and found your father. He was addicted to drugs and disowned by his family since he was only thirteen years old. Living on the streets, alone and afraid. He saw an angel in your mother too. A fair-skinned, lovely Peruvian angel. They were so deeply in love and she tried so hard to save him. But she couldn't do it. And then they had you before he slipped away, taken by an epidemic that even an angel could not erase.

And when you were born, you entered a world of women. You have been working so hard to please them, to perform well at home as the only boy in the house, and as the child of immigrants at school. You run extra hard in gym class—the place where you are the most insecure. So unsure of your body, afraid of how others see you. You are afraid of the authority figures, the parents, the grandparents, the uncles, the godfathers, the teachers, the nuns. You are nervous of how they see you. So you pour your heart and soul into making straight A's—you'll do anything to see your exhausted mother beam. But when you are older you will realize you don't have to be the best of the best in every single class to make your mother smile. Damaging your grades will not damage her love for you. She smiles when you bring her straight A's not because of the A's. She smiles because *you* are smiling. She has so much on her mind, and she is always working so hard, but seeing you smile will always make her smile.

You keep hearing the same refrain she must have heard when she came to America. *If you work hard and follow the rules, it will all work out.* But being a transgender first-generation American like you means you are usually going against all the rules. No matter how many A's you make, you are still breaking the rules. You were born to a family who defies borders, and in a body that resists rules. When you got kicked out of Catholic school for kissing your crush Anthony on the cheek, you were not breaking *your* rules. You were breaking *their* rules. You felt shame when the teacher lectured your mother. You felt so guilty that you scrubbed the chalkboard as you listened. As if to clean up your mess. But you have not made a mess. I am not ashamed of you.

So forget their rules. Go to that place where you can love yourself, where you see yourself as you are. Close the door in your mother's bathroom and feel safe in that mirror, wearing her makeup, wrapping your hair in your T-shirt. Turn on the boom box and blast the R & B, the Selena, the JLo. I wish you could open the door and let your mom and sister in on all the fun. I wish you didn't have to go to bed hoping and praying every single night that you would wake up the next day a girl. I wish you didn't have to ask yourself *Was I born in the wrong body? Was I born in the wrong country?*

Trust yourself, listen to yourself. I love that your beauty icons do not exist in magazines. They are right in your own family. If you were to emulate anyone, it would be Melissa, your oldest cousin, with her edgy beauty, her gorgeous tattoos, and her Peruvian face. Or your mother—her name is Carmen, a name you will borrow one day—with her smart business clothing and her lovely smiling face that seems to be made of pure light.

You have found what makes you feel beautiful. It is not the socks your grandmother gives you for Christmas every year because no one knows how to buy clothing for you. It is not even your obsession, Buffy the Vampire Slayer herself, Sarah Michelle Gellar. It is your beautiful mother, her name, her face. It is driving to the beach with her in her sports car, turning up the pop music, feeling the wind in your hair. When you grow up, you will look like her. Your uncles will say, *Oh my god, you even act like her.* All of the pieces of the puzzle will come together, and you will feel authentic one day. And you won't have to wear makeup to be pretty. You won't have to dress sexy to be a woman. You don't have to change to be *you*.

You can hold on to where you came from. What made you, you. A line of strong Peruvian women. Always come back to the love that brought you here. Come back to it, even when you think they won't accept you. Even when you fear they are ashamed of what makes you different. If you need love, there is no one better than your family. Invest in your bond with them, and help them understand who you really are.

Sometimes it will be hard for your mother to watch you grow up and become who you are. In her eyes right now, you are your dad's only son. Your dad is gone, and she is still in love with him. So losing her son will be hard. But it's okay to hold your mother accountable. It is her job to love you. And when you need her because you miss your father so deeply, or because you feel alone—she *will* be there for you. Tell her you need her. Her mothering will kick in and she will help her child. Not her gay son. Or her trans daughter. Her *child*.

And if you are nervous about coming out when you get older, here's my advice. Be very perceptive and even more brave. Braver than you are every single time you get grouped with the boys at school and have to converse with them in their foreign language of boyness. Braver than when you have to undress near them before gym. Braver than the time they put your locker right next to the boy you are madly in love with, and the gym coach called you out for crushing on that boy. Pointing his finger at you so everyone would laugh. And everyone would know.

Here's what you must do to bravely come out: When you are older, bring home your most confident and "out" friend, the one who inspires you to be yourself. Invite him to sit next to your grandmother at dinner. Allow him to shine for everyone to see. Watch the faces of your family members as they soak him in. As they see him for who he really is—a proud, funny, loud gay man. How do they respond? Measure the amount of work you will have to do to open their hearts and minds to really see you too.

And then *do* it.

I *know* you can do it.

Be proud of who you are. You will be explaining yourself to curious or nervous people for the rest of your life. Be visible. This will change the world. Help other kids see themselves in you. There are so many more like you. You are not alone.

Find a way to walk proud. To be comfortable in your skin. Find the girl in the bathroom mirror. Celebrate her. *Build something*, just like your grandmother said.

Go to Peru for the very first time, and bring your grandmother to the party celebrating your magazine cover in her country. The cocktails, the lights, the Peruvian celebrities all around. The meet-and-greet with hundreds of your fans in a country you've never even been to. But it is *your* country too. You share it with your grandmother. It is the country where she will see you for the first time as Carmen Carrera, the Peruvian-American model and activist. You will find yourself in every breath you take there. You will feel your power when you speak to the LGBTQ kids there. You will feel the spirit, the soul, the connection to this place and to yourself.

Imagine this. One day you will go to the judge, file the paperwork, jump through all their hoops, undergo all their evaluations, write the check, and wait for the paper to come in the mail. On February 21, 2017, you will open the envelope that contains your new birth certificate, your legal gender, your legal name. You will open the door to a whole new life. You will answer your own question. No, you were not born in the wrong body, you were just born to be born anew.

Welcome to the world, Gabriella Costa-Roman.

Honoring your father with the name Roman and your mother with the name Costa. Because she named you Christopher, meaning *bearer of Christ, the one who carried the Christ child across the river.* And Gabriella means *woman of God.* Congratulations, you no longer have to carry him on your back. You are finally allowed to be you.

But you're already allowed to be you. Right now. I promise. So get comfortable. Get excited. A beautiful world is waiting for you.

Love,
Gabbi xoxo

A formidable talent to be reckoned with, **Uzo Aduba** is an award-winning actress whose work spans television, film, and theater. Aduba currently stars as Suzanne "Crazy Eyes" Warren in the critically acclaimed Netflix original series *Orange Is the New Black*.

Uzo Aduba

MY NIGERIAN PARENTS WERE very committed to giving me and my four siblings a well-rounded American upbringing. We grew up in a small New England town and were encouraged in whatever we did, as long as we worked hard. I have a freakishly strong work ethic, and it comes from my mother. In school, I was in track, theater, choir, and was also a competitive ice-skater outside of school. There could not have been a sport more foreign to my mother, but she was always so steadfast in her support. I can still see her sitting through my practices in the rink, dressed in more layers than all the other parents and gripping the sides of her arms to keep warm. Nigerians, in my experience, are always cold in Massachusetts.

She was and still is a graceful and dignified woman. She always carried herself in a very different way from most American moms I knew. She never talked down to us or tried to mimic our speech the way some parents do when they converse with young children. She seemed to glide around the room, speaking to us like we were her royal subjects. And I mean that in a good way, because she always seemed positively regal to me. She had two master's degrees that she had acquired in Nigeria before I was born. She used to tell us that her university was the Harvard of Nigeria and that it was no accident she had been accepted there. I never doubted her for a second.

She raised us to speak Igbo, which is my parents' native language, but she was also very serious about our English. She speaks the loveliest, most refined English of anyone I know. She has the vocabulary and syntax of a professor, and that beautiful, lilting Nigerian accent, which sounds so gorgeous to me. So much better than my own American accent. But of course, as a child I was sometimes embarrassed of her accent. There weren't many African-Americans in our town, much less immigrants who walked around sounding like royalty. She was a rarified unique thing. But back then, I would roll my eyes every time she rearranged a sentence to avoid ending on a preposition. And her vocabulary was so expansive. Sometimes she would use an exotic, multisyllabic word like *persnickety* or *deciduous* or *gallivanting*, and I would argue with her that she was making up words.

She would blink her eyes slowly and smile at me. "Go look it up in the dictionary, my dear."

When I would try to correct her pronunciation or suggest she use more informal language around my friends, she would refuse to adjust.

"Mom, no one talks that way," I would whine and plead.

She would not appear even the slightest perturbed: "I speak the Queen's English. You people are the ones not speaking proper English."

Even though her way of talking annoyed me, I would immediately defend it when anyone else ever pointed out her quirks. Inside I knew it was part of her strength and power.

"That's the Queen's English," I would say to the offender. "She speaks it correctly. We don't."

I got a lot of blank stares.

The full name she gave me is Uzoamaka, which of course no one could ever say correctly. I became fed up with teachers butchering the pronunciation and kids making fun of it, so one day, I approached her in the kitchen while she was cooking (which is where she is located in so many of my childhood memories). I proposed she start calling me Zoe instead.

"Why?" she said with such elegant disdain.

"Because no one can say Uzoamaka!" I said.

Without even looking up from the giant pot she was stirring, she replied, "If they can learn to say Tchaikovsky and Michelangelo and Dostoevsky, then they can learn to say Uzoamaka."

I didn't know what a Dostoevsky was, but I knew it was the end of the conversation about Zoe.

She was proud of our Nigerian heritage and made it a priority that her children would have a chance of feeling this pride too. She and my father took us to Igbo meetings every Saturday in nearby Boston so we could hang out with other Nigerian-Americans in the area. We'd eat big feasts of Nigerian food, and kids would gather for language lessons. We got an education in Nigerian culture and history. And best of all, we got to play with other Nigerian-American kids, the likes of which I never saw in my own town or school.

I used to marvel as I'd look around the room to see all the adults dressed in traditional Nigerian clothing. My parents were very integrated into American life, adopting a regular Western wardrobe most of the time, but they still delighted in wearing traditional Nigerian clothing too. Compared to regular drab and denim American garb, Nigerian clothing is bright, colorful, and alive. The women would wear *ashoke*—beautiful woven cloth fabric skirts, or wrappers as we call them, and blouses in bright jewel tones. On their heads they wore *ichafu*—fabric wrapped in a sculptural way around their heads.

There was always, *always* jewelry—not a woman without it. The necklaces and earrings were made of gold, sapphire, or thick chunky strings of coral. Nigerians aren't afraid of color, style, and rich fabrics—Ankara prints in vibrant African patterns and motifs; intricate, heavy laces; and other fine, textured cloths. To my eyes, a roomful of Nigerians dressed in traditional clothing always looked magical, joyful, and regal. And being among other Igbo people on the weekends made me feel as if I were rooted in something bigger and greater than myself or the small town I lived in.

Although I embraced my Nigerian self at home and on the weekends, I still struggled with being different at school. Like most kids, I preferred to blend in. I used to hate the prominent gap between my top front teeth. Of course, kids made fun of me for it, calling my two front teeth Chiclets. My mother was always asking me to smile when she took photos, but I never wanted to open my mouth enough for the gap to show. As soon as all my friends at school began getting braces, I begged my mother over and over again to get me braces to help close the gap. She never entertained this idea, but I wouldn't let up. She finally grew tired of my persistence and sat me down to explain.

"Uzo, I will not get you braces and here's why. You have an Anyaoku gap."

She went on to tell me the history of her family—a lineage of Anyaokus people who were known and revered for this gap. She told me that it pained her to see me embarrassed by it, because it was actually considered a sign of beauty and intelligence to her people. Parents would pray their children would be born with it. People *want* it. She looked me deep in the eyes and with her lovely, thick accent proclaimed:

"Uzo, you have history in your mouth."

And then she revealed to me that she had been sad all her life that she had not been born with the gap. After this revelation, I didn't immediately begin loving my teeth. I didn't even stop asking for braces. But it did blow my mind to imagine my mother as sad or desperate about anything. It was hard to picture her as anything less than the serious and indomitable force she always presented. I knew she had endured a great deal in her life, but these hardships only made her seem even more otherworldly. For example, I knew she had survived polio as a child, which caused her to develop "K leg." Her lower leg was extremely thin and slanted, making it impossible for one of her heels to properly touch the ground. And yet, she insisted on running track and playing tennis as a teenager. When the headmaster of her boarding school called my grandmother and urged her to force her daughter to accept the fact that she was "a cripple," my grandmother wasn't having it. She told the headmaster that her daughter could do anything she wanted if she worked hard enough. Sounds like the same thing I always heard as a kid. And sure enough, my mother kept at it and ended up a college champion in tennis. It almost made sense to me that one of her heels didn't properly touch the ground. Neither one of her feet touched the ground in my imagination. She could probably do anything she wanted if she set her mind to it.

Like her mother before her, she was an unbreakable statue-of-a-woman to me. She and my grandmother had even lived through war and displacement in Nigeria, but it still never registered what that really meant, or what effect it had on me.

I didn't get the chance to know my grandmother very well before she died. The first memory I have of her is kneeling to bathe my newborn baby sister, Chi-Chi, in our bathroom. I was only three years old at the time, but I can still picture the smile on her face and the colorful sweater she was wearing to shield her from the balmy eighty-degree weather that August in Massachusetts.

She lived in Nigeria all her life, but she was staying with us for several months as part of the Igbo tradition called *omugwo* in which a grandmother comes to help her daughter in the months after a new baby is born. Even though my mother was an experienced parent by the time Chi-Chi was born, *omugwo* honors the idea that it truly does take a village to raise a child. Or five children in my mom's case. Women in Igbo culture are not left all alone with the demands of a newborn baby. The grandmother sometimes stays a full year to help with childcare, keeping house, and cooking nourishing foods for the breastfeeding mother. My mother told me that she never once saw or even heard of postpartum depression in Nigeria, perhaps because the community of support for mothers is part and parcel of the childbirth and mothering experience.

After my grandmother's stay for *omugwo*, I didn't see her again until my first trip to Nigeria when I was eight years old. My grandmother had asked that her entire family gather in Nigeria to visit her. She had children all over the world—in the United States, the United Kingdom, and Australia—and she was insisting she see *all* of them and *all* of her grandchildren *this* year. Most of the family was going for Christmas, but my mother had just gone the previous year with my infant baby brother. It was a big schlep with a baby and all her children, and since she had just recently visited, the decision was made that she would skip the trip. Chi-Chi and I would go with my father the following August.

I was very excited to travel to the place my parents came from. It would be my first time on an airplane, and that alone was thrilling. I didn't have a strong grasp of geography, but I knew I would be crossing an ocean and that all those people we always talked to on the phone would be on the other side of it. I couldn't wait to meet my cousins. I had no idea what I was walking into, but I can still remember the unforgettable feeling of stepping out of the air-conditioned Pan Am plane into that heat. *That heat.* It washed over me. It felt like opening an oven door. It was sensory overload for me, because there is almost nowhere in the United States like that. There was an overwhelming and sometimes unforgivable smell there. The smell of heat, yes, but also the smell of burning wood, fire, work, and soil. The earth there was a surprising shade of bright red that I hadn't ever seen in nature.

And color was all around us in Nigeria. Everyone spoke the language. Everyone ate the Nigerian food that tasted so much better than it did when we tried to re-create it back home, having to substitute ingredients. My eight-year-old brain was hit with the strange reality that all of this—the food, the language, the clothing—was a real way of life here. This is a *real* place where people move through the world this way *all the time*. These people weren't dropped out of the sky—like me, coming in from an airplane across the world. This was my mother's *home*. She grew up getting to be here and live this way every. Single. Day.

And this was my home too.

I was wildly aware that my thoughts were moving quickly. I was feeling myself connecting with something new. I journaled very diligently at this time in my life, and it was almost too much for my young self to be able to write fast enough to keep up with my racing thoughts.

On the day we went to visit my grandmother where she was staying at my aunt's house, my father brought our video camera. In Nigeria, electricity isn't reliable, and it happened to be completely out the day we visited. As the sun set, we arrived at my aunt's house and surrounded my grandmother at her bedside. We spoke by the dim lights of kerosene lanterns. As chance would have it, the light on our camcorder also wasn't working, so when the room grew darker, the footage my father shot wasn't visible. He captured mainly just darkness and audio recordings of our conversation. But I still remember what I saw. My grandma was very old. She was diabetic and very tired—but she still had an energy and intensity that came through. She had a scarf tied around her head, and her hands looked so worn. So weathered. The lines and wrinkles in her hands told stories of her life that I wanted to know. She didn't feel real to me. I was in awe.

We were the last of all her grandchildren to come home to visit her. They sat her up, and she began speaking to Chi-Chi and me in Igbo.

"I'm your grandmother. You look so good."

We may have smiled in the dark room, or maybe just widened our eyes.

"How's your mother?" she asked.

"She's good," we managed to say.

"Are you being good for her?"

"Yes," we said.

"Good. Continue to be good to her. Tell her that her mommy loves her. And that I miss her."

As these words came out of her mouth, I remember being astonished. Floored. *This is my mother's mommy.* Somehow it hadn't ever occurred to me to imagine my solid-as-a-rock mother as a child—who had a mom. As far as I was concerned, my mother's life had begun at the age of twenty-five, when she came to America. I had never seen photos of her as a little girl—or any evidence whatsoever of her childhood. I never had the experience of going through artifacts of her life the way you often do when you visit a grandparent. Most of their personal keepsakes, papers, photos, and heirlooms had been lost over the years due to the circumstances of war. My grandparents had fled from the north back to the southeast, where Igbos are from. They lived in a time and place where people were oppressed by war, homes burned down, family members killed or slowly starved out of entire regions.

That night, when I went back to the place we were staying, I journaled about the entire experience. It felt so special and important to me. I wrote about what it felt like to see my grandmother, what she was wearing, what she said to me and Chi-Chi, how my thoughts turned to my mom when I saw her. The next morning, we drove to visit my cousin Ijay, and when she opened the door, we were greeted with shock. My grandmother had died that morning.

It was Chi-Chi's birthday, and we had to say goodbye to the woman who had bathed her as an infant, the woman who had bathed our mother as an infant. I thought about these things carefully on the plane ride home.

I don't remember how my mother was told that her mother had passed away. I don't know what her exact response was or how she handled the fact that she had missed one last chance to say goodbye. But I know it must have been hard for her to bear that kind of regret for not going to Nigeria with us. We gave her the videotape—which was heartbreakingly just an audiotape—of my grandmother, and I showed her my journal entries. These were the last accounts she had of my grandmother. She placed them in a safe-deposit box along with other items dating no earlier than her twenty-fifth birthday.

Chi-Chi's birthday party was to take place the weekend after we returned. One day, she and I were playing when Mom called Chi-Chi into the kitchen, where she was cooking. We ran in to our mother and saw her standing in front of the stove. She had her eyes closed for a moment and she breathed deeply, as if to gain composure.

"Chi-Chi." She paused.

"Would it be okay if we don't have your birthday party this year?" Another pause.

"Mommy's really sad."

She looked so broken. All of the sudden my immovable, fierce mother was just a human. A daughter. A little girl who had lost her mom.

When you are the child of an immigrant, as I am, you never experience the youth of your parents. You never see them as kids who are in the sweeter side of a parent-child relationship. You can lose this window into their humanity. They are the saviors, the dreamers, and the sacrificers. Not the innocent or vulnerable people.

Several years later, when I was older, my mother unexpectedly recovered a few of her old family photos from a relative. I finally got to see a black-and-white photo of her as a child. In the photo she is four years old, sitting for a formal portrait with six of her siblings. Their faces are all stoic—the way you had to be in those times when you were being photographed by a professional. Her two sisters' dresses match hers, and her tiny little arm is wrapped protectively around the baby seated to her right, my godfather Ifeanyi. Even as a baby, she looked like a strong, protective little mama. I felt as though I was looking at someone I knew so well, and yet meeting a very important part of her for the very first time.

My mother was also able to show me a few other items she'd recovered—an old report card that was of course full of A's, and one of her championship tennis trophies. There was something about seeing her name engraved on the little silver plate at the base of the trophy. This simple tarnished artifact helped me believe details about her life that had formerly seemed like legends or tall tales. And even today, I am still constantly recalibrating my tenderness for my mother, seeing her as a person and not just the strong, brave, and unchangeable force who raised me.

I am grateful to know her as a whole person now, one who has had pain and youth and fault. And in fact, this only deepens my delight in worshipping her for the royalty that she is. I still relish the act of mimicking her beautiful accent (which I do often) and seeking her approval for my adult goals and accomplishments. I can see my mother in myself all the time. We butt heads, sure, but we are so much alike. "We're of the same rib," she used to always say to me, when I was young and didn't understand this phrase.

But I see this now more than ever. Not only do we look exactly alike—I am constantly approached at parties and told "You must be Noyem's daughter"—but we understand each other so well. And people we are close to tend to relate to us the same way—as trusted and valued listeners. It is not an understatement to say that my mother and I are the same person. And it is because of her that I have even a fraction of the strength she has. It is because of her that I am proud of my Nigerian heritage. Many people know my name now. It flashes across TV screens, and no one questions it. Because I don't. It is because of my mother that I am no longer embarrassed of the gap between my teeth. I will always be honored to share her history—our history—with my smile.

My mother may not have a lot of remnants from her childhood—or many keepsakes to pass down to me. But she has given me a greater inheritance—my soul, my spirit, my strength, and my Nigerian pride.

When I was a senior in high school, I was asked to give a speech at my graduation ceremony. My parents were so proud that I was living up to all they had worked for. They planned a huge graduation party for me where we would invite all of my classmates, and their parents—as well as all our family and friends, many of whom are Nigerian.

When my mother asked what kind of food I wanted to serve at the party, I surprised her by choosing Nigerian dishes like *jollof* rice, *egusi* soup, *moi moi*, and coconut rice instead of hamburgers and hot dogs. When my mother asked me where I would like to buy my graduation dress for the ceremony and party, I surprised her again.

"Mommy, I want to wear traditional clothes. And I want all our family and Nigerian friends to come dressed in Nigerian clothes too."

"Why?" she asked. Probably masking her excitement, because she is an expert at masking any hasty or sudden emotion.

"I want all my friends to see us. I want them to know exactly who we are and where we're from. And I want us to stand proud in that," I said.

On the day of the ceremony, I remember standing at the podium, looking out into the audience and spotting that Nigerian cluster of vibrant greens, purples, reds, and yellows among the sea of my school colors—white and blue. After, at the party, my school friends were in awe of my Nigerian guests, who walked around proud as peacocks in their traditional clothing. They had seen *Coming to America* maybe, but never real Africans up close and personal. I remember my friends telling me how gorgeous and regal we looked. I was proud to be the one to show them the beauty and richness of our culture.

It was a wonderful, fun party. I was walking on air because I had made my mother proud in more ways than one. I remember seeing her gliding around the party, her feet barely touching the ground as she tended to guests and food, wearing her white lace *ashoke* with a jewel-green *ichafu*, positively beaming from the inside out. It was my big day, of course, but *she* was the queen of that party.

Linda Sarsour is an award-winning racial justice and civil rights activist, seasoned community organizer, and mother of three. She is most known for her intersectional coalition work and for building bridges across issues and racial, ethnic, and faith communities.

Linda Sarsour

I WAS BORN INTO a community of radical love. It echoed through my home and down the streets of my neighborhood. Sunset Park was a noisy, happy place, filled with Palestinian, Dominican, Mexican, Ecuadoran, and Honduran families. A place where families and neighbors were one in the same. You did for your neighbor just as you would for an immediate family member. You knew their names, what they liked to eat, what music they listened to, and who they prayed to. Your block was your home. Your hood was your village. I didn't know at the time that this kind of love could be considered radical. Unusual. Powerful.

I am a Palestinian-American Muslim woman who wears a hijab. So I've been made painfully aware that some people ruffle when I use the word *radical*. But when I describe the loving place I grew up in, it is a word that truly applies. Brooklyn is a place I love like a human being. It is the place where I learned the meaning of radical love.

I was my mother's first child, born in a hospital in Brooklyn, delivered by a Muslim Palestinian immigrant, Dr. Ahmad Jaber, who whispered in my ear the call to prayer just moments after I was born. Like all Muslim babies, the first sounds I heard upon entering the world were words of love. I was welcomed into life, into my neighborhood, into my family with great enthusiasm. Even though my parents should have been disappointed to have a baby girl instead of a boy, they were overjoyed at my arrival. In Arab culture, everyone wants a son first and foremost, because boys can carry on the family name. It is customary to hope aloud that your first child will be a boy. People in my culture do not shrug and say, "Oh, we don't care about the gender—as long as the baby's healthy!" No. They pray openly and unabashedly for a son. But my parents had a girl, and my name was to be Linda. Inspired by a pop song that was very popular all over the Middle East at the time about a man who loved a girl named Linda.

My dad was also a man who loved a girl named Linda. As his oldest child, I was his pride and joy. His love was so vocal that for several years into my childhood, people in the neighborhood used to call him Abu Linda (*the father of Linda*). This nickname made his eyes twinkle, his spirit shine. He loved nothing more than his children. In a span of ten years, my mother gave birth to five daughters and two sons. The five daughters came first—one after the other, five of us in a row. Every time my mother would have another daughter, people would say, "Poor lady, inshallah [God willing] next time it will be a boy." Not my dad. He would be so elated every time my mother had a daughter that when he would come home from the hospital acting so giddy, our neighbors and family would rise up from their seats thinking surely Dad's glee meant that this time it was a boy. Then my dad would tell them my mother had given birth to another girl, and it always left them puzzled.

The moment my mother delivered her fifth child into the world—the last of her five girls—she closed her eyes.

"Is it a boy? Is it a boy?" my mother asked the doctor, wincing with hope and expectation.

"You have another beautiful princess!" Dr. Jaber announced joyfully.

"It's a girl?!" she could not believe the odds that she had brought a *fifth* girl into the world, and she made no secret of her longing for a boy.

"I don't even have a girl's name prepared!" she said in complete desperation. "I thought for sure it would be a boy this time! What am I supposed to name her?!"

"*Hela*. You should name her Hela," he said, using the Arabic word for *welcome*. "We must let her know she is welcome in this wonderful family, and this marvelous world."

"Yes, you are right. She is Hela," my mother cried.

Hela was welcomed into this world just like the rest of us were—with nothing but sheer exuberance from my father. While my mother recovered from labor, resting in bed with her baby, he would make his excitement known to anyone who would listen in the hospital, in the mosque, in the streets. My father did not have an easy life, but you would not have known this from his constant, visible joy. The way he saw it, he was so blessed to have so many healthy children—girls and boys—in a country so full of opportunity. He and my mother had left their village in Al Bireh, Palestine, where they lived under military occupation. My father came here with just a fifth-grade education and a few hundred dollars. But he and my mother wanted to start their family in a safe place, with better opportunities. They arrived in Brooklyn to find that several other people from their village back in Palestine had come here too. My father hit the ground running very quickly, opening a corner store in Crown Heights where he often worked sixteen-hour days. His love for his family was unquestionable and extreme. He would have worked even more without complaint if it meant he could provide better for his family.

We were not an unusual family in our neighborhood. There were dozens of other Arab families, along with the Dominican, Mexican, Ecuadoran, and Honduran families. They all worked hard, raised their children, supported their neighbors, and gave back to the community. During the daytime, the kids would all gather to play tag, Wiffle ball, and dodgeball in the street. We'd sit for hours on end on the front stoops. When it got really dark, all the moms and grandmothers would come outside and call us home for dinner or bed. We had block parties all throughout the summer filled with music from our different cultures. We used to teach one another dances like salsa and debka.

The Palestinian-Americans were very close-knit. The community was always there for one another when someone was in need or when someone had something to celebrate. We would have concerts with Palestinian folklore, dancing to raise money for Palestinian orphans and refugees; festivals in the park that showcased our heritage and brought our community together for celebration and networking.

My father's love for celebrating Palestinian culture with his children and community was—like everything else he did—inexhaustible. And his support of all his children—boys and girls alike—was also very clear. It is true that in Muslim families, women are often the backbone, the foundation, and not so much at the forefront. But my father never kept his daughters at home. He always integrated us into social activities and encouraged us to participate in anything that could help us learn or have fun. He routinely brought us to classes in the community where we could learn more about Palestinian folklore and history and practice speaking our Arabic. My dad rooted for us to learn Palestinian folk dance, and cheered me on when I played the lead role in the plays or walked in the Arab fashion shows. My uncle, my mother's brother, was our Palestinian folklore instructor, and I was the youngest member of the dance troupe. Because my uncle lived with us at the time, I got a lot more practice and became one of the best performers. I loved it so much that I even became an instructor when I was older and taught Arab-American girls debka, performing all over New York City. Many of the Muslim parents didn't want their daughters dancing in public, but my parents were happy to see me doing what I loved. And my father was always the guy in the front row, blocking everyone else's view with his giant 1990s video camera on his shoulder, taping every moment and angle of the performance. He used to stay up all night making copies of the videotape to distribute among the other parents in our community who didn't have cameras of their own.

People sometimes ask me now how a Muslim woman like me can be a feminist, because they are under the impression that those two things are incompatible. But I was brought up to believe I was loved, important, and integral to our community.

My Muslim immigrant father set the standard for me that girls and women are just as important to the village as anyone else. People imagine that Muslim communities turn their backs on women or subjugate them to lesser roles, but this was not my experience. As a child, I never felt less than my brothers or male cousins. I was Linda, the daughter of Abu Linda. My name meant something to the most important man in my life. It never even occurred to me that women couldn't speak in public or that women were any less important in our community—or any part of the world, for that matter. I was always surrounded by my sisters, female cousins, and other mothers in my neighborhood, and we weren't a passive bunch. We all looked out for one another.

In my family, I was the little mama. By the age of ten, I was already the oldest of seven children. My parents were never ashamed that my English was better than theirs. They leveraged this for the good of our entire family. With my father working sixteen-hour days, my mom needed my support. She had an eleventh-grade education and is a very smart woman, but still needed help filling out forms in English, assisting my siblings with homework, and speaking to bill collectors, doctors, and teachers. I did all of these things for my parents. I was always helping my six younger siblings. This gave me a sense of responsibility and empowerment at a very early age. There were definitely times I wasn't sure I wanted this role, but it built up my confidence, which I would need later in life.

And no matter how critical my English-language skills were for our family, my parents never allowed me to forget Arabic. I used English at home only when absolutely necessary. My parents wanted us to be fluent in their mother tongue, and so they made a house rule to speak only Arabic to them. I remember running home from school to tell my dad a story about something exciting that had happened that day. I would let the words rush quickly from my mouth, forgetting the rule, only to be stopped by my father:

"Linda, tell me the whole story again. But this time in Arabic," he would say with a smile.

I resented this at the time, but now as an adult I am grateful to be bilingual and to pass on the mother tongue of my ancestors and parents to my children. Our language is one thing that connects the past with our future—our grandparents with our children. I always knew I would have children. I wanted to become a mother. I was surrounded by them, in awe of them. And every mother in our community was a mother to all. The woman who lived next door was just as concerned about my well-being as my own parents were. My friends' mom could correct me if I was misbehaving. Other aunties—which is what you called almost any of your mother's female friends—were welcomed and even expected to comment on me, my grades, my attitude, my accomplishments, and my shortcomings. In my community, we didn't see ourselves as just singular individuals or singular families. We were connected to something bigger. There was and still is a collective that we all feel like we are a part of. It was not just logistics—it was a way of thinking.

This was the village mentality that I thought all Americans shared. But as I grew older, I found that I was fortunate to have been born into my neighborhood, and maybe I had even taken it for granted. Not everyone has this village experience. It is a thing of the past in many cities. People have said goodbye to the village life in exchange for the global life. More and more people have embraced being alone in their homes—a stranger to their neighbors—but digitally connected to people across the world.

I am grateful and proud of the way I grew up. As a child, I never questioned that I was loved, safe, and connected to a village within a larger city in a country I loved. The first time I realized life wasn't as good for everyone else was when I was in high school. Some of the kids at my school came from different neighborhoods in Brooklyn. Their streets had been shattered by crime, drugs, police corruption, and gang violence. They would show up at school with stories of their friends being shot or jumped. Every morning when we arrived at school, we were greeted by security officers who waved their wands across our bodies and asked us to run our book bags through the scanners. These were the only metal detectors I'd ever encountered besides at the airport. But some of the other kids of color would comment about being stopped and frisked within their communities by NYPD all the time.

When I finished high school, I wanted to dedicate my life to helping kids who didn't have the same kind of support and love I had experienced growing up. I had seen the movie *Dangerous Minds* in high school and wanted to be just like Michelle Pfeiffer—the bighearted badass teacher showing kids how to love poetry, one another, and themselves. It made sense to me to work outside my own village—where I had it so good—to help kids in other neighborhoods. I enrolled in community college in Brooklyn to get my English degree. I was going to become the adult who told all the disenfranchised kids of Brooklyn that they mattered.

And then 9/11 happened. I was twenty years old. A new wife, young mother, and college student. I loved my country, and I loved my people. But suddenly the two seemed at odds. After that horrific attack on our city and our fellow Americans, my Muslim community began to be regarded as a group of suspects—just by virtue of our language, our ethnicity, and our faith. Muslims were now very unwelcome in many places. They became subject to racial profiling and police surveillance. I watched with my very own eyes in Sunset Park as law enforcement agencies raided coffee shops and businesses. I watched women cry and say, *Somebody picked up my husband and I haven't seen him in five days and he never called me.* I knew so many Muslims who had fled their home countries to escape the very situations they were now encountering in America.

So this was the catalyst in starting my life's work as an activist leader—my love for my people. I wasn't going to let this happen to Muslims, to America. I knew my love would fuel me through the fight. I started working with women in the community whose husbands had been detained, connecting them to legal services, translating for them. I began to volunteer with the Arab American Association of New York, an organization my cousin had helped found with Dr. Jaber, the man who had delivered me and my siblings. He was also a very well-respected leader in the community and imam in the mosque. I followed my cousin's lead, seeing her as a role model and mentor, and as yet another person confirming that I was allowed and expected to use my voice to help. It was just like Dr. Jaber used to always say: "Women are going to lead us one day. We must give young women the space to practice leading."

A few months after 9/11, I attended a citywide meeting at a mosque where various Arab-American leaders were coordinating efforts to defend Muslim-Americans across the city. When I entered the large room, I bent down to take off my shoes. As I stood up, I looked up to see thirty men in the room, all staring at me. I paused, realizing I had almost never been in a room of men only. Demographically this had never even been a possibility. There were always so many people around, so many of them girls or women. I kept my head high and crossed the room to where I saw the one familiar face, Dr. Jaber, who had resumed conversing passionately with another man. I could see by their frequent gestures and facial expressions that Dr. Jaber must have been defending my presence to this man.

I approached quietly, not wanting to interrupt or show disrespect.

"Is everything okay?" I asked.

Both men stopped talking to look to me.

Dr. Jaber broke the silence: "No, there's no problem here. You're a part of this meeting, Sister Linda, and we are going to sit down now and start."

This was not a moment when I thought of Dr. Jaber or even myself as radical. We had made these other Muslim men—all very good and principled men—take a pause and question themselves. But they accepted me and moved on. We had work to do.

And we believed what Dr. Jaber said, my cousin and I, my sisters and I. There are millions of Muslim women who are powerful and independent. Women who are going to lead us one day. We did not consider this idea to be radical, just as we did not consider my dad's love and pride for his daughters to be radical.

But what was—and still is—radical is the strength of our commitment to take care of one another. Our community had such strong ties that it was going to take a lot to break us. We are, in fact, stronger than I knew. As my activist work continued into my twenties, I began to see that the community I belonged to transcended my gender, my religion, and my village. I was part of a much *larger* village. Muslims could not fight this fight alone. We were aligned with so many others who shared our struggles. There were many young black and brown people who faced injustices every day—long before 9/11 when I felt it most in my community. These fellow Americans had been dealing with being stopped, frisked, interrogated, arrested, and even killed just because of the color of their skin. There were undocumented people living every day afraid of being separated from their families. If I hadn't grown up believing that my neighbors are my family, I may not have cared, but it was in my nature to care about all of these groups of people.

I do not believe that it is every man for himself, every woman for her child. Because my parents did not believe this. My neighbors did not believe this. And my community will not stand for this.

This is the radical love that has powered me through my decades of work. I used to think it was hope that fueled me—my hope for social justice and civil rights. But I have realized what truly fuels me is love. I love my people so much. I will lay my life on the line for my people. I would do that for my own children or for other people's children. I am a mother, and mothers know this radical love.

As our country has become more and more divided, I have had to weather personal attacks on my sincerity, my feminism, my faith. And my patriotism. My life has been threatened, my children and family have been intimidated by mainstream journalists, internet trolls, counterprotestors, and random passersby on the street. My children have been taunted for being Muslim, accused of being terrorists, belittled for who their mother is. They have seen Muslims attacked in their city, they have heard stories of Muslims killed for their beliefs. Right here in America. They have seen their president ban Muslims from entering this country. Sometimes at my low points, because I am only human, I can feel very "done" with this mess. I can feel hopeless and *done*.

But I am *never* done with my love for my people. The love that was given to me the moment I was born isn't going away until the day that I'm no longer on this earth.

This is radical love. It was passed down to me by my mother, by my father, and by so many fellow citizens of Brooklyn and America. This is the kind of love that will wake you up from hope. Hope can feel empty because you can't move toward something that is imagined. You can't work for something you are dreaming of and waiting for. But you *can* work for something that you see and feel every day. *Love is something you can see and feel every day.* When I go to my neighborhood, I know it is there. I am so lucky to be a member of this community, this family, and this movement that was born of radical love.

Congressman **Joaquin Castro** is a native of San Antonio and represents Texas's Twentieth Congressional District, serving on both the House Permanent Select Committee on Intelligence and the House Committee on Foreign Affairs. His twin brother, Julian, served in President Barack Obama's cabinet and as mayor of San Antonio. Congressman Castro and his wife, Anna Castro, have two children, Andrea and Roman.

Joaquin Castro

THROUGH HER STORIES, MY grandmother helped me imagine. She told incredible tales about her life and what might have been. As children, we tend to powerfully believe what the grown-ups we love tell us. Santa Claus and the Easter Bunny are real until your parents reveal them as imaginary. My favorite story that my grandmother Victoria told was a true story—that took place when she was a child in San Antonio, Texas. She saw a woman, dressed all in white with a small white dog beside her, who motioned Victoria to move closer, pointing down at a spot in the open field she had to cross on her way to retrieve water for her family. Victoria had seen the lady pleading in the field before. Scared, she always walked past. But she told some neighbors about the woman, and eventually one of them dug into the ground where the woman kept pointing and unearthed great treasure—enough to buy that very land.

That's one story my grandmother would tell us every so often when she imagined the things that could have been. She was old by then, a heavyset woman who stood under five feet tall, whose salt-and-pepper hair never succumbed to total whiteness even at the age of eighty-two. By this point, she could no longer work. In fact, she could barely walk. Yet sometimes, in the first days of every month, just after her $335 Social Security check arrived, she would open her cordovan purse and look inside. The purse usually stayed under the sofa. I don't remember where she bought it but it carried no designer label or tag. It snapped together with gold-colored clips, and the faux leather was chipped on the sides, giving it a look that might pass as antique in the hands of the wealthy women whose homes she used to clean. But on San Antonio's west side, the place where we lived, it wouldn't be mistaken for anything other than cheap. With what little she had, she would give my twin brother, Julian, and me, her only grandchildren, ten dollars to go to the store and buy whatever we wanted. It was Big Red and Cheetos for us. She always wanted Fritos and Fresca—or Sprite if they didn't have Fresca. We would race back to the house and at least for the day didn't complain about missing *Diff'rent Strokes* or *The Dukes of Hazzard* when she wanted to watch *Cantinflas* or Lawrence Welk—or some other show that ten-year-olds would never enjoy.

Victoria Castro was born in Coahuila, Mexico, sometime around 1914. She told us that her parents owned a small store during the time of the Mexican Revolution. Her father, Victoriano, left to fight in the war and never made it back home. Her mother, Anastacia, cared for my grandmother and her younger sister, Trinidad, until Anastacia developed tuberculosis, an especially lethal disease in Mexico at the time. Victoria talked often—wistfully but also angrily—about her final days by her mom's side at the hospital. Throughout her life she never forgave her grandmother, who took her away from her mom days before she succumbed to the disease. Perhaps her grandmother didn't want the young girls to see the final ravages of tuberculosis on their mother's body. Maybe she figured they might get sick as well. Whatever the reason, Victoria never understood it or accepted it. All she could come back to is the goodbye she never got with her mother.

The closest relatives who could take in the orphaned young girls were north of the border in San Antonio, Texas. Like the Irish who, upon arriving in cities such as Boston and New York, were greeted by signs that read NO IRISH NEED APPLY, my grandmother encountered signs above Texas establishments that read NO DOGS OR MEXICANS ALLOWED. She settled with relatives on San Antonio's heavily Mexican-American west side in a home that at times housed three generations of extended family. She never made it past elementary school, and spent most of her life working as a maid, babysitter, and cook.

By the time Julian and I came along she had raised my mom to be the first in their family to go to college. And after forty years as a legal resident, she become a citizen during the Camelot years of America's first Catholic president, John F. Kennedy. The young girl who came to America with nothing, disconnected from her origins and formally uneducated—taught herself to read and write in Spanish and English. I would watch her hunch over Agatha Christie novels with a large magnifying glass, and then I'd borrow it to burn candy wrappers in the Texas sun for amusement.

By a combination of historical accident and familial dysfunction, Victoria Castro was the only grandparent I ever knew. What I know of my other grandparents—which is very little—is just a precious inventory of random facts. My mom, Rosie, was Victoria's only child—the product of a relationship with a man many years her junior. I don't believe I ever met Rosie's father, Edward Perez, but either in my memory or imagination he once gave my mom $200 to pass along to Julian and me. My own parents were together for ten years but never married. Legally they could not since my dad, Jesse Guzman, was married with five children when his marriage fell apart and he started a new life with my mom. His mother, Trinidad, died from liver failure—perhaps from drinking—five years before I was born. His father, whom I only met once or twice, served in the Army Air Forces during World War II. People sometimes talk about the deep roots and long branches of family trees; they hold family gatherings with custom-made T-shirts where multiple generations share stories and quibble about the details. I wish I'd had a chance to know all my grandparents, but Victoria's story is the only one I have to tell, a single branch disconnected from its roots.

My mom, Rosie, was the first person in our family to get involved in politics. By the time I was born, in 1974, my parents were deeply committed to the Mexican-American civil rights movement. They helped run candidates for office, organized marches, and stayed up all night at favorite hangouts talking with friends about the oppressiveness of "the system" toward people like us. I used to fall asleep to the sounds of a living room full of my parents' friends laughing, arguing, and talking about issues I wouldn't be able to grasp until years later. Choco, Danny, Irma, Bill, Lucille, Manuel, George. Some of them are still close friends, some have passed away or disappeared from our lives long ago. My mom's fiery passion for politics, for taking injustice head-on through democratic means, was in stark contrast to my immigrant grandmother. Victoria never took much of an interest in politics.

She never could've imagined that her grandsons would someday lead the American city that gave her refuge as a young, orphaned girl. Despite having such a difficult life, with complicated roots, she always tried her best to just enjoy her everyday life. She didn't concern herself with the daily grind of politics the way her daughter did, the way her grandsons still do. It is hard for me to imagine a life where public service was not my calling. Growing up with parents who lived and breathed politics, I came to believe that when government works right, it can create opportunities in people's lives.

Many in government believe that America should fundamentally change its immigration laws. Rather than the poor and huddled masses welcomed by the Statue of Liberty, many argue that we should measure a person's value before admitting them. *What can they do for us?* That's the new standard. By this logic, computer scientists, chemical engineers, laboratory researchers, and other "high-skilled" immigrants would predominate. Our nation undoubtedly benefits from the fact that brilliant, accomplished people want to make a life here. But our success has never depended upon it. America did not cherry-pick her way to greatness. Instead, we created a system—an infrastructure of opportunity—that enables the pursuit of the American dream through hard work. Just as there's an infrastructure of streets and highways that helps everyone get to where we want to go on the road, in America there's an infrastructure of *opportunity* that helps us get to where we want to go as a society. Good schools, a strong health-care system, and well-paying jobs are pieces of that infrastructure. My mom and so many others fought hard over the years in the civil rights and women's rights movements, for example, to make sure that everyone has access to the American infrastructure of opportunity.

Today, many are afraid of immigrants, of providing them this access. But do they realize there is something far scarier than being the country *everyone* wants to come to? What if we become the country *no one* wants to come to? Fifty years ago, if you asked someone living in Europe, Asia—or anywhere else, really—where they would go if they had to leave their home country, the answer was clear. For all the work we still had to do on civil rights, voting rights, and women's rights, the answer was almost always *the United States of America.* Because here, the world saw an infrastructure of opportunity with ample room for the high-skilled and the hardworking; the refugees and the dreamers.

But under the standards many are proposing now, my grandmother would never have been allowed into the country. She would have been deemed completely worthless.

Victoria deserved the same opportunities as the rest of us. She belonged in a country that allowed her to pursue her dreams. Yet, her life also made me realize that we can't just measure the American dream in material terms. Measured only by those standards, my grandmother and so many people never achieved the American dream. When my brother, Julian, gave the keynote address at the 2012 Democratic National Convention to urge his fellow Americans to reelect our nation's first African-American president, he talked about the American dream exactly as Victoria's grandson understood it:

> In the end, the American dream is not a sprint, or even a marathon, but a relay. Our families don't always cross the finish line in the span of one generation. But each generation passes on to the next the fruits of their labor. My grandmother never owned a house. She cleaned other people's houses so she could afford to rent her own. But she saw her daughter become the first in her family to graduate from college. And my mother fought hard for civil rights so that instead of a mop, I could hold this microphone.

My grandmother sparked my curiosity and imagination through the stories she told me and the love she gave me. She was the branch in a family tree that left me otherwise disconnected from my past. My grandmother showed me that people who start out with nothing—those who would be considered worthless under new immigration standards—can be the seeds that bear significant contributions to American society. She passed the baton to my parents so that I could one day have it too. She helped me imagine a better country and believe in the dream for the next generation after me.

And she also continues to remind me that all of us here in this country are equally deserving of health and happiness—whether we are immigrants or indigenous people; whether our ancestors have been here for generations or whether we just arrived. For years I never knew whether my grandmother came to the United States legally. I never asked or even thought to. But the day before Julian spoke at the Democratic National Convention, a genealogist researched our family's history and published what she'd found in the *Huffington Post*. A copy of the document that allowed Victoria to enter the United States demonstrated the thin line in the 1920s—and for most of America's history—between documented and undocumented. Under the description for the purpose of her visit are scrawled the words *To Live*.

America Ferrera

Dear Reader,

I grew up believing I was alone in feeling stuck between cultures. I didn't know other Americans shared my experience, because I never saw my story told. I tried shaping an identity that would make sense to other people by shedding pieces of myself and attempting to assimilate.

Ironically, the opportunities to fulfill my dreams were the ones that required me to embrace my unique identity. I didn't get my career-making roles in *Real Women Have Curves*, *The Sisterhood of the Traveling Pants*, and *Ugly Betty* in *spite* of who I was, I got them *because* of who I was: someone who didn't fit easily into any preexisting mold. All the labels that I had been told my whole life would keep me from success—brown, short, chubby, too Americanized, too ethnic-looking, et cetera—were the very aspects that made me perfect for the roles that would make my dream career a reality.

I learned quickly that my particular challenges gave me the power to connect to others. Everywhere I went I met people who also felt underrepresented, unseen, and like they didn't fit in to fixed boxes. I found something I never could have imagined as a child: a larger community that, like me, struggled to find identity between the cracks of cultures. Finding community and a sense of belonging emboldened me to not only own my experiences but to also celebrate them and to create from them.

I invited my friends, peers, and heroes to share their stories in this book so that we might build community; so that we could identify our whole selves within a larger culture that tends to leave important pieces of our stories out; so that our voices would amplify one another's as we declare who we actually are. We are kids with no key chains, daughters carrying history in the gaps of our teeth. We are the sons of parents who don't speak of the past, inheritors of warriors' blood and mad bargaining skills. We are the grandchildren of survival: legacies, delivered from genocide, colonization, and enslavement. We are the slayers of "impossible." We stand on the shoulders of our ancestors' dreams wearing the weight of their sacrifice on our backs. Our love is radical; our unstraightened hair, a tiny revolution. We are here to survive, to thrive, to live. We connect to our roots clumsily, unknowingly, unceasingly. We call ourselves "American" enthusiastically, reluctantly, or not at all. We take fragments of what was broken, severed, or lost in history, and we create whole selves, new families, and better futures. We live as citizens of a country that does not always claim us or even see us, and yet, we continue to build, to create, and to compel it toward its own promise.

Dear reader, there is great power in your story, especially in the pieces that have never been seen or told before. Please add your voice to ours so that we can see ever more authentic reflections of our realities in the culture that surrounds us. I am grateful and proud to be a part of this growing generation of Americans rewriting and reshaping the narrative to include our lived experiences.

Truly yours,
America

ACKNOWLEDGMENTS

DEAREST CONTRIBUTORS, thank you for accepting my invitation to share a piece of your life. You brought your history and hearts to these pages, and I am forever grateful that you believed in the power of this book.

Cayce Dumont, my endlessly talented collaborator and coconspirator, this book would not have been possible without you. Thank you for so patiently and lovingly working with each contributor, including myself. You helped me find and illuminate the soul of this book. From beginning to end you were a fierce advocate for my vision and you were the one who brought it all together.

David Kuhn, thanks for being an amazing book agent and for patiently waiting ten years for me to finally fall in love with a book idea. Oh, and thanks for coming up with the idea for the book and not giving me a chance to say no. To Kate Mack, my other book agent, thank you for your advice and steadfast support in helping with so many details throughout this process.

Carrie Byalick, my manager and favorite BOSS, you make everything more fun. Thank you for encouraging my true voice through this process and for your constant creativity and inspiration.

My fabulous team of publicists at IDPR—Molly Kawachi, Brianna Smith, and Lindsay Krug—you ladies are all class and I love you. Thank you for everything, always.

To my lawyers Jodi Peikoff and Michael Mahan and the rest of my Peikoff-Mahan family, no one loves their lawyers more than I love all of you. Thank you for taking care of me my whole career (and for receiving all my mail).

Tom Carr, thanks for always managing the business and helping me find ways to do the things I love.

I am very grateful to all the people at Simon & Schuster and Gallery Books, including Carolyn Reidy, Jennifer Bergstrom, and Jennifer Robinson for believing in this project as much as I do and helping me get it into the hands of readers; Aimée Bell, Lisa Litwack, Jaime Putorti, and Davina Mock-Maniscalco for making the book look beautiful; Stephen Fallert, Elisa Rivlin, Monica Oluwek, Caroline Pallotta, and their teams for carefully tending to so many details behind the scenes.

Thank you especially to my editor, Alison Callahan, who helped shape this book beautifully. Alison, thank you for believing this would work and for making it even better. And my very special thanks goes to Brita Lundberg, Alison's editorial assistant, who has been endlessly helpful, smart, creative, and kind.

Many thanks to my former assistant Jessica Chou. Jessica, thanks for being there in the early days and for contributing your many talents and boundless creativity to the recruiting process!

A special thank-you to my longtime creative coach, Kim Gillingham, for helping me find my path to writing. Kim, I am so grateful for the decade of your wisdom, guidance, and friendship.

Finally, thanks to Ryan, my phenomenal partner in life. Your love and support make all things possible. Your creativity is a constant source of inspiration to me. Thank you for always believing I can do whatever I set out to do, and thanks for being my witness in this life.